Cakes & Pastries

Cakes &

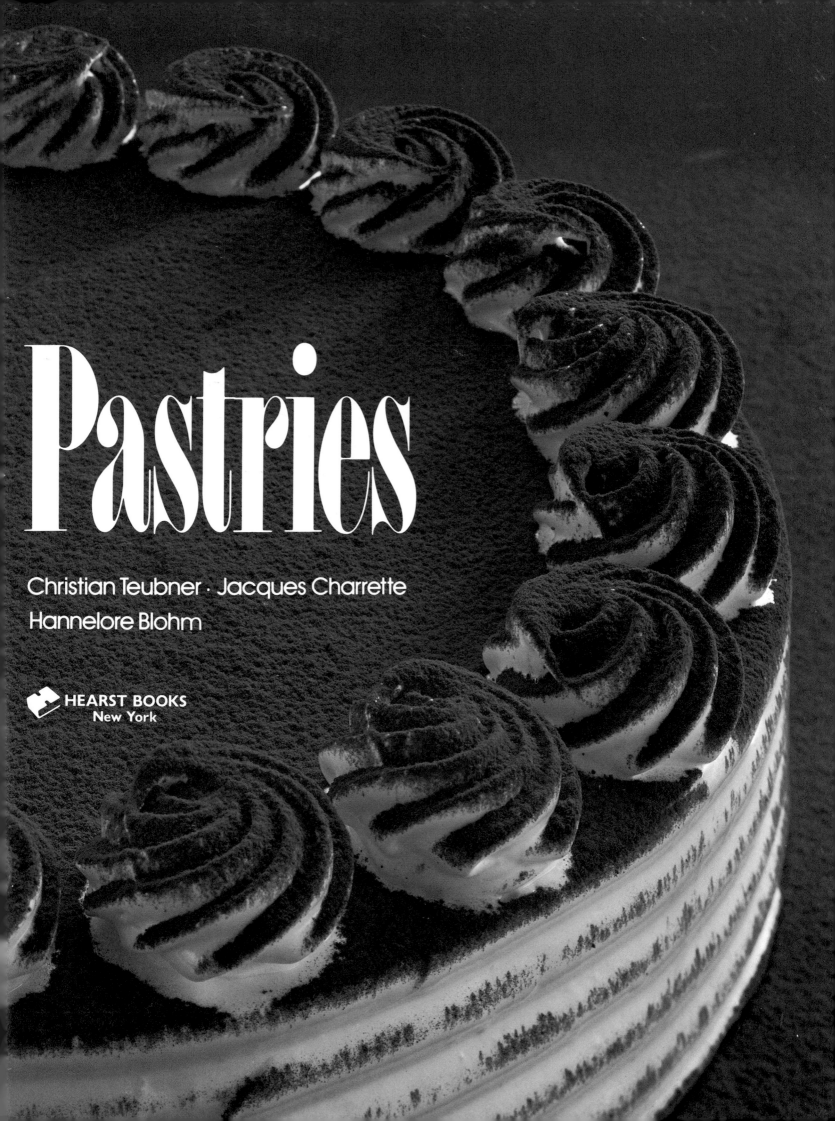

Pastries

Christian Teubner · Jacques Charrette

Hannelore Blohm

HEARST BOOKS
New York

Library of Congress Catalog Card Number: 85-60081

ISBN: 0-688-04218-X

Printed in Spain

First U.S. Edition
1 2 3 4 5 6 7 8 9 10

Contents

Foreword

Cakes and Pastries is the latest volume in a splendid series of which the first two—*The Great Dessert Book* and *Pâtés and Terrines*—are currently available. This book is the ideal manual for both the amateur home cook and the professional. The first chapter describes the major ingredients used in patisserie, briefly covering their history and useful facts about their use in baking. The next section is devoted to the basic recipes which are the foundations upon which everything else is structured. Each basic method is illustrated by clear step-by-step photographs and numbered instructions. Sponges, meringues, shortcrust, puff and choux pastry as well as yeast dough are all covered. Their accompaniments in the form of creams, custards, buttercreams, and icings are all described in mouthwatering detail. There is also a section on chocolate and its use in decorating gâteaux as well as a piece on cake decorations that can be bought ready-made.

"Cakes and Company" encompasses plain cakes of the loaf or cylindrical type and also a small section on traditional British cakes. Baking with fruit of all kinds—either in a pie, tart, small tartlet, or on a baking sheet—shows how they can be used to provide delectable desserts using whatever fruit is in season at the time.

The chapter on cheesecakes also has recipes that use yogurt as a delicious alternative to the slightly heavier curd or cream cheese that is used elsewhere. "Baking with Yeast" and "Baking for the Morning" contain a large selection of sweet bread, brioche, croissant, and Danish pastry recipes. Also included is the well-known Gugelhupf cake—originally a German favorite whose popularity has spread throughout the world.

Large cakes and gâteaux from several European countries, among them the famous Sachertorte, the Black Forest Gâteaux, Dobostorte, a Millefeuille, and many more, are next in line. For morning coffee or afternoon tea the "Small Cakes" chapter is particularly appropriate as quantities can be adapted to fit the occasion. A selection of two or three kinds of small cakes, cream slices, or Swiss rolls would form the focal point of any gathering.

The recipes in the final chapter are specifically designed for the time around Christmas and Easter and other traditional festive celebrations. These recipes are gathered together from all over Europe: from as far afield as Russia through Italy, Germany, France, and Britain.

The book ends with a useful glossary, an illustrated description of how to divide a large cake into a number of portions, and finally a helpful guide to equipment and utensils.

7

It has been our aim in this book to provide a reliable guide to the art of cake and pastry making for all our readers, be they complete beginners studying the basic recipes or experienced cooks seeking guidance on a particular problem. Since the early days, just after the discovery of sugar, patisserie has developed into an important area in the general arena of cookery. While other areas have flavor as their prime consideration, cake and pastry makers have placed an equal emphasis on taste *and* appearance. The emphasis on the visual presentation of cakes and pastries relies to a large extent on the materials with which the patissier works, for these are particularly suited to the modeler's art. Take doughs for instance, these can be shaped or plaited; marzipan, which is an ideal modeling material; or the various butter-creams used for decoration—all are materials, which used imaginatively, offer almost limitless possibilities to the creative. The license that this offers does not always, however, produce tasteful creations and taste is often at odds with imagination. Since "confectioner's style" is not always synonymous with a good taste we have kept decoration as simple as possible in this book. This is because we place less weight on intricate decoration than we do on flavor. This is not to say that those who prefer more intricate decoration should be denied the opportunity of indulging their tastes, but the prime consideration of any cake maker should be to make the freshest, crispest pastry

and the lightest,
most delicious fillings.
As in the previous books
in this series—*The Great Dessert
Book* and *Pâtés and Terrines*—we
have tried to follow the basic guidelines of
providing reliable and relevant technical
information, and in this we have been helped
by a number of international experts. Once again
we have used the basic recipes as a starting point
and these have been presented as clearly as possible
in a series of photographs. Building on these basic recipes,
it is a short step to successfully making much more complicated
cakes or even producing one's own original creations.

We wish you every success

Christian Teubner · Jacques Charrette

Christine Reuland, Füssen
Hannes Ehrenreiter, Intercontinental, Vienna
Maurice Stocker, Intercontinental, Geneva
Ernst Bachmann, Intercontinental, London
Susan Greenway, Intercontinental, London

Nothing But The Best

Cake and pastry making has been raised to the level of a sophisticated art in many countries, especially in Europe with its history of making use of dairy products. To obtain the best results you must use the very best ingredients.

Over the last two hundred years the area of baking and patisserie has made great advances seen principally in efforts to better quality by improving the rather coarse and primitive ingredients of the past. Better methods of milling, for instance, allowed millers to provide finer flour. This alone improved the results of both professional bakers and housewives. In addition, advances in world trade provided the confectioner with the finest ingredients from all parts of the world. But difficulties still remained with regard to quality, and those who wanted first-class products required more than a little experience. One egg could be very different from another, milk had no standardized fat content, and in dealing with millers you not only needed to know something about flour, you also had to be able to trust the miller.

Changes wrought by the Industrial Revolution were not confined to iron or textile production. Agricultural producers were not slow to take advantage of new methods in marketing their products. Acceptance of the new industrially produced goods was a gradual process, with the self-sufficient country areas clinging longest to old traditions. But it was only a matter of time before the standardized food products captured the market, rationalizing the job of the professional cook and making life much easier for the housewife, who now had such products as baking powder at her disposal. There is no doubt that in recent years the food industry has developed high quality products, but care is still needed when shopping. It is the individual who must make up his or her mind which semi-manufactured products can be used without affecting quality or which may even improve quality.

Baking is no different from any other area of cooking, and as in other sectors only the best and freshest products can guarantee good results. This does not mean, however, that in cake and pastry making one has to ignore the aids offered by the food industry as a matter of course. Take marzipan, nougat, or fondant icing. These are examples of manufactured products that not only make the job considerably easier, but whose quality it is often difficult to duplicate in the kitchen. So it is a matter of knowing how to successfully combine natural products and modern time-saving aids. If a sound knowledge of methods is combined with this then success is ensured.

Flour – the basis of baking

Dictionaries define flour as "a foodstuff obtained by grinding grain cereals." Any type of grain, wheat, rye, barley, rice, or maize can be milled to produce flour. Different grades of milling produce either coarse or superfine flour. For cakes and pastries we are mainly interested in wheat flour, with rye flour being used for a few specialized recipes such as gingerbread.

The role of wheat as the main foodstuff of the world is not confined to the present day. It has been closely linked with the history of mankind since the earliest times when man the hunter began to form settlements and to take up agriculture. The various methods of grinding grain into flour had their origins in these early days and have gradually evolved to produce the very latest techniques of flour production.

To understand flour properly you must know something about wheat grain and its internal structure. A cross-section through the grain shows the large kernel (endosperm) in the center, then the honey-comb aleuron layer that is rich in minerals and lies just below the skin of the grain. The grain itself is enclosed by a fiberous layer known as bran. At the bottom of the grain is found the germ-bud, which is rich in vitamins and fat. All the goodness in the grain, its protein, vitamins, phosphorus, and minerals are found within the endosperm.

How is wheat flour produced from grain? In answering this question we will attempt to avoid becoming bogged down in technicalities and stick to a simplified explanation of the process used today. The grain is first cleaned and then crushed by rollers. In the milling of wheat there is considerable slack between the rollers, for if the grain is crushed too finely much of the goodness in the outer layer would be lost. The grinding process that follows is known as "groats" or "wheat" milling, a technique marked by the distance separating the rollers that, as we have said, ensures the careful crushing of the grain, followed by a gradual process of grinding in several stages. The grain is first coarsely ground into groats and then the groats are ground into flour.

In order to keep the properties of the flour constant, and to achieve uniform quality, various types of wheat are combined for grinding. There are two basic kinds of wheat: hard and soft. Hard wheat when milled produces a strong flour that is mainly used for bread and doughs; soft-grained or weak wheat is suitable for cakes and general use. Whole-wheat or whole-meal flour is made from the entire grain of wheat, and bread made with this flour is quite dense, with a nutty taste. Wheat-meal flour contains between 80 and 90 percent of the wheat with some of the bran and germ having been removed.

Strong plain white flour is usually a blend of soft and hard wheats. Unbleached plain flour has a better flavor than the bleached variety, which has been whitened artificially. Plain flour is the refined and bleached product of soft wheat. It has a light, short texture in baking because soft wheat flours contain only a small amount of gluten. It is particularly good for cakes and shortcrust pastry.

These different types of flour are to be found in any shop. If more specialized flours, such as potato flour, were needed you could try buying from a health-food shop or delicatessen, which should offer a wide range of high quality flours. This book however only requires the usual types of flour as are generally sold.

The gluten in wheat flour

Gluten is a sticky, rubberlike substance that is present to a larger or lesser degree in all types of flour. As previously mentioned, flours made from hard wheat produce the largest amount of gluten. Fine plain flour has the lowest gluten content.

The proteins that make up gluten are found in varying quantities in different types of wheat. In warm, dry climates the gluten content is increased and also it is higher in hard or strong wheats. In yeast dough, for instance, the gluten content of the flour is important. Since gluten can absorb water, it binds the liquid in the pastry and gives it its elastic quality. In baking, the liquids bound by the gluten evaporate into steam allowing the air in the pastry to expand. At around 160°F, the gluten coagulates and combines with the starches in the flour to give pastry its crumbly texture. The pastry or cake mixture has risen and become firm and will not now fall.

A further factor determining the quality of flour is its feel. It is a sign of quality if you can feel the "graininess" of the flour between your fingers for this shows that the flour is rich in gluten and that it has been properly milled. With modern grinding methods all flours should be of high quality in this respect, but you can also recognize quality flour by its color—a bright, creamy white. Flour is sensitive to smells and will pick up other odors so it should be stored in a dry, ventilated cupboard. When flour is stored too long the fat in the flour goes bad giving the flour a rancid taste and smell.

Cornstarch and other edible starch

The gluten content of the flour, and the extent to which the gluten is developed during preparation, determines to a certain extent the finished texture of baked goods. For example, in a yeast dough a strong flour with a high gluten content is used and the gluten is developed during the kneading stages. This gives a tough dough lightened by the yeast working to produce gas which is then trapped within the mixture.

For sponges and light cakes a low-gluten flour is necessary for a more crumbly result. The addition of sugar, and the fact that the cake mixture must be handled lightly to prevent the gluten from toughening, goes to make a soft, crumbly mixture. To further reduce the effect of the gluten in wheat flour a proportion of cornstarch or other starches can be introduced into the mixture.

Other edible starches which can be used for some cakes or light pastry doughs include rice flour, potato flour, and arrowroot. The use of these ingredients is not particularly common in simple cakes, but they are required to give the fine texture expected of certain special sponges and pastries.

Yeast

Yeast consists of micro-organisms, tiny living creatures that centuries of research have revealed as a type of fungus. Under the right conditions the fungus cells increase by division and it is this process that makes yeast a useful ingredient in baking.

The conditions that yeast needs consist of air, moisture, warmth, and nourishment (in the form of sugar for instance), and the fungus cells find everything they require in dough. In these conditions the cells divide very quickly, changing the sugar into alcohol and carbon dioxide. This in combination with the gluten in the flour causes fermentation. This produces many tiny, gas-filled bubbles in the dough that increase the volume of the dough considerably. To prevent the dough "asphyxiating" air must be beaten into it. The more oxygen you can incorporate into the mixture the lighter the finished product will be.

Fresh yeast has a pleasant, rather sour smell and taste, is pale beige in color, and should be crumbly and not greasy. It should be stored in the refrigerator where it will keep for a couple of weeks or it can be frozen for several months. Dried yeast will keep for several months if stored in a cool, dry place. Half the quantity of dried yeast should be used to that of fresh as it is more concentrated.

Yeast is by no means a modern raising agent. It was used in baking as long ago as the sixteenth century. The bakers of Nuremburg are said to have discovered its effects by using the yeast provided by the town's brewers. It was the French chemist and biologist Louis Pasteur (1822–92) who discovered that yeast consisted of micro-organisms, but it was the Nobel Prize winner for chemistry, Eduard Buchner (1860–1917), who first separated yeast into its component parts and isolated the enzyme zymase that causes fermentation.

Besides yeast, which is a biological lightening and raising agent, there are also chemical agents.

Baking powder, carbonate of ammonia, and potash

Baking powder is a mixture of sodium carbonate, cream of tartar (or tartaric acid), and a separator, usually rice or potato starch. Under the combined effect of air, moisture, and warmth carbon dioxide is produced that again causes fermentation. It is the function of the separator to prevent the two other ingredients working prematurely—it therefore acts as a kind of insulator. It also absorbs moisture in the air when the baking powder is not in use. The inclusion of either cream of tartar or tartaric acid gives either fast or slower raising.

When baking in large quantities, in a patisserie for example, a raising agent known as ABC (ammonium bicarbonate) is often used. This works in the same way as baking powder. A much more traditional raising agent is carbonate of ammonia. This is a white salt that used to be obtained from horns and hooves (hence its alternative name, hartshorn). It is a mixture of substances formed by ammonia and carbonic acid. It decomposes in the air and must be stored in a tightly sealed tin, but it is soluble in water with no decomposition and is usually added to a cake mixture in dilute form. It acts in the same way as the above raising agents. With deep cakes some ammonia may remain at the end of the baking process and this gives a highly unpleasant taste. This is the reason why carbonate of ammonia is usually recommended only for thin spicy cakes (gingerbread). Potash (potassium carbonate) is another long-established raising agent. This white powder has no smell, but tastes rather caustic and is again recommended only for thin cakes.

Milk

The land of milk and honey . . . this phrase tells us much of the importance of milk, which forms the basis of a range of dairy products such as cream, curds, yogurt, and butter. Milk has always existed, and it became important to mankind from the time when he first learned to milk a nursing animal, be it a cow, goat, sheep, ass, camel, horse, or buffalo. We know that in Babylon, the rich land between the Euphrates and the Tigris, milk was used for human consumption five thousand years before Christ. Excavations in the Babylonian city of Ur produced clay tablets that record the raising of milk cattle in 3,000 B.C. Relief sculptures depict the separate stages in the treatment of milk. Other races too—Egyptians, Greeks, Romans, Germans, and the nomadic horsemen of central Asia—were all heavily involved in milk production and the production of dairy products. Curds flavored with honey or herbs was a delicacy of the German tribes and the forefathers of Genghis Khan made kefir (a soured milk) and dried milk. For the latter the cream was skimmed off and dried in flat bowls in the sun: It was as simple as that in those days.

Modern dairy science is the result of technical developments over many centuries but most particularly in the nineteenth century. As early as 812 the Emperor Charlemagne gave his court precise instructions on milk, butter, and cheese production. In 1679 the Dutchman Leeuwenhoek, who also discovered the microscope, identified the fat globules in milk. The invention of the steam engine and the subsequent development of railways was of considerable importance to the dairy industry as milk could be transported quickly and efficiently from the country to the city. The introduction of condensed milk took place in 1849. 1853 brought the invention of condensed milk by evaporation at low temperatures, and in 1859 the protein content of milk was discovered.

Milk of constant quality

Progress in food technology, the desire for the most constant quality possible, and the need for health control, resulted in stringent regulations for the production of milk for the general public. Anyone who has ever drunk a glass of milk direct from the farm will have found that it is different from treated milk. In the case of milk this has little adverse effect in cake making where it has to be heated anyway, but in the case of cream, which is normally used fresh as a filling or accompaniment to cakes, modern production methods have brought a considerable diminution of flavor.

A nutritious product

Cow's milk—the only type of milk that need concern us in baking—consists of 87 percent water. The remaining 13 percent consists of highly nutritious substances such as fat, milk sugar (lactose), casein, globulin, albumen (which coagulates to form a skin when milk is boiled), a number of important minerals and vitamins, as well as enzymes and hormones. Thus milk contains all the main substances that the human body requires combined with a high nutritious value.

It is milk fat that gives milk its creamy color. It consists of tiny globules, each enclosed by a skin of protein that are dispersed in the liquid. Milk sugar gives milk its sweet taste and when bacteria are present produces lactic acid. This in turn combines with the calcium in the milk that was previously combined with protein. The protein is thus freed and rises to the top and the milk becomes thick and sour. Proteins in milk that are important to the human organism can be roughly divided into casein, globulin and albumen. Of all the minerals and trace elements found in milk, calcium and phosphorus are the most important to man; however, the human body also needs potassium, sodium, magnesium, iron, and iodine. Milk is particularly rich in vitamins and its high content of the vitamins C, B_2, B_6, B_{12} is extremely important to growth.

Cow's milk, as it comes from the farm, is tested in the dairy for purity, quality, and presence of antibiotics or other chemical impurities. When it has passed these tests it is cooled to $39°F$, before being separated by centrifuges into skimmed milk and cream. Depending on whether the end product is to be full-fat, low-fat, or skimmed milk, the correct amount of fat is then replaced. The milk is then pasteurized, a process invented by and named after Louis Pasteur, for heating the milk sufficiently to kill off potentially dangerous bacilli but not so much as to destroy its nutritious qualities. Some milk is also homogenized, a process that makes the tiny fat globules even smaller so that they do not rise to the top when the milk is left to stand—i.e., no cream forms on the top of the milk. This milk is no lower in fat content, the fat is merely more finely distributed. Alongside methods of making milk keep better (sterilization, for example), various methods of milk conservation have been developed. This has produced the familiar condensed milk, both sweetened and unsweetened, as well as low-fat condensed milk. As the name indicates, this type of milk has been condensed to make it thicker.

Another type of condensed milk is obtained by evaporation; this is dried milk. Here again various fat contents are available in the form of dried full-fat milk, dried cream or dried skimmed milk. If you have to use dried milk in baking it should be mixed dry with the flour or diluted and used in the normal way; however, it is better to use fresh milk if possible.

Cream – something special

The very word *cream* has a special festive sound. It has always been used for entertaining, as a special treat at such times as birthdays, when cakes or desserts would be topped with whipped cream, and even today cream has lost none of its specialness. Anything made with cream or served with whipped cream has added goodness and flavor. Cream makes anything special. Rich Egyptians even took cream with them on their travels and the Greeks prized it highly. To come back to modern times, as we have said in the section on milk, the separation of the milk in a centrifuge produces large quantities of cream, for untreated milk usually contains more fat than is put back into the skimmed milk. Cream is thus the "skimmed" milk, fat. Regrettably, real "fresh cream" (untreated) is no longer generally available and its excellent flavor remains only a memory. Pasteurization (now a legal requirement) takes away the natural fresh taste of the cream and sacrifices flavor in favor of a purer product that will keep better. Creams vary in thickness and richness and there are laws governing the minimum butterfat content of creams: light cream 18 to 30 percent, whipping or heavy cream 36 to 40 percent, sour cream (soured with lactic acid) 18 to 20 percent, and half-and-half 10½ to 12 percent. The higher the butterfat content the less likely cream is to fall, and only whipping or heavy cream will whip successfully. Whipped in a chilled bowl and preferably in a cool room, cream should be of the right consistency and double or triple in volume after whipping. Take care not to overwhip or the cream will become granular in appearance and this cannot be rectified once it has occurred. As with milk, cream needs to be stored in a cool place or in the refrigerator.

For and against butter

It is not necessary here to go into the arguments between the medical profession and the butter producers about the merits and otherwise of fat, but it is an incontrovertible fact that butter improves both the flavor and consistency of patisserie. Many housewives prefer to replace butter with other fats, not only for economic or health reasons, but also because, with improved ingredients and production techniques, they can now give similar or in some cases better results. They are usually easier to work with and keep longer. Every cook will have to make up his or her own mind whether to use butter exclusively or whether to turn to other fats where possible. The argument concerns not only butter and margarine but other traditional fats too, such as oil, lard, and suet, each of which still has a place in some areas of cooking.

Butter has existed almost as long as the milk from which it is made. In the Bible Proverbs XXX, verse 33 reads "the churning of milk bringeth forth butter." In the Near East and Mediterranean it was long used as an ointment rather than a foodstuff, for with their olives and other oil-producing fruit the people of these regions had no shortage of fats. In cooler climes such as Europe, and Scandinavia in particular, butter was used much earlier as an edible fat. Butter was used as a food in Western Europe around A.D. 600. In the Middle Ages butter was prohibited on fast days because it was considered a luxury. Butter has the longest list of ingredients of all fats: it contains all the fatty acids that the body needs but cannot produce itself, together with proteins, minerals (particularly calcium and phosphorus) trace elements, and vitamins A, D, and E. Of all the fats butter is the most nourishing and the most easily digestible. Since its melting point is below body temperature butter fat is quickly absorbed by the body.

For centuries butter was made in a churn with either a rotating beater or a wooden disk on a handle that was pushed up and down. In this way cream was beaten and "pressed" until the globules of cream fat came together to form butter and separated from the "butter milk." The ball of butter was then kneaded and shaped. Many of the old molds are still around today and show the artistry with which the butter was presented. Today butter is still churned but in automatic, continuous machines.

Modern butter production guarantees absolutely constant quality. Today the various types of butter are produced by a process of pasteurization and are differentiated by the amount of salt added. Lightly salted butter is often ideal for shortcrust or yeast pastry that, in fruit flans for example, can take a little salt. A variation on butter that keeps well is butter fat. You can make it yourself by "rendering the butter down." The butter is melted so that the water it contains is evaporated and any bacteria are killed by heating, but the process also lowers the butter's protein, lactose, and salt content. Stored in a cool place in earthenware containers butter fat will keep for up to a year. Butter itself is extremely susceptible to heat, light, and smell, and is best stored in an airtight container in a cool, dark place.

Butter makes light pastry and much more besides, but other fats are just as necessary in baking. After butter comes margarine, which is available in three types. Block margarine is firmer and more elastic than butter and withstands kneading and beating better. It is excellent for shortcrust and flan pastry, for it gives a less crumbly pastry that keeps better. Creamed margarine is excellent for making custards and cream desserts for it whips well, has no taste of its own, and has good binding qualities. It whips easily with eggs, sugar, or *crème patissière*.

Spreading margarine should be elastic but of spreading texture. These qualities, which are especially desirable for puff pastry or croissant dough, are also present in suet or suetlike fats. Although these fats are easier to use than butter, they cannot give the delicate butter flavor we associate with, for example, puff pastry (and this becomes more noticeable if the pastry is not completely fresh). A large number of vegetable fats and oils have their uses in pastry making. They are particularly useful for deep frying cakes like doughnuts, for they can reach relatively high temperatures without burning. Lard is excellent for deep frying too. High quality lard can also be used in shortcrust pastry to make fruit flan cases.

Eggs

For thousands of years the egg has been a fertility symbol, the source of life, in every culture imaginable. In the myths of India or Ancient Egypt, in the religious ceremonies of Central America or Europe, people regarded the egg as a sign of fertility, of renewed life for nature and for themselves. And these associations have some truth in them for the egg provides one of the best possible sources of nourishment. An egg contains everything the body needs: protein, fat, carbohydrate, vitamins, minerals, and trace elements. The best in terms of nourishment and digestibility is the hen's egg, and it is this type alone that is discussed in this book. Eggs are an indispensable part of cake making. They are fundamentally very simple things with few component parts: shell, white, and yolk, but the essential differences between the yolk and the white and, the ease with which they can be separated, are important factors in their uses in the kitchen.

A Grade A large egg weighs about 2 ounces and has a nutritious value of between 75 and 90 calories. Egg white whisks easily and makes cakes lighter. During baking it solidifies to lock in the air. The effect of heat also produces several proteins. Egg yolk can be used as a glaze to improve the look of your baking. Because of its high lecithin content egg yolk emulsifies well, especially in mixtures rich in fat or sugar, in cream desserts and, naturally, ice cream. Adding egg yolks to cakes not only provides extra nourishment but also improves the texture, flavor, and color.

Because of their high nutritious and moisture content eggs will not keep long. For a long time attempts have been made to conserve eggs. At one time they were stored in a chalk and water solution, and lasted through the winter. Alternatively, they were coated with wax and stored in a cool place. Today eggs can be kept for relatively short periods in refrigerators. For longer periods there are two main methods of conserving eggs: by removing liquid to make dried eggs, or by freezing. Today, when the supply of fresh eggs is guaranteed all year round and when there are no seasonal price fluctuations, the need for these conserved products should be extremely rare. Occasionally it may make sense economically to use frozen egg white where large quantities are involved, for meringues for instance. Thaw frozen eggs or egg whites slowly (preferably under cold running water) and use them immediately.

The color of the shell, brown or white, is quite irrelevant and has nothing to do with the quality or taste of eggs. In a fresh egg the white consists of a thicker layer around the yolk and a slightly more runny part. If the egg white is completely runny it is a sign that the egg has been stored too long. The white should also be free from all impurities as should the yolk be free from flecks or impurities, but the color, pale or dark yellow, is not a sign of quality nor of the nutritional value of the yolk. Fresh eggs are first checked for external irregularities, illuminated to show up any internal impurities, and then weighed, sorted, and packed. Only Grade A large eggs have been used for the recipes in this book.

Honey

Long before the birth of Christ honey was considered the food of the gods, especially amongst the Indo-Germanic peoples. One of the earliest of man's artistic creations, a famous cave painting in eastern Spain, shows a figure searching for honey, climbing up to a cleft in the rock face where the bees had made their honeycomb. From the same period there is also evidence of beekeeping in Ancient Egypt where clay pots were stacked to form the first beehives. We also know that later the Germanic tribes made a delicious drink, mead, from honey. In the Carolingian period, around the tenth century, the "Lorscher Bees Blessing"—an exhortation to the bees to produce lots of honey in honor of the Virgin—was recorded in Old High German at a monastery in the Rhineland. As early as the time of Charlemagne, German emperor from A.D. 800 to 814, the

Emperor himself kept fifty swarms of bees and ordered the peasants to increase stocks of plants and flowers whose nectar was especially attractive to bees. Monasteries were forced to employ beekeepers since honey was used to sweeten foods and drinks and the wax was necessary for candles for both religious and secular purposes. Most medieval farms included a few beehives and honey remained the most widely used sweetener until well into the seventeenth century—for cane sugar was expensive and was available only for special occasions, even for the better-off families. Anton Tucher of Nuremburg who wrote a highly detailed book of household management between 1507 and 1517 revealed that he used very little cane sugar, but huge quantities of spices such as saffron, cloves, nutmeg, cinnamon, ginger, cardamom, almonds, and figs and honey. This book describes the great feast days in Tucher's household and reveals that it was only at the great New Year festival that "fine sugar" was used. For daily use honey was to remain the most common sweetener for a long time to come.

Honey is a sweet substance produced by bees as they take in nectar from flowers, transform it inside their bodies by enriching it with secretions, then emit it from their bodies into honeycombs where it is left to mature. Honey varies in smell, flavor, color, and texture according to where it is produced. Honey is differentiated first by the type of plant from which it is produced, so that there is clover, lime-tree, wood, or heather honey, to name but a few, and then by its geographical source. The choice of which honey to use depends on the individual's own taste. Blended honey, as well as the more exotic varieties, is readily obtainable and is reliable and consistent.

Fresh honey is clear and fluid, but with time it becomes slightly grainy, cloudy and thick. This has nothing to do with quality, however. Honey can be returned to its liquid state by slowly warming over hot water (not higher than 122°F). Sunlight encourages crystallization so honey should be stored in a well ventilated, dark cupboard.

Sugar—cane and beet

It is difficult for us to imagine a world without sugar, and yet until quite recently honey and sweet fruits were the only sweeteners available to the average man. Cane sugar is thought to have originated from New Guinea. Cane sugar was being cultivated thousands of years before the birth of Christ as Indian texts dating from 1400 B.C. reveal. From India the plant spread in every direction. Alexander the Great came across it in the Indus Valley in 327 B.C. and between A.D. 700 and 900 the Arabs brought cane sugar to the Mediterranean. Marco Polo also came across sugarcane in 1280 during one of his journeys to China. Later, sugarcane, which really only grows well in a hot, damp climate, was taken by the Spanish and Portuguese to the West Indies and Central and South America, while the Dutch established plantations in Indonesia. Eventually sugar was imported to Europe but for centuries it remained a luxury item for royalty and rich merchants.

The great revolution in cooking and baking came with the discovery of sugar beet. In 1747 A. S. Marggraf, a chemist in Berlin, discovered that the sugar obtained from beet was chemically identical to cane sugar, and his findings were later taken up by his pupil, F. G. Achard, in 1786. With financial help from King Friedrich Wilhelm III of Prussia, the first sugar beet factory was set up in Cunern in Silesia in 1802. By 1830 the cost of beet sugar was similar to that of cane sugar. Today sugar beet is grown throughout the world wherever sugarcane will not grow, even in the sub-tropics. Today around 55 percent of world sugar production consists of cane sugar and 45 percent of beet sugar.

Regardless of whether it comes from cane or beet, all sugar consists of 99 percent water-soluble carbohydrates and 1 percent water. Sugar types fall into two general categories, refined white sugar and the less fully refined brown sugar. The main types of white sugar are granulated sugar—the most common type of sugar to be found in the kitchen; lump or cube sugar is granulated sugar pressed together and used for hot drinks; caster sugar is a finer form of granulated sugar; icing sugar is very finely powdered white sugar that is the fastest dissolving form of sugar; and finally preserving sugar, which is used for making jams and jellies and has large, clear crystals.

Brown sugar can be subdivided into muscovado, molasses, and demerara. Many of the other brown sugars—often labeled light brown or soft dark brown—are actually fully refined white sugar tossed in syrup or molasses.

One other important type of sugar is called starch sugar, otherwise known as glucose syrup. This is obtained from potato or cornstarch and is a highly concentrated, refined syrup with a high glucose content. It is much used by the food industry in sweets, liqueurs, and jams. It is very elastic and binds excellently in marzipan or icings. This must not be confused with sugar syrup, which is sugar boiled in water to various concentrations, and which you make yourself.

Sugar is of course an important constituent of home baking and patisserie. Sugar as an ingredient makes cakes and pastries cook quicker; it browns, improves flavor and nutritional value, and helps food keep longer. It can be used for decoration in various ways, sprinkled onto cakes in the form of sugar crystals, dusted on as icing sugar, or to cover cakes in the form of icing. But sugar has one more outstanding quality: it conserves and gives rise to a whole range of products, jams, marmalades, jellies, candied fruit, and many more besides. Sugar is susceptible to damp and smells, so it must be stored in a dry place away from any contaminating odors.

There are also various types of syrup that can be used in baking. Golden syrup is a by-product of sugar refining. Molasses or dark treacle is the natural syrup drained from sugarcane. There also exist more basic syrups of which the most popular is maple syrup, which was used by the North American and Canadian Indians for hundreds of years. It is still used today, especially in the English-speaking world. The trees are tapped between February and late March and the sap is made into syrup. Maple syrup is used in sweets such as candy and caramels and also in cream desserts and highly spiced cakes.

Dried fruit

Since earliest times dried fruits have featured among winter provisions, particularly in temperate or cool climates where fresh fruit is available for only a relatively minor part of the year. Today, in the age of tinned and bottled fruit, freezers, and year-round supplies of fresh fruit, dried fruit has rather a hard time of it, and wrongly so, for it contains vitamins and minerals in concentrated form as well as high levels of fructose. Ripe fruit is carefully sorted and cleaned before being slowly dried in the air or, principally in California and Australia, in drying cabinets. Before drying, apples, pears, apricots, and peaches are cut into slices, rings, or halves. Plums, dates, figs, and bananas are dried whole. Fruits like apples and apricots that quickly turn brown are dipped in sulfur dioxide, and must be labeled "sulfurized."

For baking purposes dried fruit is used as fillings and toppings for pies and cakes, and is particularly associated with the fruit loaves baked for Advent and Christmas. Before use, dried fruit should be washed thoroughly and sulfurized fruit pre-boiled, and the water thrown away. Before stewing dried fruit it is usual to steep it overnight in water, as this brings out the flavor and makes the fruit swell.

We have not yet mentioned the main group of dried fruit: raisins, sultanas, and currants. These grow best in Greece, Crete, and Cyprus, in Iran, Turkey, and Spain, and in large quantities in the favorable climate of California.

Raisins can have seeds but are more usually seedless with a beautiful purplish-black color and are usually eaten uncooked. Vine raisins (with stems) come in several varieties. "Muscatel" from Spain and California, "Malagas" also from Spain, "Eleme" raisins from Greece, and "Rozaki" from Turkey. Raisins are also used for wine making, producing the popular Hungarian dessert wines.

Sultanas are always seedless, being golden yellow to light brown in color. They are the dried fruit of the extremely sweet, seedless "Sultana" grape. The finest sultanas come from Turkey and used to be known as "Smyrna raisins" as that was the part from which they were exported. Nowadays sultanas come from Greece, Crete, the Peloponnese, and of course Australia.

Currants are small, black seedless fruits with a very tender skin. The small-berried grapes from which they are made have been grown in the Greek Peloponnese since earliest times. Their name is a derivation from the town of Corinth, a port and trading town even for the Ancient Greeks.

How are these different grapes treated and dried? First the grapes are left on the vine until over ripe. Once picked they are left to dry in the open air (only a very small percentage is treated in drying cabinets). Drying takes from three to four weeks, during which time their water content is reduced to about 15 percent while the starches in the grape turn into fructose, which by the end of the process makes up around 70 percent of the dried fruit. After drying the fruit is automatically sorted by size, destalked, and washed.

Candied fruit

Everyone remembers grandmother's cooking with great pleasure. Candied orange and lemon peel and the bright colors provided by other candied fruit were a permanent feature of the cooking of our grandmothers' day.

Orange rind is not made from ordinary oranges but from Spanish bitter oranges commonly known as "Seville" oranges. The Seville orange tree (botanical name *Citrus aurantium*) used to be grown in the Orangeries of noble houses. It has small, deep-orange fruit with thick skins, the type used to make orange marmalade. Oil from the rind is also used in the making of liqueurs. These oranges are grown principally in Spain, Sicily, southern France, South Africa, and India.

Lemon rind comes from the mother of all citrus fruit, the lemon tree *Citrus medica*. This tree comes originally from the Far East, and is now grown in Greece, Corsica, Sicily, Brazil, and California.

Candied orange and lemon peels are both made by the same process. The skins of unripe fruit are halved and steeped in brine until transparent. Then they are soaked to remove the salt and placed in a concentrated sugar solution. The concentration is increased every day over a two-week period until the rind can soak up no more sugar or until the sugar content reaches at least 65 percent. If the peel is to be sold in whole pieces they are covered with a glaze of sugar, but there are also unglazed, chopped rinds available, which save the housewife a lot of time. If you buy peel in large pieces to chop yourself, however, the oils do not evaporate so quickly and the flavor and smell is better retained.

Nuts

It is difficult to imagine cakes and pastries without nuts in one form or another. We should remember that nuts are of great nutritional value and have formed part of man's basic diet for thousands of years.

Hazelnuts, botanical name *Corylus avellana*, are usually heart-shaped and medium-brown in color. They are widespread throughout the whole northern temperate zone, although cultivation for commercial purposes is mainly restricted to the Mediterranean countries, Turkey, Italy, and Spain. From Italy, with extensive growing areas in Campania, Sicily, and Piedmont, we import mainly hazelnuts in shells. Spain supplies mostly shelled nuts. Spanish hazelnuts do not go bad as quickly as other varieties for they contain only 50 percent fat (compared with 68 percent in Turkish nuts). Nuts in their shells naturally keep much longer than shelled nuts.

Walnuts (*Juglans regia*) grow in Southern Europe, through Central Asia to China. In Europe they are grown commercially in mild, warm areas. The main walnut exporters are Italy, France, Spain, Turkey, Romania, and California, the latter being the largest grower in the world. French walnuts are one of the most popular types and there are also "Welsh nuts" from west Wales.

Pecan nuts grow in the United States, usually in cotton-growing areas. The hickory tree from which they come (*Carya illinoinensis*) also gives excellent wood. Its nuts, which are sandy-red in color and an elongated oval in shape, are closely related to the walnut.

Pistachio nuts (*Pistacia vera*) flourish from the Mediterranean to Central Asia. The trees produce nuts only in alternate years and many live to over a hundred years of age. The nuts contain around 22 percent protein and 60 percent fat. Depending on variety the kernel may be pale green, yellow, or pink. The best nuts come from Turkey and Sicily.

Pine nut or kernel, the edible nut of the pine tree *Pinus pinea*, which grows principally in the Mediterranean region. The white nuts have an almondlike taste and are sometimes used as an almond substitute.

Coconut, large fruit of the coconut palm (*Cocos nucifera*). The nut floats excellently in water and this accounts for its presence on all tropical beaches and river banks throughout the world. The coconut as we know it, with its hard shell and tuft of fibers, is merely the ripe or unripe kernel of the fruit. The outer shell with its thick layer of fiber is removed at harvest. If the nut produces gurgling noises when shaken it still contains liquid (not to be confused with coconut milk) and is not yet ripe. In ripe nuts the liquid has completely evaporated. For home baking dessicated coconut (made by grating the fresh nut) is generally used. Coconut milk is sometimes used in special foreign dishes.

Peanut or groundnut (*Arachis hypogaea*) derives its name from the strange behavior of the parent plant: after pollination the flower stem droops, burrows into the ground for protection against the heat, and develops its fruit underground. In baking and sweetmaking, peanuts are used in the same way as other nuts, but they are processed commercially to produce oil.

Chestnut (*Castanea sativa*) prefers a warm climate and thrives in the Mediterranean region, Japan, China, India, Australia and the United States. They are related to the horse chestnut but should not be confused with them as the latter are not edible. Chestnuts are sold either fresh or roasted and are also available in cans and in puree form, either plain or sweetened.

Cashews look like an appendage to the Cashew apple (*Anacardium occidentale*), but are in fact the fruit while the "apple" is merely the stem! Cashews contain around 45 percent oil, 20 percent protein, and a high level of vitamin E. They come originally from Brazil, although today they are grown mainly in India and Africa. Since the oil has a rather sharp flavor they are usually shelled and then roasted in shallow trays. This is still done mainly by hand since mechanized shelling and roasting plants have only begun to be introduced in recent years.

Macadamia nut, botanical names *Macadamia tetraphylla* (rough shell) and *Macadamia integrifolia* (smooth shell), is quite an unfamiliar nut. It was discovered in Australia by John McAdam (hence its name). Trees over 15 years of age produce up to 112 pounds per tree per year. The nuts contain around 76 percent oil, 16 percent carbohydrate, and 9 percent protein. The kernels are tender and extremely flavorsome. They are usually sold shelled and roasted, either salted or unsalted.

Brazil or Paranuts get their name from the Brazilian province of Para which exports to every corner of the world. The Paranut tree (*Bertholletia excelsa*), one of the largest trees of the primeval forest, has made its home throughout the tropical forests of South America. From ten years of age the tree produces enormous pods of around 12 inches in diameter and $6\frac{3}{4}$ pounds in weight. Inside the pod may be as many as thirty nuts with extremely hard shells arranged like the segments of an orange. When the pods are ripe they fall to the ground, from where natives take them to collecting stations before they make their way to dealers or shelling plants. The nut kernel contains around 14 percent protein, 66 percent fat, essential minerals, and vitamins B_1, B_2, and C. Although they can be obtained all through the year, the nuts in their shell are most commonly seen at Christmas time.

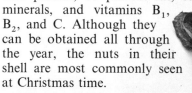

Almonds and marzipan

Sweet almonds are the fruit of a tree (*Prunus dulcis*) that originally came from Western and Central Asia. Today almond trees are grown in all temperate climates. The tree itself is quite hardy against frost but the blossoms are not, so this imposes a limit on its geographical distribution. Besides sweet almonds there are also bitter almonds from the almond tree *Prunus var. amara*, which produces pink rather than white flowers. Often, however, both bitter and sweet almonds are produced by the same tree and outside appearance gives no indication what type of fruit you have. Bitter almonds are usually smaller, more pointed, more concave than sweet ones, but this is not always the case. The bitter flavor is given by the carbohydrate amygdalin that easily separates into prussic acid. During baking the effect of heat kills off the prussic acid in the bitter almonds and they are quite safe to use in cooking.

Almond blossom in Sicily. In this region trees flower in February or March depending on altitude. The fresh green of the delightful spring landscape is then dotted with the white or pale pink blossom of the almond trees.

The almonds are ripe when the velvety outer shell splits to expose the hard shell of the nut. Almonds are usually shelled prior to export and come to our shops as shelled almonds in their cinnamon-colored skins. This thin skin is edible and in recipes that require "brown almonds" is grated with the nut to give additional flavor.

anything else could be induced to eat his delicious little marzipan cakes. Ryff even provides us with a recipe that has not really changed even today.

Anyone who feels so inclined can still make their own marzipan. The almonds are blanched, peeled (if they are in the skin), and crushed with icing sugar. Grated lemon peel and a little rose water is then worked in. When the mixture is smooth and glossy leave it to stand in a cool place for twelve hours. Then shape, decorate, and dry in a warm oven. But most people prefer not to have to go to so much trouble. Superior quality marzipan is produced commercially and most professional pastry cooks use it. It is best to use the white marzipan rather than the yellow as this produces a more professional-looking result. When buying marzipan check that it is still soft and has not dried out.

Harvesting almonds is still done by hand, at least by farmers in Mediterranean countries who have yet to introduce the mechanized methods of the large producers in California or Australia. The outer velvety husks are removed at the farm, often by children, before the almonds are dried in the warm autumn sun. Without drying, almonds would not keep, nor would they be accepted by the exporters as they would weigh heavier than dried almonds.

Almonds from Portugal, California, and Australia (from left to right). The latter two types have almost cornered the world market although they do not compare in quality with the traditional Italian varieties such as Ambrosia, Bari, or Sicilian almonds. Spain too produces excellent almonds in Valencia, Alicante, Malaga, and Mallorca.

Marzipan

is a delicacy that came to us from the Orient. We know that as early as A.D. 900 confectioners were making a sweetmeat from almonds and sugar and that it enjoyed great popularity. In later centuries the making of marzipan or almond paste was a province of the apothecary, particularly in Northern Europe. It is listed in apothecaries' books of the sixteenth century, together with sugared almonds, as a cure for sleeplessness.

Anton Tucher, a rich burgher of Nuremberg wrote in his household book of 1510 that he gave the provost of Wurzburg Cathedral two genuine crystal glasses and two marzipan cakes as a Christmas gift. Marzipan was a luxury that everyone wanted. This led to a ban in 1661 in Leipzig on giving marzipan as a christening present. Walther Ryff, who was first a doctor and surgeon in Strasburg and later court apothecary in Schwerin, published a book entitled *The Mirror and Government of Health* (published with beautiful woodcuts in 1571 in Frankfurt). Here he described how patients who could not eat

Almonds in everyday use. These prepared almonds make life much easier as shelling, chopping, etc., is extremely time-consuming. There is no noticeable difference in quality between prepared and fresh almonds although ready-prepared almonds are chopped or flaked much more uniformly than would be possible for the housewife, with the possible exception of ground almonds which can be easily ground in an electric grinder.

Cocoa and chocolate

Cocoa has been a highly prized commodity since earliest times and its importance is reflected in myths and legends. The chocolate drink of which it is the source played an important part in the lives of the upper classes among the Mayas, Incas, and Aztecs: Only the chosen few close to the king were allowed this drink, which was flavored with vanilla, ginger, and other spices. It was known as theobroma, the food of the gods. Cocoa beans were in themselves a valuable means of currency. When Cortez conquered part of Mexico in 1519 he found extensive plantations of cocoa trees, which he described to the Emperor Charles V in a letter dated October 30, 1520. He also described the drink made from cocoa beans as stimulating and extremely nutritious, having savored it at the court of Montezuma, the Mexican emperor. Besides the stimulant theobromine, a caffeinelike alkaloid, the cocoa bean contains around 54 percent fat, 14 percent protein, and 7 percent starch. Cocoa is more a food than a drink.

In 1528 Cortez brought the first cocoa beans and the utensils needed for their presentation back to Spain, and the drink was found to be delicious with the addition of cane sugar. When the princess Anne of Austria married into the French royal family the drink passed to France and in 1657 the first chocolate shop was opened in London. Chocolate made its way to Germany in 1640, but as a medicine supplied by apothecaries.

The cocoa tree (*Theobroma cacao*) is a tree of the tropical rain forest that needs protection from sun and wind together with a lot of moisture and warmth. The main areas of production all lie along the equator: Mexico, Venezuela, Ecuador, Brazil, and equatorial West Africa.

The flowers and fruit of the tree are not carried on the branches but grow on short stalks directly out of the trunk. Throughout the year any one tree will display a combination of both flowers and unripe or ripe cocoa pods. The fruits take four to six months to ripen, growing into fat cucumbers around 8 inches in length. They are chopped off the tree with a large, curved knife and taken to a collection point where they are cut open and the beans and fruit pulp removed. This is piled into large heaps in the open air or fermented in large boxes, during which time the beans lose their bitterness, increase in flavor, and turn brown. After six days the beans are washed and left in the sun for a few more days to dry before being sorted, sacked up, and transported. All cleansing, roasting, and shelling is done at source. The high fat content produces a thick paste when the beans are ground and in order to turn this into cocoa powder half the fat content, cocoa butter, must be pressed out before the mixture will dry. Drying leaves a low-fat "cocoa cake" which is again ground to give the familiar cocoa powder.

A secret recipe is used to make chocolate, in which varying quantities of sugar, extra cocoa butter (which looks like cream-colored butter), spices, and milk are added to the cocoa powder. Of course, quality depends to a great extent on the proportion of high and low quality cocoa beans (Criollo and Forastero beans) used in the original cocoa powder. After several processes in which the mixture is rolled and compressed, the mixture becomes smooth and creamy and is ready to be turned into the many forms that chocolate takes—chocolate bars or chocolates filled with nuts, fruit, cream, etc. This basic chocolate mixture also finds its way to bakers and confectioners in block form and should not be confused with its substitute, cooking chocolate. The chocolate we are talking about is pure chocolate of top quality whereas cooking chocolate, although cheaper in price and easier to use, is mainly vegetable fat with a low cocoa content. Pure chocolate is unbeatable for both flavor and smell.

Alcohol, flavoring with spirit

Is there anyone who has not experienced the wonderful smell that fills the room as cakes and pastries are set upon the table? This often includes the tempting aroma of rum, brandy, or other spirit with which the filling has been flavored or the sponge soaked. *Rum* is an ideal alcoholic flavoring for cakes and pastries. It blends well with almost any other ingredient and emphasizes the special quality of many cakes. But the rum itself must be of top quality. *Arrak* is a spirit made from rice, palm-wine, or molasses. It is good for flavoring icings and also to pour over dry cakes. *Cognac*, like all brandies, is excellent for flavoring a wide variety of cakes. A large number of *liqueurs* are excellent as food flavorings, particularly for light cream desserts and whipped cream. Fruit liqueurs especially can help bring out a particular flavor; try adding a dash of orange liqueur to an orange cream. The same applies to *fruit brandies*, the most obvious example being the combination of cherries and kirsch in Black Forest Gâteau. Raspberries with raspberry brandy produces equally good results, but it is important to use a good quality brandy, mild but full of flavor. *Wines* too are an excellent source of flavor, especially as the basis of cream desserts, but here again high quality is paramount.

Aromatics and spices

Some of the best natural aromatics are provided by the ethereal oils in the skins of citrus fruit. These were used to flavor food in the Mediterranean region for many centuries. Today it is important to scrub the fruit before use to remove the waxy coating. The peel of oranges, lemons, and limes make ideal seasoners, either grated with a fine grater or sugar cube or peeled into paper-thin strips.

Orange-flower water is obtained by distilling fresh, unopened blossoms, whereas oil, which is mainly used in the manufacture of liqueurs, is a distillation of the opened, dried blossoms. Orange-flower water is used for flavoring sponge cakes, creams, and icing.

Rose-water is a mixture of rose and water, with only 1 drop of oil per 8 fluid ounces of water. It is a by-product of rose oil production. Since rose-water has a very short life span most bakers tend to make their own from rose oil, water, and a little alcohol. Rose-water's main use is in the making of marzipan, but it is also used for flavoring sponges and icings.

Allspice, *Pimenta officinalis*, is related to the clove but comes from the New World, hence its alternative name of Jamaican pepper. It combines the flavors of cloves, pepper, and nutmeg and is used in baking mainly in spice cake and at Christmas time.

Aniseed is the dried seed of *Pimpinella anisum*, a member of the *umbelliferae* family. It is one of the most ancient spices in the world and is thought to have originated in Egypt. As well as its use in liqueurs, cough mixtures, and liquorice, aniseed is used in straws, biscuits, bread, and extensively in Christmas baking.

Star aniseed, botanical name *Illicium verum*, has been used as a spice in China for a thousand years. Because of its ethereal oils it should be used sparingly as it is stronger than aniseed. Star aniseed is usually sold in powder form.

Bitter almonds come from the pink-flowered cherry tree, *Prumus amara*, but they can also appear on white trees. Bitter almonds are used in combination with sweet almonds in any cake that requires a strong almond flavor, and of course the same applies to creams and fillings.

Cardamom, botanical name *Elettaria cardamomum*, the seed of an Indian shrub that was a popular spice in Roman times. For baking it is included in the spices for gingerbread and can be used occasionally for flavoring yeast or croissant dough.

Cinnamon is a spice that comes from two types of evergreen cinnamon tree. Ceylon cinnamon, *Cinnamomum zeylanicum*, has a thin, pale-brown bark that has a sweet, mild taste. Its excellent flavor is preferable whenever you want to use cinnamon in isolation. Cassia cinnamon, *Cinnamomum aromaticum* or *C. cassia*, the best of which is grown in Sumatra, is darker in color and stronger in flavor. This type is ideal for mixed spice, for spice cake, gingerbread, or honey cake.

Cloves are the dried flower buds of the East Asian clove tree, *Syzgium aromaticum*, which has been known in Western Europe since the Middle Ages. Ground cloves are used in baking, generally in gingerbread and Christmas specialties. Whole cloves are employed when bottling fruit and in pies, most notably in apple pie.

Coffee is an excellent flavoring for creams, fillings, and icings (especially combined with vanilla). To keep down the liquid content, instant coffee is often used. Mocha is a type of coffee bean and although the term mocha technically means flavored with coffee, it is more often used to denote a coffee and chocolate flavored mixture.

Coriander, botanical name *Coriandrum sativum*, the dried seeds are similar in taste to aniseed. In baking it is used mainly for Christmas specialties and bread.

Fennel, botanical name *Foeniculum vulgare*, was regarded as an herb to cure all ills for centuries. Like aniseed, its seeds contain ethereal oils. In baking, fennel is used to season a variety of cakes and loaves.

Ginger, botanical name *Zingiber officinale*, comes from the root of a tropical reed. Fresh or dried, preserved or ground, in any of its forms it gives baking a unique flavor. Excellent in a variety of fruit flans and essential for gingerbread.

Mace and nutmeg, *Myristica fragans*, grows in the tropical rain forests of Asia. The pretty outer coating is used to make mace while the nutmeg or seed is dried slowly. Today they are widely used in baking and desserts, although in some countries their use is restricted mainly to spice cake and Christmas baking.

Pepper, *Piper nigrum*, is one of the oldest tropical seasonings. In baking only white pepper is utilized, in pepper cake and in the spices that go into gingerbread.

Poppy seed, *Papaver somniferum*, comes from Asia Minor. Its main role today is a source of oil. In baking, the seeds are used whole for decoration or ground in flan fillings.

Saffron, *Crocus sativus*, is an ancient Asiatic plant that provides both a spice and a colorant. The spice itself comes from the stamens of the flower. Small cakes, especially sponges, are often colored with saffron.

Vanilla, *Vanilla planifolia*, is an orchid from the tropical forests of Mexico. The best vanilla now comes from the islands of Madagascar, Reunion, and Mauritius. To produce the spice the unripe fruit pods are gathered and fermented. Vanilla is widely used in cake mixes, cream fillings, and is delicious with chocolate.

Basic Recipes

The ingredients and methods used to make basic cakes and pastries are described in this chapter. Many of them are sufficient in themselves and are delicious just as they are. Others greatly benefit by the addition of fillings, icings, and decorations. These are the finishing touches whose practice provides one of the most interesting aspects of home baking, and whose mastery can help to raise the standard of home cooking to a professional level.

In this chapter you will find easy-to-follow, step-by-step instructions for making the basic pastries and sponges. These are the methods that will be referred to in later chapters of this book. It is no good buying the best ingredients unless you know how to use them properly, so these first recipes should be tried and mastered before you move on to the later chapters.

The use of traditional cooking methods and fresh ingredients is essential to this chapter. This does not, of course, rule out the use of kitchen machines such as electric whisks or food processors, but it must be emphasized that all cooks should have an idea of how a particular mixture or dough should look and feel—and this is best gained by literally trying your hand at it first.

It is useful to remember to assemble all the necessary equipment before you begin to bake. Read through the recipe before starting to make sure that you have all the required equipment and ingredients. If the pan or baking tray is to be lined with parchment paper or greased and floured, do this first. This will prevent any delay before baking once the mixture is ready—a point that can be important with a whisked mixture that could fall if left for too long before cooking.

The oven should always be preheated; depending on the type of oven, it will generally take from 15–20 minutes to reach the required temperature. Remember that the shelves should be placed at the right position in the oven before switching it on. As a general rule yeast and pastry mixtures should be cooked toward the top of the oven, cakes and tarts should be placed toward the center, while meringues should be cooked as low down in the oven as possible to prevent browning during the long cooking time. Do not open the oven door during the early cooking stage and avoid opening it too frequently during the course of baking.

Baking is an exact science

Successful baking depends primarily on following the instructions provided and above all on the correct proportions of the separate ingredients. Never try to rely on the judgment of your eye or hand. Accurate weighing scales are an essential for good results. It is helpful to buy a pair which shows both American Standard and metric measures. The same accuracy is necessary with liquids. For larger quantities you will need a glass measuring cup. A glass cup will enable you to see clearly that the right amount of liquid is reached. Plastic cups are similarly useful but can be distorted by heat and hot liquids, thereby often altering in shape and accuracy. The common measurements such as teaspoon or tablespoon are always for a level, not heaped, spoonful. A set of measuring spoons is an essential addition to kitchen equipment and will show accurately a $\frac{1}{4}$ teaspoon to a tablespoon. Very small quantities, such as salt or spices, are best indicated by "pinch."

Basic equipment

There are naturally a few pieces of equipment that are essential for baking, one of these being an oven. This does not mean you have to have the sort of expensive oven used by professional chefs: A reliable oven without fancy trimmings will do the job just as well. Anyone with a serious interest in learning to cook should forget about electric mixers and food processors to start off with, for it is only by working with your hands that you can get a real feel for the products you are using. Eventually experience will show which processes can be done by machine without affecting the quality of the final outcome.

A good set of basic equipment should include the following. For mixing pastries and doughs, a flat, plastic, or preferably marble, worktop. A marble sheet is particularly useful when working with sugar or chocolate. A large wooden rolling pin. The plain rolling pin (without handles) is best. Basins and bowls. A set of three round-bottomed bowls in assorted sizes is all you need for beating cake mixtures in, although the more rounded stainless steel or copper bowls, 10 to 12 inches in diameter, are better still. These allow lots of room for using a balloon whisk and have the added advantage of being able to go directly on the stove without having to stand in water. Several smaller basins are useful for mixing icing, melting chocolate, etc.

Whisks in various sizes. Balloon whisks are useful as well as an electric whisk. You will also need three or four wooden or plastic spoons (or spatulas) in different sizes.

A wooden-framed sieve may sound old-fashioned but is ideal (though regrettably it can be difficult to find nowadays). A sieve like this makes easy work of sifting together flour, cornstarch and other ingredients, whereas it can be a long process in a small plastic sieve.

Knives needed for baking include a serrated knife (10 inches long), a fruit knife, and particularly two or three palette knives in assorted sizes. These are the pastry cook's universal tool. A flexible palette knife is by far the best thing to use to ice a large area. A chopping knife will also be necessary to chop dried fruit, etc. You should aim at good quality even with your small kitchen utensils: pastry brush; plastic or hard rubber spatula with wooden handle for scraping mixing bowls; plain and fluted pastry cutters and wheel. Also, piping bags in various sizes and a selection of plain and star nozzles.

These are all the essential utensils. There are a host of small implements used in cake decoration but these are by no means necessary. With a little imagination you can produce excellent designs with the minimum of piping nozzles and cutters. Just think of the effects that can be achieved with a piping tube made solely of parchment paper. Nor do you really need a large number of cake pans, although with the large choice and different varieties that are available it seems almost impossible to avoid amassing quite a collection.

Baking pans

Baking pans make an important contribution to the final result in baking, and you don't necessarily have to go for the most expensive. For sponges, yeast mixtures, and most cakes you can now get very inexpensive pans in aluminum or tinplate, both of which are excellent conductors of heat, or in sheet-iron. Pans with a nonstick plastic coating are now widely available and these give excellent results in the oven. Traditionally, the best materials for baking pans used to be copper and good-quality ceramic. These were fired at over $1,832°$F and are excellent for deep cakes. They can sometimes be obtained today and one advantage is that both copper and ceramic containers are extremely attractive to display in the kitchen.

For sponge bases there are a variety of pans you can use. The most popular for home use are springform pans. Professional chefs use plain aluminum rings, which are simpler and better since they produce a more even sponge. French chefs prefer ordinary pans with slanting edges, and with these it is essential to cover the base with parchment paper so that the sponge will come out easily once you have cut around the sides.

Flan rings, which can be covered with parchment paper on the bottom and placed on a baking sheet ready to be filled with batter, are preferred to springform pans by most professional bakers. (See step-by-step instructions on page 29.) Once the sponge cake has been baked, it can be removed from the flan ring easily by peeling off the paper and running a knife around the inside of the ring.

Although electric mixers can be helpful in the beating of cake batters, professional chefs prefer to use a hand-held whisk. The correct method for beating a mixture with a whisk is illustrated on pages 28–29. When beating by hand, the mixture is whipped in a vertical direction first and then beaten horizontally in a circular motion to loosen batter that may stick to the sides of the bowl. This method provides the best results. On the other hand, an electric mixer rotates in a horizontal direction only. Although the speed of the beaters can be varied the direction in which the beaters move cannot. Since the beaters of the average electric mixer are smaller than the balloon whisk used to beat cake mixtures, the mixture on the sides of the bowl is not mixed adequately. As a result, an electric mixer does not do as good a job of mixing as can be done with a hand-held whisk, and therefore the results are not as satisfactory. Large professional electric mixers have beaters that rotate both vertically and horizontally. In addition, the shape of the bowl makes it possible for the mixture around the sides of the bowl to be moved back in toward the center of the bowl, and the results are close to those achieved by hand mixing.

The oven

It is worth considering carefully the type of oven that you require. Generally it is better to buy a larger oven if possible because otherwise there can be problems when entertaining or at such times as Christmas when the oven is in almost constant use. Nowadays one can buy either free-standing or built in cookers; those with one or two ovens (the smaller of which often converts to a grill); and the choice will be between gas, electricity, or a convection oven. The manufacturer's instructions should be read through and carefully followed to ensure good results. However the majority of ovens will vary slightly and there can be slight irregularities in the temperature and the only way to get to know your oven is to test-bake various kinds of pastry and cake mixtures.

Preheating the oven?

This is a question that comes up repeatedly and that has been revived once more by the convection or hot air ovens. One should work on the basic principle that the oven should be at the required temperature when the baking goes into the oven. You will need to check on the manufacturer's instructions how long your oven takes to preheat since it varies from model to model. Electric ovens take 10 to 20 minutes to reach temperatures around 400°F; gas ovens take only a few minutes, while the circulatory ovens are even quicker. It is essential to preheat the oven and all the recipes in this book work on this assumption. Equally problematical can be some manufacturers' instructions to take advantage of the after-heat of the oven— i.e., to turn off the oven before the food is completely done and to allow it to finish cooking in the slowly cooling oven. This is a highly questionable way of saving energy and can have an extremely adverse effect on your baking. Be sure to take food out of the oven and not merely to turn the oven off at the end of the recommended time. There are a few exceptions to this rule but if this is the case it will be made clear in the recipe in question.

Correct temperatures and baking times

In principle all baking recipes should be followed as closely as possible and this is certainly true of the measuring of ingredients and method of preparation. The weak link in any recipe, however, is always the recommended temperature and baking time. The problems with ovens, as discussed above, may affect the recommendation made in the recipe and experience alone can show when this is the case. The longer the baking time the more necessary it will be to check times and temperatures from experience. With any new recipe you try it is a good idea to make a note of the exact temperature and baking time, even though this may involve writing in the margin of a brand new cook book. The next time you make the same recipe you will be glad for the guidance this provides. Small and very thin cakes and pastries can be cooked more or less "by sight"; this means that when you think the cakes will be almost ready you keep an eye on them until they look done. If your oven has a window this is quite simple as you can see when the cakes are done without having to open the door. If there is no window you will have to keep opening the oven door to have a look at the cakes. Don't worry too much about this as cakes are not likely to fall during the final stages of baking.

Genoise Mixture

(a basic sponge mixture)

Sponge mixtures, of which the Genoise sponge is the most well known, can be mixed warm (see step-by-step photos) or cold. When they are mixed cold, egg yolks and egg whites are added separately. (See small photos on page 29 for Dobos Mixture.) The higher the sugar content, the denser and firmer the sponge will be. Reducing the amount of sugar will make a sponge lighter, but also more fragile. When sponges are mixed warm instead of cold, the sugar dissolves more quickly and the eggs are more easily incorporated into the mixture. The egg whites will bind better with flour and cornstarch during baking, and the final result will be a dense and stable sponge. The recipe below makes an excellent light sponge with success more or less guaranteed!

5 eggs
2 egg yolks
¾ cup sugar
½ teaspoon grated lemon peel
1 cup cake flour
¼ cup cornstarch
6 tablespoons melted and clarified butter

10-inch deep flan ring or springform pan

Preheat oven to 375°F

1 **Place eggs**, egg yolks, sugar, and lemon peel in large mixing bowl over (not in) pan of barely simmering water. Let mixture stand until eggs are just warm to the touch, about 5 minutes.

2 **Beat mixture** over warm water with balloon whisk until thick and lemon-colored, about 3 minutes. Beat vigorously and in a steady pattern.

3 **Remove bowl** from pan of water and place on flat work surface. Continue beating until mixture is cool, 10 to 12 minutes. Mixture should be thick and tripled in volume.

4 **Sift flour and cornstarch** onto sheet of waxed paper. Fold paper in half lengthwise and gradually sprinkle flour mixture over egg mixture, folding it in thoroughly with spatula.

5 **Gradually add warm clarified butter** in slow, steady stream, stirring with spatula. Stir until butter is thoroughly incorporated and no streaks remain. Mixture should be smooth and uniform.

6 **Fold large sheet of parchment paper** in half to make double thickness. Place ungreased flan ring on paper and fold and crimp paper around base of ring to seal. Place on baking sheet.

7 **Pour batter into ring slowly.** Check for air bubbles and stir down if present. Ring should be filled to within ¾ inch of rim.

8 **Smooth surface of mixture**, pushing some of mixture toward outer edge of ring to prevent center from rising during baking and to produce flat surface on cake.

9 **Bake sponge in preheated oven** 30 to 35 minutes or until center springs back when lightly pressed. Let stand 5 minutes.

10 **Sprinkle clean baking sheet** with flour to prevent sponge from sticking and turn sponge upside down onto baking sheet to give sponge flat top. Cool completely. Peel off paper and run sharp knife around inside of ring to release sponge. Sponge can be cut into several layers and filled and frosted as desired.

Dobos Mixture: This recipe is an example of a fat-free sponge that is mixed cold rather than over a pan of simmering water. Ingredients: 9 eggs, separated; 2 cups confectioners' sugar; 1¼ cups cake flour, sifted. Beat egg yolks and 1 cup confectioner's sugar in large bowl until thick and lemon-colored. Beat egg whites in separate large bowl until stiff peaks form. Gradually add remaining 1 cup confectioners' sugar and continue beating until stiff and glossy. Stir about one quarter of beaten egg whites into egg yolk mixture until well blended. Fold in remaining egg whites alternately with sifted cake flour. Cut six to eight sheets of parchment paper, depending on how many layers you want to make. Draw 10-inch circles on sheets and place parchment sheets on baking sheets. Divide sponge mixture into six to eight portions. Spread one portion of sponge mixture over each parchment circle, covering circles completely and spreading mixture evenly. Bake layers as promptly as possible, one after the other, in preheated 425°F oven about 6 to 8 minutes. (You will have to watch these thin layers very carefully to prevent them from burning.) Layers must be baked promptly because batter will lose volume and begin to weep if allowed to stand too long. Remove layers from baking sheets as soon as they come out of oven. Cool without removing paper. Follow directions for removing paper in recipes (pages 142–143).

Chocolate Genoise

The step-by-step instructions on right are an excellent example of a sponge cake mixed cold. The egg yolks and egg whites are mixed separately in the usual manner but, in this case, the fat and flavoring are added ahead of the beaten egg whites. Since many flavorings such as nuts and chocolate contain fat, it is important to add them at the correct time. Nuts, melted chocolate, and melted butter must be added to the egg yolk mixture before the beaten egg whites are folded in. If the fat is added after the beaten egg whites, as in the Genoise sponge, the egg whites will begin to collapse. To make a light sponge cake, it is important to fold the beaten egg whites into the egg yolk mixture as gently and thoroughly as possible. When the egg whites are folded in properly, the volume of the mixture will increase considerably, and the result will be a light sponge cake.

8 eggs, separated
$\frac{3}{4}$ cup sugar
$\frac{1}{4}$ cup ground nuts (walnuts, pecans, or almonds)
$\frac{1}{2}$ teaspoon vanilla
$2\frac{1}{2}$ ounces unsweetened chocolate
6 tablespoons melted and clarified butter
$\frac{1}{3}$ cup cake flour
1 cup fine dry bread crumbs

10-inch springform pan

Preheat oven to 375°F

Classic Chocolate Mixture

Mix either warm (see below) or cold, following steps illustrated for Genoise Mixture on pages 28–29.

7 eggs
1 cup sugar
1 cup cake flour
$\frac{1}{2}$ cup unsweetened cocoa
$\frac{1}{3}$ cup cornstarch
5 tablespoons melted and clarified butter

10-inch springform pan or deep flan ring

Preheat oven to 375°F

Warm eggs and sugar in large bowl over pan of barely simmering water. Beat mixture until thick and lemon-colored. Remove bowl and beat until mixture is cool. Sift flour, cocoa, and cornstarch, and gradually fold into egg mixture. Fold in melted butter. Pour into parchment lined pan and smooth top. Bake 35 to 40 minutes or until center springs back when lightly pressed.

1 **Place egg yolks**, half the sugar, ground nuts, and vanilla in large mixing bowl.

2 **Beat egg yolk mixture** with balloon whisk in circular motion until mixture doubles in volume. If you prefer, use an electric mixer set at medium speed.

6 **Gently fold in remaining beaten egg whites**, stirring as little as possible. Combine flour and bread crumbs and sprinkle over batter. Fold in until mixture is smooth and uniform.

7 **Line bottom of** springform pan with circle of parchment paper. (Do not grease sides of pan because greasing will cause cake to pull away from sides of pan and fall during baking.) Pour sponge mixture into prepared pan.

Sponge Roll

4 egg whites
$\frac{1}{2}$ cup granulated sugar
8 egg yolks
$\frac{1}{4}$ teaspoon salt
1 teaspoon grated lemon peel
$\frac{2}{3}$ cup cake flour
3 tablespoons cornstarch
confectioners' sugar
$1\frac{1}{2}$ cups flavored whipped cream, page 52, or buttercream, pages 54–55

16 × 12-inch jelly-roll pan

Preheat oven to 450°F

In this recipe the beaten egg whites are not folded into the egg yolks. Instead, it is mixed the other way around. Bake the sponge roll 8 to 10 minutes, but check it after 6 minutes.

1 **Beat egg whites and granulated sugar** until stiff peaks form. Stir egg yolks, salt, and lemon peel together until blended. Gradually fold egg yolk mixture into beaten egg whites. Sift flour and cornstarch and fold into mixture.

3 **Melt chocolate** in top of small double boiler set over (not in) pan of simmering water. Stir until chocolate is melted and smooth. Remove top of double boiler and pour melted chocolate into egg yolk mixture in thin, steady stream.

4 **Stir until mixture** is thoroughly blended and uniform in color. Pour melted butter into mixture in slow, steady trickle. Stir until blended. Beat egg whites in large bowl with remaining sugar until stiff peaks form.

5 **Spoon about one third of beaten eggs** on top of chocolate mixture and stir with wooden spoon. Stir in circular direction, turning bowl in opposite direction. Blend egg whites thoroughly into chocolate egg yolk mixture.

8 **Smooth top of mixture** with small plastic scraper, making surface flat or allowing it to slope up sides of pan slightly (see Genoise sponge, page 29). Bake 35 to 40 minutes or until center springs back when lightly pressed. Cool as directed for Genoise sponge. Sponge cake may be cut into several layers and filled and frosted as desired.

2 **Line bottom of jelly-roll pan** with parchment paper. Spread mixture evenly over bottom of pan with long bent spatula or pastry scraper. Bake in preheated oven 8 to 10 minutes or until center of cake springs back when lightly pressed.

3 **Sprinkle towel** with confectioners' sugar. Run tip of knife around inside edge of pan to release cake. Invert cake onto towel. Peel off paper and roll cake in towel, jelly-roll style. Alternatively, leave cake flat and cover with damp towel.

4 **Unroll cake when completely cool.** Spread flavored whipped cream or buttercream over cake to within ¼ inch of edges. Reroll without towel and dust with confectioners' sugar or spread with icing.

Sponge Mixture

for Marguerite cake

There are three methods for preparing sponge cakes:

1. Warm melted butter is added to other ingredients as the final step in preparing the mixture. This is the method used to make Madeira Cake and other plain cakes.

2. The mixture is prepared in four steps. Egg yolks are beaten with sugar; flour and cornstarch are creamed with butter; egg whites are stiffly beaten. Finally the three mixtures are combined in the order given in the recipe.

3. The butter is creamed with part of the sugar, and egg yolks are beaten in gradually. Beaten egg whites are folded into the mixture with flour and cornstarch. This is the method used in the following recipe for Marguerite Cake.

Marguerite Cake

butter and sponge cake crumbs for pan
1 cup (2 sticks) butter, softened
3½ ounces (½ of 7 ounce package) almond paste
¾ cup sugar
½ vanilla bean
6 eggs, separated
1 cup cake flour
9 tablespoons (½ cup plus 1 tablespoon) cornstarch

10-inch daisy pattern cake pan or decorative cake mold

Preheat oven to 375°F

Grease pan and sprinkle with sponge cake crumbs. Beat butter, almond paste, and ¼ cup sugar in large bowl until mixture is smooth and soft. Scrape pith from vanilla bean and stir into butter mixture. Add egg yolks gradually and beat until thoroughly combined. Beat egg whites with remaining ½ cup sugar until stiff peaks form. Stir about one third of beaten egg whites into butter mixture, stirring until completely blended and mixture is lightened. Sift flour and cornstarch and fold into butter mixture alternately with remaining beaten egg whites. Spoon mixture into prepared pan and smooth surface.

1 **Beat butter**, almond paste, and ¼ cup sugar in large bowl until smooth and fluffy. Scrape pith from vanilla bean and stir into butter mixture. Add egg yolks gradually, beating until well combined.

2 **Beat egg whites** with remaining ½ cup sugar until stiff peaks form. Stir about one third of beaten egg whites into butter mixture until well blended.

3 **Sift flour and cornstarch**. Fold into butter mixture alternately with remaining beaten egg whites.

4 **Grease pan** and sprinkle with sponge cake crumbs. Tap out excess crumbs. Spoon mixture into prepared pan.

5 **Smooth top of mixture** with spatula, bringing mixture slightly up at outer edge to prevent center from rising during baking. Bake in preheated oven 45 minutes or until cake tester inserted in center of cake comes out clean. Cool in pan on wire rack 15 minutes. Invert from pan and cool completely on wire rack.

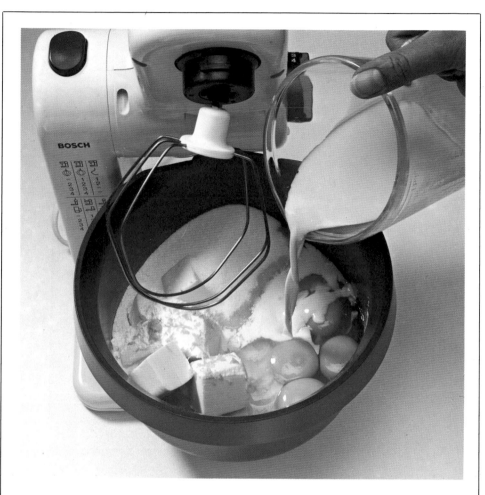

Quick Sponge Cake

This is another basic sponge mixture, but one that is much simpler to make than the Marguerite Cake on page 32. The addition of baking powder is what makes this cake so popular and easy to make.

With modern kitchen equipment (standing mixers, hand mixers, or food processors) a basic sponge mixture for a Madeira or marble cake can be made in a matter of minutes. The only drawback is the unavoidable taste the baking powder gives the cake, but it is outweighed by the advantages of this quick method. The flavor of the cake can be varied by adding ingredients such as nuts or dried fruit. The consistency of the cake can be changed by substituting cornstarch for part of the flour.

There are two ways in which the mixture can be prepared. In one method, the butter, sugar, eggs, and flavorings are beaten until light and fluffy. The flour and baking powder are sifted and then added alternately with milk to the creamed butter mixture. In the second method all the ingredients are mixed in one step.

Ingredients for basic recipe: 3 cups all-purpose flour; 4 teaspoons baking powder; $\frac{1}{2}$ teaspoon salt; 4 eggs; 1 cup (2 sticks) butter, softened; $1\frac{3}{4}$ cups sugar; 1 teaspoon vanilla; $1\frac{1}{4}$ cups milk. Sift flour, baking powder, and salt into large mixer bowl. Add remaining ingredients. Beat at low speed 2 minutes until all ingredients are well blended, scraping down sides of bowl occasionally. Increase speed to high and beat 2 minutes, scraping down sides of bowl occasionally. Fold in nuts or dried fruit, if using. Divide mixture evenly between two greased and floured 10-inch round cake pans. Bake in preheated 350°F oven 40 to 45 minutes or until centers of cakes spring back when lightly pressed. Cool in pans on wire racks 10 minutes. Remove from pans and cool completely. Fill and frost as desired.

Meringue Layers

Meringues are one of the most important basic mixtures used in cakes and pastries. They can be varied by changing the amount of sugar or by flavoring them with coffee, chocolate, ground almonds, or ground hazelnuts. Meringues can be used as a topping for fruit flans, or can be piped and used for decoration.

> 1 cup egg whites (about 8 egg whites)
> 1 cup superfine sugar
> 2 cups sifted confectioners' sugar

Prepare meringue according to step-by-step photos. Flat meringue bases should be baked about 3 hours at 225°F with oven door slightly ajar. Dry in oven overnight with oven turned off. This recipe will make four 8- or 9-inch bases. Pipe meringue onto parchment paper with ½-inch plain tip (#7). Meringues can be stored in airtight containers one to two weeks in a cool, dry place.

1 **Although a balloon whisk** is best for beating egg whites, an electric mixer will make the job much easier. Set mixer at medium speed and beat until egg whites begin to form soft peaks. Add superfine sugar gradually and increase mixer speed to high.

2 **Turn mixer to lowest setting** while sugar is added in order to prevent sugar from spraying out of bowl. After each addition of sugar, turn mixer back to high. Repeat process until all superfine sugar has been incorporated.

3 **When all superfine sugar has been added,** turn mixer to medium speed and continue beating until egg whites are smooth, white, and shiny. They should be firm enough to remain in bowl when bowl is turned upside down. Rub a little meringue between your fingertips; it should be smooth and not grainy.

4 **Fold in confectioners' sugar** with wooden spoon. Mixture will not fall at this stage, so you can fold vigorously.

5 **Fit large pastry bag** with ½-inch plain tip (#7). Fold down sides of bag to make cuff. Spoon meringue into bag with rubber spatula, shaking meringue down into bag. Twist top of bag closed. Pipe meringue into four 8- or 9-inch bases.

Japonais

Meringue mixture with almonds or other nuts

This mixture has a variety of uses in gâteau and smaller cakes. Many different butter creams (mocha being used traditionally), as well as lighter flavored creams or whipped cream all go well with this sweet, crispy base. Japonais is basically a meringue mixture with lightly toasted, finely ground almonds or hazelnuts added. Depending on how solid you want the Japonais mixture to be the amount of almonds can be up to two-thirds of the combined weight of egg white and sugar. Cornstarch or flour (in very small quantities) are used as a stabilizer.

Japonais Layers

A Japonais layer is basically a meringue flavored with lightly toasted, finely ground almonds or hazelnuts. This mixture has a variety of uses in baking. Many different kinds of buttercream (mocha is the most traditional), as well as lighter-flavored creams or whipped cream go well with this sweet, crispy base. This recipe will make three 8- or 9-inch bases.

$\frac{2}{3}$ cup egg whites (about 6 egg whites
1 cup superfine sugar
$\frac{2}{3}$ cup toasted, finely ground almonds or hazelnuts
3 tablespoons cornstarch
$\frac{1}{2}$ cup sifted confectioners' sugar
$\frac{1}{2}$ teaspoon vanilla
1$\frac{1}{2}$ cups mocha buttercream, page 55

Preheat oven to 325°F

Place egg whites in absolutely clean wide bowl. Beat until white and frothy. Add a little superfine sugar and beat until stiff. Gradually beat in remaining superfine sugar until it has completely dissolved. Mix ground almonds, cornstarch, and confectioners' sugar and fold into beaten egg whites. Add vanilla. Spread or pipe three 9-inch rounds onto parchment paper. Leave oven door ajar to allow steam to escape and bake 35 to 45 minutes or until golden brown. When baked at this temperature, which is quite high for meringues, bases will be nice and crisp. At this temperature bases will take about 35 to 45 minutes or less to bake.

1 **Beat meringue** as directed on page 34 (opposite). Superfine sugar must be completely dissolved. Egg whites should form stiff peaks when beaters are lifted and remain in bowl when bowl is turned upside down.

2 **Mix finely ground almonds** with cornstarch and confectioners' sugar. Fold into meringue with wooden spoon. Add vanilla. Mixture should be of uniform consistency.

3 **Draw three 9-inch circles** on parchment paper and spread meringue mixture over circles with small spatula or palette knife. Alternatively, pipe mixture onto paper. Piping is time consuming but will ensure even thickness.

4 **Bases can be trimmed** with sharp pointed knife while still warm. Cut around bottom of 9-inch springform pan to make even edge. Alternatively, allow bases to cool, fill with buttercream, and refrigerate. Trim edges when chilled.

5 **Place first base**, right side up, on clean work surface. Spread with buttercream. Place second base on top of first and spread with buttercream. Top with the third base, bottom side up. Spread remaining buttercream over top and around sides of cake.

6 **Sprinkle cake with finely ground almonds** or hazelnuts and lightly press nuts into buttercream with small spatula or palette knife. A traditional Japonais cake has a small dot of pale pink fondant in the center. Small Japonais cakes can be made in the same manner by making 3-inch meringue bases.

Choux Paste

Choux paste is a pastry that is made on top of the stove. Milk or water, butter, salt, and sugar are brought to a boil. The flour is added all at once and stirred until the mixture forms a fairly firm, elastic ball that comes away from the sides of the pan. The eggs are beaten in, one at a time, off the heat, until the mixture is smooth, glossy, and of piping consistency. It is piped or spooned into shapes for éclairs, cream puffs, profiteroles, large rings, or cakes such as the Flaky Choux Cake on page 149. Finally it is baked and then filled.

1 cup milk
½ cup (1 stick) butter
1 pinch salt
1 teaspoon sugar
1½ cups sifted all-purpose flour
5 to 6 eggs

A crisp mixture made with water:

1 cup water
½ cup (1 stick) butter
1 pinch salt
1 teaspoon sugar
1½ cups sifted all-purpose flour
5 to 6 eggs

Preheat oven to 425°F

Cream puffs are a classic, cream-filled choux pastry. The less fat there is in the pastry, the better it will rise. The more steam there is in the oven during baking, the higher the pastry will rise. Choux paste is both light and moist. To create steam in the oven, place a shallow pan of boiling water in the bottom of the oven when you put in the baking sheet. Close the oven door quickly so the moisture does not escape. Bake choux paste in preheated oven 15 to 20 minutes. Lower oven temperature to 400°F and bake 10 to 15 minutes or until golden brown. Do not open the oven until the end of the baking time or the pastry will fall and become doughy and unusable.

1 **Place milk, butter, salt, and sugar** in medium-size saucepan and bring to a boil. Add flour all at once. Stir until mixture comes away from sides of pan and forms a ball. Remove mixture from heat.

2 **Transfer mixture** to bowl and cool slightly. Beat in 1 egg. Do not add second egg until first egg is completely incorporated into mixture. Add remaining eggs in the same way until mixture is smooth and glossy and the right consistency for piping.

3 **Spoon mixture** into pastry bag fitted with large open star tip (# 8A). Pipe large rosettes onto greased baking sheets leaving space between each cream puff because choux paste will swell. Keep piping bag vertical and end piping exactly in center of each rosette.

Shortcrust Pastry

The term "shortcrust" applies to several kinds of pastry. Basic shortcrust pastry is usually made with flour, fat, sugar, and egg, and may be mixed by hand or with an electric mixer. It is used to make a variety of things including pies, flans, tarts, cookies, and cake bases. Many pastries are actually shortcrusts made with salt or sugar; butter, oil, suet, lard, or margarine; sweet spices such as cinnamon or cardamon; or savory spices like paprika or curry.

All shortcrust pastries have the same quality: They are crumbly and tender. It is the high fat content and low ratio of liquid to flour in the pastry that makes it special and, by definition, a shortcrust pastry or short pastry.

One of the most popular shortcrust pastries is the unsweetened, or very slightly sweetened, classic "pâte brisée." It is made with butter by the "cut in" method (see below) and can be relatively neutral in flavor or lightly salted. It is excellent for making fruit flans, nut tarts, pastries with sweet fillings, cake bases, or piecrusts.

Sweet shortcrust pastry is called "pâte sucrée" or "pâte sablée" (sand pastry). It is ideal for any sweet pie or tart.

There is also a shortcrust pastry that is made in a method similar to the method used to make a sponge mixture. It is piping consistency. Shortcrust variations are almost limitless.

Shortcrust dough, with the exception of piping shortcrust, should be kept in the refrigerator wrapped in waxed paper, plastic wrap, or aluminum foil. Tightly wrapped, it can be refrigerated safely for up to eight to ten days. It also freezes well and can be frozen for up to three months. Shortcrust pastry can also be frozen after baking. When a baked product is to be frozen, it should be slightly underbaked. After thawing, it should be reheated briefly to bring out the full flavor of the pastry.

The recipes in this section can be cut in half or may be doubled, depending on the quantities required.

Cut-in Pastry

Pâte Brisée

The name of this pastry comes from the method by which it is made. The fat is cut into the flour with a pastry blender or two knives, using a "scissor cutting" action. Standard proportions are two parts flour to one part fat. It is ideal for lining tart pans and, since it contains very little sugar, it is also ideal for fruit pies and tarts.

$1\frac{1}{2}$ cups all-purpose flour
2 tablespoons sugar
$\frac{1}{2}$ teaspoon salt
$\frac{1}{2}$ cup (1 stick) butter
1 egg yolk, beaten
2 to 3 tablespoons ice water

Stir flour, sugar, and salt in medium-size bowl. Cut in butter with pastry blender or two knives until mixture resembles coarse crumbs. Add egg and 2 tablespoons ice water. Toss mixture with fork until dough begins to bind together. Add remaining water only if necessary. Gather dough and shape into slightly flattened ball. Wrap and refrigerate or freeze until ready to use.

Shortcrust Pastry, Mixer Method

The mixer method is excellent for making pastry that contains a large amount of fat. The fat can be mixed with the flour quickly without overworking the dough and making the pastry too brittle. (Of course this dough can also be made by hand if desired.)

$1\frac{1}{2}$ cups (3 sticks) butter, softened
$\frac{1}{4}$ cups confectioners' sugar
1 teaspoon salt
2 eggs
2 tablespoons milk
$3\frac{1}{2}$ cups all-purpose flour

Cream butter, confectioners' sugar, and salt in large mixer bowl at medium speed until light and fluffy. Beat in eggs and milk until well blended. Remove beaters and insert pastry hooks. Add flour all at once, and beat at low speed just until flour is incorporated. Divide dough in half, wrap, and refrigerate or freeze until ready to use. This dough is soft, but nonetheless easy to use.

Sweet Shortcrust Pastry

Pâte Sucrée

This is the recipe for the wonderful French flan or tart pastry called Pâte Sucrée. The quantity given will make enough pastry to line four 10-inch tart pans. Bake as much as you need, wrap the balance, and store it in the refrigerator or freezer until needed. Remove the butter from the refrigerator about 15 minutes before you plan to use it. It should be firm, but not too cold.

5 cups all-purpose flour
2 cups sifted confectioners' sugar
1 teaspoon salt
1½ cups (3 sticks) butter
2 eggs
1 to 2 teaspoons vanilla or 1 to 2 teaspoons grated lemon peel (optional)

3 **Gradually work flour** in toward center of well with long thin spatula or fingers working flour into butter mixture.

6 **Form dough into large flat ball** and wrap tightly in plastic wrap, waxed paper, or aluminum foil. This will keep dough from absorbing odors in refrigerator and keeps it from drying out. Refrigerate 1 hour.

1 **Sift flour** onto large flat work surface. (Marble is best if available.) Make wide well in center of flour. Place confectioners' sugar and salt in well. Cut butter into cubes and add to well with eggs and vanilla or lemon peel, if using.

4 **Chop dough with large knife** or long thin spatula. Work from the outside in toward the center until all flour has been fully incorporated into butter mixture. Dough should be the consistency of large bread crumbs. Work quickly to prevent butter from getting too soft.

7 **Sprinkle cold work surface** lightly with flour to prevent dough from sticking. Remove as much dough from refrigerator as needed and roll out to desired size with lightly floured rolling pin. Work quickly to prevent dough from becoming too soft.

2 **Knead butter with fingers** and work butter, sugar, eggs, and flavoring together until somewhat crumbly.

5 **Gather dough into ball** and knead just until it binds together. The more quickly this is done, the lighter the pastry will be. If dough is too crumbly and will not bind together, work a little lightly beaten egg white into dough.

8 **Fold dough over rolling pin**, carefully lift off work surface, and place on ungreased baking sheet. Trim dough after it has been placed on baking sheet because it will stretch when lifted. Prick surface of dough all over with fork to prevent dough from puffing up during baking.

Cinnamon Almond Flan

Flans and tarts that are filled with soft or runny fillings cannot be made with flat pastry. The pastry must have sides to hold the filling in place. To prevent the sides of the pastry from collapsing, the pastry is prebaked with a "substitute filling" that is removed after prebaking. This is known as "baking blind." The procedure is to line the unbaked pastry with waxed paper, parchment paper, or aluminium foil, and fill it with pie weights or dried beans before baking.

1 recipe Cut-in Pastry (Pâte Brisée), page 37
10 tablespoons butter
3 eggs, separated
$\frac{3}{4}$ cup sugar
1 teaspoon cinnamon
$\frac{1}{8}$ teaspoon ground cloves
$\frac{1}{8}$ teaspoon salt
$1\frac{1}{4}$ cups finely ground almonds
1 cup sponge cake crumbs
sweetened cocoa for sprinkling

10-inch fluted tart pan with removable bottom

Preheat oven to 375°F

Line tart pan with pastry and bake blind 10 minutes. Remove paper and pie weights and return to oven. Bake 5 minutes. Set aside to cool. Beat butter, egg yolks, sugar, cinnamon, cloves, and salt in large bowl until light and fluffy. Beat egg whites in separate bowl until stiff peaks form. Stir about one quarter of beaten egg whites into butter mixture to lighten. Fold in ground almonds and sponge cake crumbs. Fold in remaining beaten egg whites. Pour mixture into cooled pastry and smooth top. Bake in preheated oven 40 to 45 minutes or until center is set. Cool completely in pan on wire rack. Remove from pan and sprinkle cocoa over top of flan. Pipe sweetened whipped cream on top of flan, if desired.

Baking blind is the term used when pastry is prebaked without a filling. Roll out dough, wrap around rolling pin, and unroll over tart pan. Press pastry into pan with small ball of leftover dough. Trim pastry even with rim of pan. Prick bottom of dough, line with parchment paper, waxed paper, or aluminum foil, and fill with pie weights or dried beans. Bake 10 minutes in preheated 275°F oven. Remove lining paper and pie weights. Return to oven and bake 5 minutes. Set aside to cool before filling.

To make decorative design on top of flan, roll top with knobby puff pastry rolling pin. This will give flan a small checked effect and finish it off nicely. Add piped sweetened whipped cream, if desired.

Linzertorte

Pastry made with ground almonds or other nuts is so good it almost melts in the mouth. The natural fat content of nuts often causes this kind of pastry to get too crumbly. If this happens, it will be difficult to make the lattice top for the Linzertorte. Therefore, it is important to work as quickly as possible when using a nut pastry. The more quickly you work, the less likely you are to have problems.

2 cups ground almonds
3 cups all-purpose flour
1½ cups (3 sticks) butter
3 egg yolks
2 cups confectioners' sugar, sifted
⅛ teaspoon ground cloves
⅛ teaspoon cinnamon
½ teaspoon vanilla
grated peel of 1 lemon
1 cup seedless raspberry or red currant jam
1 egg yolk beaten with 1 tablespoon milk for glaze
1 to 2 tablespoons sliced almonds for sprinkling

10-inch deep flan ring

Preheat oven to 400°F

Prepare, shape, fill, and bake torte as illustrated in the step-by-step photos.

Bake in preheated oven 15 minutes. Lower oven temperature to 325°F and bake 65 to 70 minutes or until pastry is nicely browned. Cool torte completely in flan ring on baking sheet. Ground hazelnuts may be substituted for ground almonds, if desired.

Light Linzertorte

¾ cup ground almonds
1¾ cups all-purpose flour
12 tablespoons (1½ sticks) butter
1 cup confectioners' sugar
4 egg yolks
⅛ teaspoon salt
1 tablespoon grated lemon peel
1 cup seedless raspberry jam

10-inch deep flan ring or springform pan

Preheat oven to 400°F

Prepare and bake torte according to step-by-step photos for Linzertorte. Sprinkle top with almonds or dust with confectioners' sugar.

1 **Place ground almonds** on clean work surface. Sift flour over almonds and make wide well in center. Cut butter into cubes and add to well with egg yolks, sugar, cloves, cinnamon, vanilla, and lemon peel.

2 **Break up butter cubes** and work butter, sugar, egg yolks, and flavorings together with fingertips to make smooth mixture.

6 **Break off piece** of reserved dough in refrigerator and combine with dough trimmed from flan ring. Shape into ½-inch rope, about 31 inches long. Roll into spiral, place spiral on flat plate, and press around inside edge of flan ring as illustrated.

7 **Spread jam over dough**, inside rope, with plastic pastry scraper. Be careful not to get any jam on edge of dough.

3 **Gradually work in flour** and ground almonds, squeezing mixture to make large crumbs. Knead dough lightly and shape into flattened ball, working quickly to make sure dough binds together and does not become crumbly. (Crumbly dough will be difficult to use in making lattice top.)

4 **Wrap dough and refrigerate 1 hour**. Divide dough in half, rewrap half, and return to refrigerator. Roll out remaining piece of dough on lightly floured surface to 11-inch circle, ½-inch thick.

5 **Line large baking sheet** with parchment paper. Place rolled dough on parchment paper. Cut with 10-inch deep flan ring. Remove excess dough and set aside.

8 **Roll refrigerated dough** into twelve ½-inch thick sticks, each about 10 inches long. Arrange six strips evenly spaced over jam, cutting each strip to fit. Arrange remaining six strips at right angles to first strips to make lattice top.

9 **Brush pastry** with beaten egg yolk mixture to glaze. Don't allow glaze to touch sides of flan ring because this will cause torte to stick to ring. Sprinkle sliced almonds around inside edge of torte. Bake in preheated oven 15 minutes. Lower oven temperature to 325°F and bake 65 minutes or until pastry is golden brown.

Puff Pastry

Light, deliciously crisp, and so tender it melts in the mouth! This is what good puff pastry should be—a magnificent treat with rich, buttery flavor.

A great deal of care and precision are required to make puff pastry, and there is no way it can be made in a hurry.

Refrigerate flour to be kneaded into butter to prevent butter from getting too soft. Rinse hands under very cold water and dry well before kneading flour and butter together. If hands are too warm, they will make butter too soft. It is important to prevent pastry from sticking to work surface when rolled. Sprinkle work surface and rolling pin lightly with flour before rolling. Reflour rolling pin as necessary. If butter breaks through pastry, flour broken places generously. Roll gently until broken spot is the same thickness as rest of pastry. Wrap and refrigerate 1 hour before rolling and folding again. Pastry can be kneaded by hand or in heavy duty electric mixer fitted with pastry hooks. The bulk of time necessary to make puff pastry is taken up in making turns, which must be done by hand, and allowing pastry to rest. To keep track of number of turns that have been made, mark pastry with corresponding number of fingers after each turn. Thaw frozen pastry in refrigerator 24 hours before using. Pastry will keep, tightly wrapped, in refrigerator three to four days.

Pastry (about 3 pounds):
3¾ cups (approximately) unbleached all-
purpose or bread flour
2 teaspoons salt
1 cup ice water
1 pound (4 sticks) unsalted butter, chilled

2 **Knead dough until smooth and glossy.** Wrap dough in plastic wrap and refrigerate 30 minutes. Remove butter from refrigerator and dice. Sprinkle butter with ⅓ cup flour. Knead butter and flour until well combined and butter mixture is same texture as dough. Do not overknead or butter will get too soft.

3 **Roll out pastry** on lightly floured surface to 20- by 14-inch rectangle. Shape butter mixture into 12- by 10-inch rectangle. Place butter in center of pastry and brush edges of pastry with water.

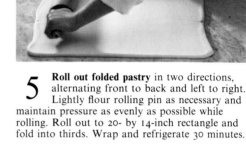

5 **Roll out folded pastry** in two directions, alternating front to back and left to right. Lightly flour rolling pin as necessary and maintain pressure as evenly as possible while rolling. Roll out to 20- by 14-inch rectangle and fold into thirds. Wrap and refrigerate 30 minutes.

6 **To make single turn**, fold pastry in thirds. Fold as evenly as possible to keep edges straight. Precision and care in making turns are very important.

1 **Sift flour onto marble slab** and make well in center. Dissolve salt in ice water. Slowly pour salted ice water into well and mix flour and water with one hand. Work from center to outer edge. Use dough scraper to bring in more flour.

4 **Fold sides of pastry** over butter (see photo) overlapping slightly in center. Press edges firmly to seal in butter.

7 **To make double turn**, roll out pastry to 20- by 14-inch rectangle, fold both sides in to meet at center. Fold sides in half again to make 4 layers (see photo). Wrap and refrigerate 30 minutes. Repeat rolling and folding four more times, making two single turns and two double turns.

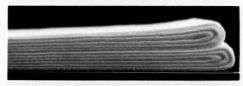

8 After making one single turn and one double turn, layers of pastry and butter should be even (see photo). Butter melts when pastry is baked, leaving air between layers of pastry.

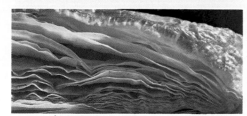

9 After making third turn, layers in baked pastry are very thin, but still distinguishable. The pastry still needs one more double turn.

10 This puff pastry case is made of delicate flaky layers. After the fourth turn, the layers are hardly visible when the pastry is baked. If the turns have been made carefully, the pastry will rise very well.

Puff Pastry Case

1½ pounds puff pastry
1 egg yolk beaten with 1 tablespoon water for brushing

½ pint strawberries, pureed
2 to 3 cups sweetened whipped cream

8-inch and 10-inch deep flan rings

Preheat oven to 425°F

Roll out pastry to about ¼-inch thickness and slightly larger than 10-inch flan ring. Place on lightly floured metal base. (1) Place 10-inch flan ring on top of pastry and cut around inside edge with very sharp knife. Remove ring and excess pastry. (2) Place 8-inch flan ring on center of pastry circle and cut around outside edge of ring. Remove ring. Gather reserved pastry scraps and shape into ball. (3) Roll out scraps to ⅛-inch thickness and place on ungreased baking sheet. Brush lightly with water. Place 10-inch flan ring around cut pastry circles to hold them in place and carefully slide pastry circles off metal base onto pastry on baking sheet. (4) Remove flan ring. Remove pastry from center of pastry circle. (5) Place 8-inch flan ring inside pastry ring to support pastry as it rises during baking. Trim excess pastry around outside of pastry circle. Prick pastry inside flan ring with fork to prevent base from rising during baking. (6) Brush pastry ring with egg yolk mixture. Do not get any egg yolk mixture on flan ring or pastry will stick to ring and not rise evenly. Refrigerate 30 minutes. Bake 15 minutes or until pastry is golden brown. Remove from baking sheet and cool on wire rack. Fold strawberry purée into whipped cream and spoon cream into case.

Quick Puff Pastry

This quick variation of classic puff pastry has an unusually flaky texture because the butter is incorporated quickly, but not completely, into the pastry. Although this pastry does not rise as high, or as evenly, as classic puff pastry, it makes an excellent base for cakes.

Pastry (5 pounds):
$7\frac{1}{2}$ cups all-purpose flour
$1\frac{3}{4}$ pounds (7 sticks) unsalted butter
2 teaspoons salt
$1\frac{2}{3}$ cups water

Preheat oven to 425°F

Prepare pastry according to step-by-step photos below. Remember to roll pastry evenly in only two directions, back to front and left to right. As with classic puff pastry, the pastry must be handled very carefully. It must be turned as carefully as it is rolled out.

Roll out pastry into rectangle. Fold short sides of pastry over in thirds. This is the first single turn. Refrigerate 10 minutes. Roll into rectangle again; fold short sides in to meet at center. Fold sides in half again to make 4 layers. This is the first double turn. Refrigerate 10 minutes. Repeat single turn. Refrigerate. Repeat double turn. Refrigerate.

Dutch Cherry Cake

3 Quick Puff Pastry bases
1 jar (16 ounces) dark sweet cherries
2 tablespoons granulated sugar
$\frac{1}{8}$ teaspoon cinnamon
1 tablespoon cornstarch
$\frac{1}{4}$ cup red currant jelly
Fondant, page 60
$2\frac{1}{2}$ cups heavy cream
5 to 6 tablespoons confectioners' sugar
additional drained cherries for decoration

Prepare cherry filling while pastry bases are cooling. Drain cherries, reserving liquid. Place cherry liquid in saucepan. Add granulated sugar, cinnamon, and cornstarch and stir until blended. Place saucepan over low heat and cook, stirring, until mixture thickens and comes to a boil. Stir in cherries and simmer 1 minute. Remove from heat and cool.

1 Sift flour onto work surface and make well in center. Dice butter and place around edge of flour. Sprinkle butter with a little flour. Sprinkle salt in well and pour in water carefully.

2 With one hand, work as much flour and water together as possible without including any butter. Stir several times to make soft dough.

3 Work in butter until well incorporated, kneading to mix well. Roll out pastry and make two single turns and two double turns (see instructions above). If time is short, reduce or eliminate resting time in refrigerator.

4 Remember to roll pastry from front to back and left to right only. When all turns have been completed, divide pastry into three equal-size pieces, each about $1\frac{2}{3}$ pounds (26 ounces). Wrap and refrigerate or freeze two pieces of pastry until ready to use.

5 Line baking sheets. Cut one (26-ounce) piece of pastry into three equal-size pieces. Roll out each piece to $\frac{1}{8}$-inch thickness and place on baking sheet. Place sides of 10-inch springform pan upside down over pastry pieces and cut around outside edges with sharp knife. Refrigerate bases 15 minutes.

6 Prick pastry bases all over with fork. Bake in preheated oven 15 to 20 minutes or until golden brown. Place sides of springform pan over pastry bases while still warm and cut around inside edge of pan with sharp knife. Cool bases completely on rack before filling.

Dutch Cherry Cake has a light filling spread between crisp layers of puff pastry. The separate layers of pastry and cream are clearly visible, and it is easy to see whether or not the pastry has been prepared carefully. The rings of cherries and whipped cream in the bottom layer should be evenly spaced.

1 **Select flattest pastry base** and place upside down on work surface. Heat red currant jelly until just melted and brush over pastry base. Let stand until set. Brush fondant over jelly and let stand until set.

2 **Cut fondant covered base** into sixteen wedges with long bladed knife.

3 **Beat cream with confectioners' sugar** until firm. Place one pastry base in bottom of 10-inch springform pan and spread with thin layer of cream. Spoon about 1½ cups whipped cream into pastry bag fitted with large plain tip and pipe around pastry edge. Pipe two more rings onto base about ½ inch apart.

4 **Spoon cherries** between rings of whipped cream. Pipe whipped cream into center. Top with remaining plain pastry base and gently press down.

5 **Set aside 1 cup whipped cream.** Spread remaining whipped cream over pastry base. Smooth top with pastry scraper. Gently drop cake onto work surface to eliminate air bubbles.

6 **Run tip of knife** around inside edge of pan and carefully remove sides of pan. Smooth sides of cake. Place fondant covered pastry wedges on top of cake. Spoon reserved whipped cream into pastry bag fitted with small open star tip and pipe one rosette on top of each wedge. Decorate with cherries.

Basic Yeast Dough

Although a complete chapter in this book is devoted entirely to baking with yeast, the two most basic yeast recipes are included in this section. Yeast dough is one of the most versatile of all doughs and forms the basis for a variety of cakes and pastries, from a simple braided loaf to the finest croissants. The typically slightly sour taste and airiness of the dough are produced by the yeast cells that reproduce under warm, moist conditions. The yeast causes fermentation that turns the starch in the flour into glucose and then into alcohol and carbon dioxide.

Yeast dough can be made by two very different methods. In the first method, known as the conventional method, the yeast is diluted in lukewarm milk and immediately mixed into the flour and other ingredients to form a dough. In the second method, the sponge method illustrated in the step-by-step photos, the yeast is mixed with milk and a little flour to make a preliminary dough. This produces better, quicker fermentation than the first method and therefore the dough can be made more quickly. The remaining ingredients are not mixed in until the preliminary dough has risen.

Basic recipe for yeast dough prepared by "sponge method":

about 4 cups all-purpose flour
1 package active dry yeast or 1 cake (0.6 ounce) fresh yeast
$\frac{1}{4}$ cup sugar
1 cup warm milk (105° to 115°F)
$\frac{1}{4}$ cup ($\frac{1}{2}$ stick) butter, melted and cooled
2 eggs
1 teaspoons salt

1 **Sift flour**, place half of flour in large bowl, and make well in center. Add yeast (if using fresh yeast, crumble first) and 1 teaspoon sugar to well. Add milk and stir to dissolve yeast, working in a little flour. Sprinkle small amount of flour over yeast mixture.

2 **Cover bowl** and set aside in warm, draft-free place 10 to 15 minutes or until cracks appear in layer of flour over the yeast mixture. (This indicates yeast is active.)

3 **Beat remaining sugar**, melted butter, eggs, and salt until well blended. Add to bowl with 1 cup flour and beat vigorously with wooden spoon until smooth and well blended. Stir in enough remaining flour to make smooth dough that comes away from sides of bowl.

4 **Turn dough out** onto lightly floured surface and knead in enough remaining flour until dough is no longer sticky. Continue kneading until dough is smooth and elastic, 8 to 10 minutes.

5 **Lightly grease clean bowl with butter**. Place dough in greased bowl and turn to coat surface of dough. Sprinkle top with a little flour. Cover bowl with clean towel and set aside in warm, draft-free place until doubled in bulk, 1 to 1$\frac{1}{2}$ hours.

6 **When dough has risen sufficiently** it is ready to be punched down, shaped, and baked. Dough will have lighter texture if it is kneaded again 3 or 4 minutes before shaping. Shape and bake dough according to directions on page 108.

Croissant Dough

Yeast dough with extra butter

This basic croissant dough is a cold yeast mixture that is worked in the same way as Puff Pastry, page 42. By making a series of turns, fine layers of butter are incorporated into the dough. The end result is a crisp, layered pastry with its own individual taste of yeast dough and butter.

about $7\frac{1}{2}$ cups unbleached all-purpose flour
$\frac{1}{2}$ cup (1 stick) butter, softened
2 teaspoons salt
$\frac{1}{2}$ cup sugar
4 eggs
3 packages active dry yeast or 1 package (2 ounces) fresh yeast
$1\frac{3}{4}$ cups warm milk (105° to 115°F)
$1\frac{1}{4}$ pounds (5 sticks) unsalted butter, chilled
$\frac{2}{3}$ cup additional flour

Sift flour onto work surface and make well in center. Add $\frac{1}{2}$ cup softened butter, salt, sugar, and eggs. Sprinkle yeast over milk, stir to dissolve, and let stand 10 minutes. Pour yeast mixture into well. Work all ingredients together starting from center and working flour in gradually. Knead dough vigorously until smooth and shiny. Wrap and refrigerate 2 to 3 hours. Remove $1\frac{1}{4}$ pounds chilled butter from refrigerator, sprinkle with $\frac{2}{3}$ cup additional flour, and knead butter and flour until well blended. Shape butter mixture into 10- by 8-inch block. Remove dough from refrigerator and roll out on lightly floured surface to 20- by 16-inch rectangle. Place block of butter in center of dough. Brush edges of dough with water. Fold dough over butter, enclosing butter completely. Roll out dough to 28- by 16-inch rectangle. Fold dough into thirds (single turn) and refrigerate 20 minutes. Roll out pastry to 28- by 16-inch rectangle. Fold sides of pastry in to meet at center. Fold sides in half again to make four layers (double turn). Repeat rolling and folding pastry four more times, making two single turns and two double turns (see Puff Pastry, page 42). Refrigerate pastry 30 minutes between each turn. Roll out pastry and cut into croissants or other shapes.

Fine Fillings

For as long as cakes have been in existence there have been a variety of fillings to enhance their flavor. Even in early medieval times there was a "porridge," a "fine monastic specialty" that consisted basically of barley, oats, or millet boiled in milk, but that could be varied in many different ways: by being colored with pollen or flower petals to make it look more appetizing: mixed with dates, raisins, figs, and nuts; made lighter with eggs; sweetened with honey; or made richer with cream. However it was not until the nineteenth century that delicate gâteaux with delicious fillings and decorations were invented. Cake makers and pastry cooks competed with one another to bring out new and different creations. While patissieres cooked for the coffeehouse, the best restaurants have always employed a pastry chef, and still do so today.

If pastries and cakes are the basics of baking, then the fillings are the creative luxuries. There are many cakes and pastries that need no extra touches. Take nut cake, for example, poppy-seed cake, or the traditional rich fruit cake that is iced only in honor of special occasions such as weddings or birthdays.

Simple fillings, like jams, fruit jellies, and marmalades, require no special preparation and are therefore not included in this chapter. Other fillings suitable for small cakes made from puff pastry or yeast dough can contain fresh or preserved fruit, nuts, or poppy seeds and these are all included in the appropriate recipes. In addition, creams and custards provide the basis for many filling variations that you can use as the basis for your own creations, and these will be dealt with in this chapter.

Light, airy creams are suitable for filling gâteaux, sponge rolls, or cream slices. The simplest and lightest of these is cream itself. Double cream gives the best consistency for a cake filling. It is important to whip it correctly: stiff enough to hold its shape but not over whisked to look "granular" in texture. Whipping cream can also be used as a filling for light cakes; however, it does not retain its whipped consistency for many hours but tends to weep very slightly and lose body if left for a long time. Vanilla cream is another light filling: Made with sugar, cornstarch, egg yolks, vanilla pods, and milk, this is none other than the familiar custard. Mixed hot with whisked egg white we get the delicate Chiboust Cream. Custards made with fresh cream are other light fillings, and these include Bavarian Cream, which goes with almost any flavoring—fruit, nuts, or chocolate—or the various wine creams, which are excellent with citrus fruit.

Following these are the heavier buttercreams, led by the less rich vanilla buttercream, a mixture of butter and custard. Next come the light buttercreams with eggs, sugar, and vanilla, and Italian buttercream, which is made lighter with meringue. One of the richest of all fillings is French Buttercream, *crème au beurre nature*, made from boiled sugar, vanilla, egg yolk, and butter. One of the best fillings is Canache Cream, an exquisite mixture of melted chocolate and fresh cream. Now it is up to you to make the most of the choices available. You have only to develop the art of combining the various ingredients to enhance each of them to the fullest and to create wonderful delicacies.

1 **Place ¼ cup sugar and cornstarch** in medium-size bowl. Separate eggs carefully, because any traces of egg white in custard will form lumps when custard is boiled. Add egg yolks to bowl with ½ cup of milk.

Simple Vanilla Custard

Crème Pâtissière

Simple Vanilla Custard or Crème Pâtissière is really an elegant French custard. It is made by boiling milk and sugar and binding it with starch. The traditional flavoring is vanilla. The addition of egg yolks is an improvement to the basic recipe and helps to thicken and enrich the custard. It is essential to this recipe.

With or without vanilla, this custard is a basic filling and has many uses. The addition of beaten egg whites to the hot custard forms the basis of the deliciously light Crème Chiboust. It also forms the basis of German Buttercream, French Almond Cream, and a whole variety of other fillings. If it is to be used cold as a basic

custard, it will remain smooth if it is stirred as it cools. The difficulty is that stirring will thin the custard. Alternatively, the surface of the custard can be sprinkled with confectioners' sugar or covered with a piece of waxed paper to prevent a skin from forming. If necessary the cold custard can be pressed through a fine sieve and stirred until smooth. If the custard is to be refrigerated, the bowl must be covered to prevent the custard from absorbing odors. Do not refrigerate custard longer than 2 days.

½ cup sugar
5 tablespoons cornstarch
4 egg yolks
2 cups milk
1 teaspoon vanilla

2 **Beat mixture with small balloon whisk** until all ingredients are thoroughly blended. Place remaining 1½ cups milk and remaining ¼ cup sugar in medium-size saucepan over low heat. Bring just to boiling point.

3 **Gradually pour cornstarch mixture** into hot milk in slow, steady stream, beating constantly. Bring mixture to a boil over high heat, beating constantly.

4 **Cook custard** to eliminate taste of cornstarch, stirring constantly 3 to 4 minutes or until mixture thickens. Constant beating will prevent custard from burning and sticking to pan.

5 **Remove custard from heat** and pour into bowl. Add vanilla and beat vigorously. Dust top of custard with confectioners' sugar. As sugar melts it will help prevent a skin from forming on surface of custard. Set custard aside and cool to room temperature.

6 **To be sure cooled custard** does not have any lumps, use pastry scraper to press custard through inverted fine mesh sieve set over bowl.

7 **Beat custard vigorously** with balloon whisk until smooth and creamy.

Crème Chiboust

Prepare Simple Vanilla Custard according to the recipe, page 50, using only 2 tablespoons of sugar. It must be exactly the same temperature as the Italian meringue with which it is combined.

Italian meringue:
6 egg whites · $\frac{3}{4}$ cup sugar · $\frac{1}{4}$ cup water

Beat egg whites in large mixing bowl until soft peaks form. Beat in 1 tablespoon sugar. At the same time, bring remaining sugar and water to boil in small saucepan over moderate heat. Boil syrup until temperature registers 244°F (firm ball stage) on candy thermometer. Add sugar syrup to beaten egg whites in slow, steady stream, beating constantly. Fold in hot vanilla custard just until blended.

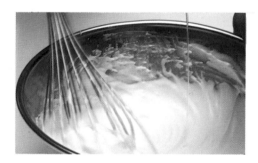

1 **Beat egg whites** with balloon whisk or electric mixer until soft peaks form. Add 1 tablespoon sugar and beat until stiff. Add sugar syrup in slow, steady stream, beating constantly.

2 **Fold hot vanilla custard** into Italian meringue with wooden spoon just until combined. (Cakes or pastries filled with Crème Chiboust must be refrigerated until ready to serve.)

Whipped Cream

Flavored whipped cream is one of the quickest, easiest, and most popular cake fillings you can make. Heavy cream and whipping cream are the same thing, the only difference being the name placed on the carton by the producer of the cream. Both are required by law to have a fat content of 36 to 40 percent. Most cream that is sold today is ultrapasteurized to prolong its shelf life. Although this means the cream can be kept in the refrigerator for a few weeks instead of just a few days, unfortunately it also means the cream will not have nearly as fine a flavor as cream that has not been ultrapasturized. Never buy cream without checking the expiration date on the container. If the date of purchase is too close to the expiration date, the cream may not be fresh enough to store until you are ready to use it, and when you try to whip the cream, it may turn to butter.

To whip cream properly, place the bowl and the beaters in the refrigerator to chill thoroughly. Whip the cream until soft peaks form. Add 2 tablespoons confectioners' sugar and 1 teaspoon vanilla or 1 tablespoon brandy for each cup of cream being whipped. Continue to beat until the cream is firm. Be careful not to overbeat or the cream will start to turn and cannot be rescued. Refrigerate whipped cream until ready to use. Refrigerate any cake or pastry that has a whipped cream filling or icing.

Cream will double in volume when whipped. If you need 2 cups of whipped cream, use 1 cup of heavy cream.

Flavored Whipped Cream

Whipped cream can be flavored in many ways. Flavorings such as vanilla, almond extract, chocolate, cocoa, chopped or ground nuts, or small quantities of brandy or flavored liqueur are all appropriate. Use the following table as a guide for flavoring 2 cups (1 pint) of heavy cream.

3 tablespoons confectioners' sugar and 3 ounces melted semisweet chocolate
$\frac{1}{4}$ cup confectioners' sugar and 2 tablespoons powdered instant coffee
$\frac{1}{4}$ cup confectioners' sugar and $\frac{2}{3}$ cup toasted chopped hazelnuts
$\frac{1}{4}$ cup confectioners' sugar and 2 tablespoons brandy or flavored liqueur

When larger amounts of flavoring are added to whipped cream, the cream should be stabilized with gelatin, an excellent stabilizer because it is tasteless and will prevent the cream from separating. To stabilize 2 cups of cream, place 1 tablespoon unflavored gelatin in 1 tablespoon cold water. Scald $\frac{1}{4}$ cup cream and add to gelatin mixture. Stir until gelatin is completely dissolved. Refrigerate until chilled but not set, about 20 minutes. Whip remaining cream until soft peaks form and add gelatin mixture with flavoring. Finish whipping.

Whipped cream can also be combined with a basic custard when used as a cake or pastry filling. The flavoring for this kind of cream is often a fruit purée or juice, wine, or a combination of fruit and wine. The flavor and acidity of citrus fruit goes best with white wine, but light red wine can also be used. The disadvantage to using red wine is that it turns the cream a rather unattractive color. This cream may be kept, covered, in the refrigerator for several hours.

Orange Wine Cream

Orange sauce can be made in advance and kept in the refrigerator. When sauce is needed, place it in the top of a double boiler set over (not in) a pan of barely simmering water until heated through. Remove top of double boiler and set sauce aside to cool before adding whipped cream. The quantities given below are enough to fill and frost a 10-inch cake.

3 large navel oranges
1 cup white wine
1 cup sugar
4 egg yolks
3 tablespoons cornstarch
8 leaves gelatin or 2 envelopes unflavored gelatin
2 cups heavy cream

1 **Wash and scrub oranges** thoroughly under hot running water. Pat dry with paper towels. Grate peel into saucepan. (Be careful to grate only thin outer peel because white pith has a bitter taste.)

2 **Squeeze oranges** and measure $\frac{3}{4}$ cup juice. Set aside 2 tablespoons wine. Add remaining wine, orange juice, and sugar to saucepan. Cook over low heat about 10 minutes, stirring.

3 **Strain orange sauce** into stainless steel or enamel saucepan to avoid danger of having sauce oxidize. Bring sauce to a boil.

4 **Beat egg yolks** with reserved 2 tablespoons wine until well blended. Beat in cornstarch. Gradually beat cornstarch mixture into gently boiling orange sauce, beating constantly. Cook until sauce is thickened and comes to boil. Remove from heat.

5 **Soak gelatin leaves** in cold water 10 minutes. Squeeze out and stir leaves into hot sauce until dissolved. If using powdered gelatin, soak in $\frac{1}{4}$ cup cold water 5 minutes. Add to hot sauce, stirring until dissolved. Set sauce aside to cool, stirring from time to time to prevent skin from forming.

6 **Pour sauce into large bowl** and let stand until completely cool. Whip cream until firm. Fold whipped cream into sauce gently with whisk. Refrigerate until ready to use.

Bavarian Cream

This is one of the best-known cream fillings and it is used in pastry all over the world. It is a classic dessert cream, a combination of custard and whipped cream. Bavarian Cream makes a delicious filling for cakes and sponge rolls and can be flavored in almost any way imaginable.

4 egg yolks · $\frac{1}{2}$ cup sugar
2 cups milk · 1 vanilla bean
8 leaves of gelatin or 2 envelopes
unflavored gelatin
2 cups heavy cream, whipped until firm

Prepare cream as illustrated in step-by-step photos below. This recipe will make enough Bavarian Cream to fill and frost the Sponge Roll, pages 30–31 or any 10-inch layer cake.

A combination of Bavarian cream and raspberries is the filling for this cake. The raspberries sink into the bottom layer of chocolate Bavarian cream and are then covered with vanilla Bavarian cream. The cake needs at least an hour in the refrigerator to cool and set fully.

1 **Beat egg yolks and sugar** until thick and creamy. Use balloon whisk because sugar must be dissolved slowly and it is important not to beat in too much air.

2 **Place milk and vanilla bean** in saucepan over moderate heat and bring just to boiling point. Remove vanilla bean and beat hot milk, one ladleful at a time, into beaten egg yolk mixture. Pour mixture back into saucepan.

3 **Cook over low heat**, stirring constantly, until mixture is thick enough to coat back of wooden spoon.

4 **Soak gelatin leaves** in cold water, squeeze out as much water as possible. Add to hot sauce and stir until gelatin is completely dissolved. If using powdered gelatin, soak in 6 tablespoons warm water 5 minutes. Add to hot sauce and stir until gelatin is completely dissolved.

5 **Fill large bowl with cracked ice** and cold water. Place smaller bowl over ice. Strain hot sauce into smaller bowl to remove any lumps. Remove bowl from ice and set aside to cool to room temperature, stirring occasionally.

6 **Fold whipped cream** into cooled sauce while sauce is still slightly runny and is not set. Cream is now ready to use.

German Buttercream

This is a vanilla custard with butter added to make it a buttercream. The amount of custard used makes it unusually light in texture. Relatively little sugar is added. If you want to flavor it with nuts or coffee, for example, it will be necessary to add a little more sugar and omit the vanilla.

$\frac{3}{4}$ cup sugar
5 tablespoons cornstarch, sifted
3 egg yolks · 2 cups milk
1 teaspoon vanilla
$1\frac{1}{2}$ cups unsalted butter, softened

Using ingredients listed above, prepare custard by method illustrated in step-by-step photos on page 50 through step 5. If necessary, press cooled custard through fine sieve and stir until smooth. Combine custard with creamed butter.

Egg Buttercream

This buttercream is lighter and easier to make than classic French Buttercream (page 55) because it is not necessary to make a sugar syrup. It can be flavored with chocolate, nuts, or liqueur.

3 eggs · 3 egg yolks
1 cup sugar
$1\frac{1}{4}$ cups ($2\frac{1}{2}$ sticks) unsalted butter, softened
1 teaspoon vanilla

Place eggs, egg yolks, and sugar in bowl set over (not in) pan of barely simmering water. Beat until mixture is thick and lemon-colored. It should be warm to the touch (see Genoise Mixture, page 28). Remove bowl and beat until cold. Cream butter and vanilla in medium-size bowl until light and fluffy. When mixtures are the same temperature, beat them together.

Italian Buttercream

1 cup (2 sticks) unsalted butter, softened
5 egg whites · $\frac{3}{4}$ cup sugar · 1 vanilla bean

Cream butter in small bowl until light and fluffy. Set aside. Beat egg whites with electric mixer or balloon whisk until soft peaks form. Gradually beat in 2 tablespoons sugar and continue beating until stiff and glossy. Place remaining sugar, vanilla bean, and 6 tablespoons water in medium-size saucepan and bring to a boil. Boil syrup until temperature registers 240°F (soft ball stage) on candy thermometer. Remove vanilla bean from sugar syrup. Pour sugar syrup in slow, steady, stream into beaten egg whites, beating constantly. Continue beating until meringue is cool. Fold in creamed butter.

1 **Place butter in mixer bowl** and beat at high speed until light and fluffy and increased in volume.

1 **Beat eggs, egg yolks, and sugar** in bowl set over (not in) pan of barely simmering water until warm to the touch. Remove bowl and continue beating until mixture is light, creamy, and cooled.

1 **Beat egg whites** until stiff peaks form, adding 2 tablespoons of sugar as soon as soft peaks begin to form. Add sugar syrup in slow, steady stream, beating constantly. Beat until egg white mixture is cool.

2 **Strain custard and stir until smooth**. (It should be same temperature as creamed butter.) Add custard to creamed butter, beating at medium speed, until buttercream is light and fluffy. Refrigerate until ready to use.

2 **Cream butter and vanilla** until light and fluffy. Gradually add egg mixture, beating constantly until each addition is thoroughly incorporated before adding more. Beat until buttercream is fluffy. Refrigerate 30 minutes. Use to fill and frost cakes. Frosted cakes should be refrigerated until ready to serve.

2 **Fold creamed butter** into meringue all at one time. Be sure meringue and creamed butter are the same temperature. If meringue is too warm, consistency of buttercream will not be firm enough.

Buttercream—the Versatile Filling and Frosting

Buttercream is one of the most popular and versatile fillings and frostings used in baking. It can be flavored in many ways and coloring can be added to light-colored creams when special occasions require special decorative effects.

Buttercreams are a combination of two basic ingredients, butter and sugar, made lighter by the addition of eggs, egg whites, or custard. The quality of the main ingredient, butter, determines the flavor of the buttercream because the butter taste comes through very distinctly in delicately flavored Vanilla Buttercream. It is important to use only fresh, top quality unsalted butter.

The length of time buttercream will keep is determined by the ingredients that are added to lighten its texture. German Buttercream, made with custard, will keep for a very short time. Buttercream made with whole eggs keeps slightly longer, and Italian Buttercream that contains only egg whites, will keep best of all.

Buttercream is unusually versatile and can be flavored with many different ingredients. The basic creams on these pages are all vanilla flavored, but you can omit the vanilla if you decide to make a cream with different flavoring.

These basic recipes will make enough buttercream to fill and frost a 10-inch cake. Some contain more sugar than others and, depending on the flavoring you choose, you may have to add additional sugar. This is not necessary when semisweet chocolate is used because it contains sugar. But with bitter chocolate and unsweetened cocoa you will need extra sugar. You will also need extra sugar with coffee flavoring because coffee should be sweetened to bring out its full flavor.

Liquid flavorings, such as liqueurs, may cause the cream to separate. In order to minimize the risk of having this happen, the flavoring should be the same temperature as the buttercream to which it is added.

French Buttercream

The French name for this buttercream is *crème au beurre* nature. It is a classic buttercream that can be varied with almost any flavoring.

> 1 cup superfine sugar
> 1 vanilla bean
> 6 egg yolks
> 1½ cups (3 sticks) unsalted butter, softened

This method of preparation produces a very light buttercream. Sugar syrup is beaten into egg yolks and the mixture is beaten until it is cool. If you want an even lighter buttercream, fold in 1 to 2 cups Italian meringue (see technique photo 1, Italian Buttercream, page 54).

1 **Place sugar**, vanilla bean, and ⅓ cup water in medium-size saucepan over moderate heat and bring to a boil. Boil syrup until temperature registers 240°F (soft ball stage) on candy thermometer.

2 **Beat egg yolks** in mixer bowl until frothy. Remove vanilla bean from syrup and pour syrup in slow, steady stream into egg yolks, beating constantly with electric mixer. Continue beating until mixture is cool.

3 **Cream butter** until very light and fluffy. Add egg yolk mixture to butter gradually, beating constantly. Beat until mixture is thick and fluffy.

Almond Cream

Classic *crème d'amandes* is a buttercream often used to fill puff pastry, yeast dough, and sometimes shortcrust pastry. The basic mixture can be kept in the refrigerator for as long as one week.

1 cup (2 sticks) unsalted butter, softened
2 cups sifted confectioners' sugar
4 eggs
5 tablespoons all-purpose flour, sifted
1⅔ cups finely ground blanched almonds
3 to 4 tablespoons dark rum
Simple Vanilla Custard, page 50

Cream butter and sugar in medium-size bowl until light and fluffy. Add eggs, one at a time, beating well after each addition. Each egg must be fully incorporated into mixture before adding next egg. Combine flour and almonds and fold into creamed mixture. Cover with plastic wrap or aluminum foil and place in refrigerator until ready to use. Just before using, warm slightly and fold in rum. Measure an equal amount of vanilla custard and fold in.

Simple Almond Cream

This cream is heavier and more strongly flavored than classic Almond Cream. It is made without custard.

4 ounces almond paste
¼ cup (½ stick) unsalted butter, softened
¼ cup sugar
1 egg
⅓ cup finely ground blanched almonds
1½ tablespoons cornstarch, sifted

Beat almond paste, butter, and sugar until light and fluffy. Add egg and beat until thick and creamy. Combine almonds and cornstarch and fold into creamed mixture.

Ganache Cream

The classic chocolate cream used in this cake is also called Paris cream. It has two essential ingredients: chocolate and fresh cream. The consistency of the Ganache Cream depends on the ratio in which these ingredients are combined. A light Ganache Cream is used as a filling for cakes and pastries. A much heavier cream is used to make praline.

Basic Ganache Cream can be varied in many ways. Bitter chocolate can be substituted for milk chocolate. Butter can be added to make the cream lighter. Nougat or nuts can be added as well as liqueurs. Rum, brandy, and fruit liqueurs have a strong flavor and should be added in small amounts. However, when mild-flavored liqueurs are added, the quantity of liqueur needed to provide enough flavor will also add too much liquid to the cream. Therefore, it is necessary to reduce the amount of cream used by the volume of liqueur added. It is important not to add liqueur until the cream has cooled. Heat causes alcohol to evaporate, which also means there will be a loss of flavor.

Truffle Cake
with Ganache Cream

1 cup heavy cream
14 ounces semisweet chocolate, coarsely chopped
6 tablespoons unsalted butter, softened
5 tablespoons dark rum
Chocolate Genoise, page 30
2 tablespoons Cointreau
4 ounces semisweet chocolate, grated
16 chocolate truffles
confectioners' sugar for dusting

Place cream in large heavy saucepan and bring to a boil. Remove from heat, add chocolate, and stir until chocolate is melted and mixture is smooth. Let cool, stirring with whisk occasionally. When mixture is cool, but not set, beat vigorously. Add butter and beat until thoroughly incorporated. Stir in rum.

1 **Cream butter and sugar** in medium-size bowl until light and fluffy. Beat in eggs, one at a time, beating well after each addition. Each egg must be completely incorporated into mixture before next egg is added or mixture may curdle.

2 **Combine almonds and flour** and fold into butter mixture in thirds. Each third must be thoroughly folded into mixture before next third is added.

3 **Fold in rum**. This gives cream added flavor. (If you are not using cream immediately, store cream covered in refrigerator, without rum.)

4 **Measure an equal amount** of Simple Vanilla Custard, page 50. Stir both almond cream and vanilla custard thoroughly. Fold custard into cream. (If cream has been refrigerated, warm slightly before stirring in custard.)

1 **Place cream** in large heavy saucepan and bring to a boil over low heat. Remove pan from heat as soon as cream comes to a boil. Add chocolate off heat.

2 **Beat in chocolate with whisk**. Most chocolate will melt as soon as it is stirred in. Large lumps of chocolate will melt after a few minutes.

3 **Stir chocolate cream** until smooth. Set aside to cool, stirring occasionally. When mixture is almost cold, spoon into bowl and beat vigorously with whisk until mixture is light and fluffy and doubled in volume.

4 **Add butter** to chocolate mixture, beating vigorously until mixture is smooth and fluffy. Beat in 3 tablespoons rum gradually.

5 **Refrigerate Ganache Cream** 1 to 2 hours before using. Remove from refrigerator and beat vigorously before spreading on cake.

6 **Cut cake into three layers**. Spread one layer with Ganache Cream and top with second layer. Sprinkle second layer with 2 tablespoons dark rum and spread with Ganache Cream. Place third layer on top. Sprinkle top layer with Cointreau. Spread Ganache Cream over top and around sides of cake. Sprinkle grated chocolate over top and sides of cake. Decorate top with swirls of Ganache Cream and chocolate truffles. Dust cake with confectioners' sugar.

Icing and the Art of Decoration

Although fashions may change and cake decoration may vary from the elaborate to the simple, the art of cake decoration will always be with us as part of the repertoire of a good cook. As long as professional cooks continue to make such a wide variety of gâteaux and cakes, slices, and tarts, their example will be followed and people will continue to take pleasure in decorating their home baking. The art of cake decoration does not stand still and the best pastry chefs are continually introducing new ideas.

Just as the modern ideas about afternoon tea developed from Victorian times, so did the cakes and pastries we eat at this meal develop from baking in the Middle Ages. The large cakes now known as gâteaux reached the apex of their development in the nineteenth century. As one might expect in that age of ease and luxurious living, these were elaborate cakes, richly decorated, in a host of shapes both large and small. But just as the Modernist movement had a purifying influence on the decorative excesses of nineteenth-century art, the same trend toward purity of line became evident in the area of patisserie. Gâteaux were now decorated modestly, geometrically, stylishly. The piping bag with its swirls, whirls, and rosettes was suddenly taboo. Henceforth there was to be nothing of the confectioner's skills of construction in cake decoration.

Since then contrasting styles have developed side by side. Many confectioners and chefs are proud of having developed their own individual style of decoration. And there is no doubt about the fact that many of them are real artists. Yet it is silly to argue about whether aesthetic style is better than pretty flourishes. Clearly no one finds an over-decorated cake particularly attractive, yet clearly geometric lines will always have to compete with pretty frippery. In our use of plain and fluted piping nozzles, marzipan and chocolate, and fondant and velvety chocolate icing, we have attempted as nearly as possible to skirt this debate. We have combined chocolate with nuts and croquant. We have no objection to gold and silver balls in the right place. Yet we have not decorated over-lavishly for we believe that too little is better than too much. We have attempted to explain the separate techniques without advocating any particular style. Quite the contrary. This is the area of confectionery that best lends itself to new creations and the cook should be left completely free to put his or her own ideas into practice.

Apricot Glaze

Apricot glaze is often used as a layer between the cake and the icing. It can also be used as an icing by itself.

$\frac{1}{2}$ cup sugar
1 tablespoon lemon juice
$\frac{2}{3}$ cup (8 ounces) apricot jam

Place sugar, $\frac{1}{3}$ cup water, and lemon juice in medium-size saucepan. Stir well and bring to a boil over moderate heat. Boil rapidly 3 minutes. Remove from heat. Press jam through fine mesh sieve into separate saucepan. Place saucepan over moderate heat and stir in sugar syrup. Bring to a boil and boil vigorously until mixture is transparent. Strain through sieve again.

Fondant

Place 3 cups granulated sugar and $1\frac{1}{4}$ cups water in saucepan and bring to a boil over moderate heat, stirring until sugar is dissolved. Add $1\frac{1}{2}$ tablespoons liquid glucose or $\frac{1}{4}$ teaspoon cream of tartar, stir well, and return to a gentle boil. Brush inside edge of saucepan with water to prevent sugar crystals from forming. Cook mixture until it reaches the soft ball stage or about 240°F on candy thermometer. Pour onto marble slab and work fondant with spatula until firm and white. Knead until smooth. Store in airtight container. Fondant should be warmed in top of double boiler and thinned with sugar syrup, beaten egg white, or milk. It must be stirred constantly and must not be heated above 95°F or it will lose its shine and crystallize as it dries. Fondant can be flavored with liqueurs and extracts.

1 **Place fondant in bowl** or small saucepan set in pan of warm water. Water temperature should not exceed 104°F. Thin fondant with a little sugar syrup or beaten egg white and stir until smooth. Do not allow temperature of fondant to exceed 95°F.

1 **Press apricot jam** through fine mesh sieve into saucepan. Add sugar syrup and boil vigorously 5 to 6 minutes or until mixture is reduced by one third.

2 **Glaze is ready** when it is clear and transparent. It should be used warm. When apricot glaze is used by itself it will not harden completely.

2 **When fondant** runs off spoon in thick stream, it is correct consistency to ice a cake. Brush cake with thin layer of apricot glaze first to keep cake moist and fondant shiny. Fondant can be used to ice puff pastries as well as cakes. Fondant icing for small pastries should be transparent. To make fondant transparent, dilute with additional sugar syrup.

Icing a Large Cake

Before you ice a cake with fondant you must brush it with apricot glaze to be sure the fondant will keep its familiar glossy finish as it dries. If the cake has a custard or cream filling it is necessary to place a layer of marzipan under the glaze. The layer of marzipan should be as thin as possible. Prepare the marzipan by working 1½ cups sifted confectioners' sugar into 7 ounces almond paste. Work as quickly as possible because overhandling will make the marzipan crumbly and impossible to roll out. If you find the marzipan difficult to roll, mix in a little beaten egg white to remedy the situation.

3 **Dilute apricot glaze** with a little warm water to thin out slightly. Brush warm glaze over marzipan as thinly and lightly as possible. Glaze must be warm enough to brush on smoothly but not hot enough to melt a cream or custard filling.

4 **Pour fondant over cake** when glaze is set. If cake has cream or custard filling, place in refrigerator to chill before covering with fondant.

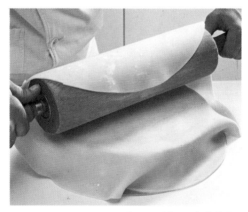

1 **Roll marzipan** until very thin and slightly larger than necessary to cover top and sides of cake. Roll around rolling pin to prevent it from stretching or tearing as it is transferred to cake.

2 **Press marzipan smoothly over edges** of cake with small spatula or palette knife. There should not be any folds or breaks in marzipan. If there are, pinch folds or breaks together between fingers and cut off excess marzipan with scissors. Smooth crack with spatula or palette knife.

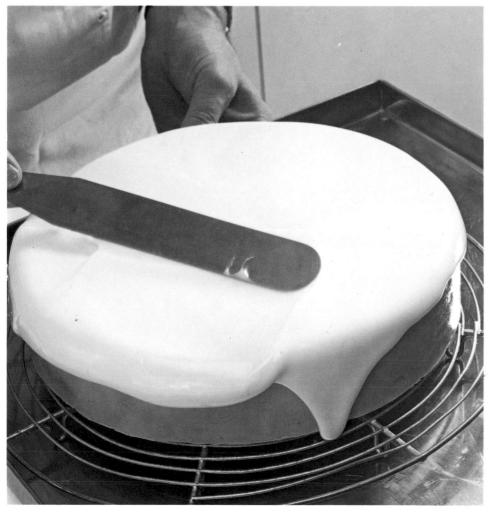

5 **Place cake on wire rack** set over baking sheet or waxed paper. Spread fondant gently and evenly with palette knife or long thin knife. Be sure icing on top of cake is not too thick so icing can run evenly down sides of cake. Use knife to spread icing evenly over sides.

Icing and Decorating Punch Cake

Both icing and decorating can be accomplished at the same time, as in this Punch Cake. It is an easy way to make cakes both delicious and eye appealing. The top of the cake is glazed and decorated with icing. The sides are not. The end product is very attractive despite the fact that the operation involves only one step.

Punch cake

1 Genoise sponge, page 28
3 tablespoons sugar syrup
3 tablespoons orange juice
3 tablespoons dark rum
1 cup red currant jelly
Apricot Glaze, page 60
6 ounces marzipan
Fondant, page 60
Piping Chocolate, page 65
¾ cup toasted sliced almonds
8 glacé cherries, halved.

Cut cake into three layers. Blend sugar syrup, orange juice, and rum and sprinkle over layers. Sandwich layers with red currant jelly. Place flat bottom of tart pan over cake and weigh down with 4-pound weight. Let stand 2 hours. Brush apricot glaze over cake. Cover with marzipan. Place fondant in double boiler and dilute with sugar syrup or rum. Proceed as illustrated in step-by-step photos

2 **Brush thin layer apricot glaze** over marzipan and around sides of cake to give shine to fondant. Brush glaze as thinly as possible.

3 **Blend melted chocolate** that is piping consistency with a little fondant, using icing spatula to mix thoroughly.

1 **Roll out marzipan** to same size as cake. Trim edge of marzipan circle and place on top of glazed cake.

4 **Pour warm fondant** on top of cake and spread with icing spatula. Work quickly to prevent fondant from setting. Do not allow fondant to run down sides of cake.

5 **Spoon chocolate fondant** into small parchment pastry bag. Cut off point of bag with scissors and pipe fondant in spiral on top of cake, starting in center of cake.

6 **Lightly draw edge of icing spatula** across cake, starting at center and working toward outer edge of cake. Wipe blade of spatula with damp cloth after each stroke.

7 **Cover sides of cake** with toasted sliced almonds. Lightly press almonds onto sides of cake with icing spatula. Decorate top of cake with halved glacé cherries.

Mocha Almond Cake

Cake:
6 eggs, separated
$\frac{2}{3}$ cup sugar
$\frac{1}{2}$ cup all purpose flour
$\frac{2}{3}$ cup finely ground blanched almonds
$\frac{2}{3}$ cup sponge cake crumbs

Filling and icing:
4 teaspoons powdered instant coffee
2 tablespoons boiling water
German Buttercream, page 54
6 ounces marzipan
Apricot Glaze, page 60
1 tablespoon strong black coffee
1 tablespoon coffee-flavored liqueur
Fondant, page 60
grated chocolate
16 candied coffee beans

10-inch springform pan or deep flan ring, bottom
lined

Preheat oven to 375°F

To make cake, beat egg yolks and sugar until thick
and lemon-colored. Beat egg whites until stiff. Fold
beaten egg whites into egg yolk mixture. Combine
flour, almonds, and cake crumbs and fold into egg
yolk mixture. Pour mixture into prepared pan and
smooth top. Bake in preheated oven 35 to 40
minutes or until cake springs back when pressed in
center. Cool on wire rack, and remove from pan.

To make filling, dissolve coffee in boiling water
and let cool. Spoon 1 cup plain buttercream into
pastry bag fitted with open star tip and set aside.
Add coffee to remaining buttercream and beat until
blended. Cut cake into three layers. Fill and cover
cake with coffee buttercream. Roll out marzipan to
10-inch circle and place on top of cake. Brush
apricot glaze over top and around sides of cake.
Blend strong black coffee and liqueur with fondant
and cover top of cake. Pipe fondant in thin
horizontal lines over top of cake at regular intervals.
Hold icing spatula at right angle to piped lines and
draw five lines at regular intervals across top of cake
with edge of spatula. Draw edge of spatula in
opposite direction between the five lines. Press
grated chocolate around sides of cake. Pipe reserved
buttercream into sixteen rosettes on top of
cake and decorate with candied
coffee beans.

Boiled Chocolate Icing

This old Austrian recipe is similar to the sweet velvety icing used on the world-famous Sachertorte. The traditional Sachertorte icing is made with $1\frac{1}{4}$ cups sugar, 9 ounces chocolate, and $\frac{1}{2}$ cup water. It is made in the same way as the recipe below. Although there is a slight difference in ingredients used, the same excellent results are achieved.

$1\frac{1}{4}$ cups sugar
4 ounces semisweet chocolate, coarsely chopped
$\frac{1}{2}$ cup unsweetened cocoa, sifted
$\frac{2}{3}$ cup water

3 **Pour icing into bowl** and beat with wooden spoon until smooth and creamy. Stirring makes icing thick and glossy.

1 **Place sugar, chocolate, cocoa,** and water in heavy saucepan. Stir until thoroughly blended. Place saucepan over moderate heat and bring to boil.

4 **Alternatively, pour half the chocolate icing** onto marble slab and work with palette knife or spatula until creamy. Stir back into remaining chocolate. This will make icing thick and creamy in the least amount of time.

2 **Cook, stirring,** until temperature registers 220°F on candy thermometer. Brush inside edge of saucepan with water to prevent sugar crystals from forming while icing is cooking.

5 **Place cake on wire rack** set over waxed paper. Pour chocolate icing over top of cake and spread with spatula covering cake completely. Let stand until icing is set. Lift cake with two wide, flat spatulas and place on serving plate.

Piping Icings

Royal Icing

1 egg white
about $1\frac{3}{4}$ cups sifted confectioners' sugar
a few drops lemon juice

The amount of confectioners' sugar given is approximate because the correct amount is determined by the size of the egg. The slightest difference in the amount of egg white used can make a substantial difference in the quantity of confectioners' sugar needed. When Royal Icing is used for piping, less icing is usually needed than the amount of icing made with 1 egg white. The consistency of the icing must be just right for piping—soft enough to pipe in a continuous line, but firm enough to hold its shape.

1 **Place egg white in bowl** and beat until foamy. Add 1 cup confectioners' sugar gradually, beating constantly. Add enough remaining sugar while beating to make icing correct consistency for piping. Add lemon juice and beat until icing is firm. Beat in more sugar if necessary.

2 **Royal Icing is ready to pipe** when it is thick and light in texture. The lines made by beaters should be clearly visible on surface of icing. Cover bowl with damp cloth to prevent surface from drying out if icing is not used immediately. Royal Icing may be tinted with food coloring.

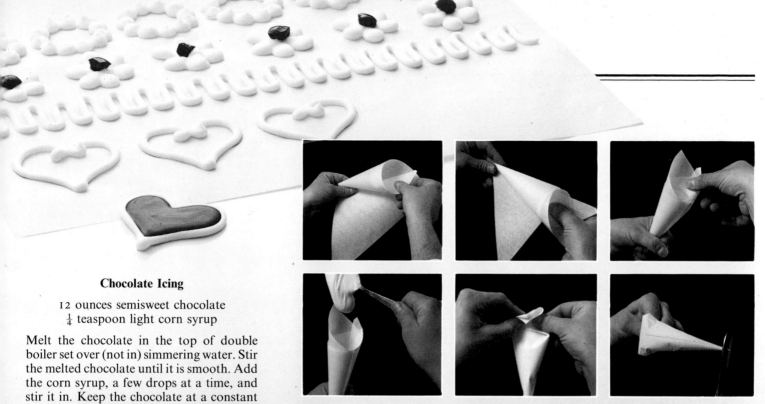

Chocolate Icing

12 ounces semisweet chocolate
¼ teaspoon light corn syrup

Melt the chocolate in the top of double boiler set over (not in) simmering water. Stir the melted chocolate until it is smooth. Add the corn syrup, a few drops at a time, and stir it in. Keep the chocolate at a constant temperature of 90°F to keep it from setting. It must be warm in order to be of piping consistency. This icing makes a flexible thread that can be piped directly onto a cake in very delicate patterns. It can also be used to make decorations that can be piped onto waxed paper or aluminum foil. When the piped decorations set, they can be removed from the paper or aluminum foil easily and transferred directly onto a cake or they may be stored carefully until needed.

A piping bag can be made with parchment paper. (1) Fold a square of paper diagonally in half. Hold the middle of the long side between your left thumb and index finger and twist the paper toward your body with your right hand. (2) Keep twisting, holding the pointed end in your left hand. (3) Fold in the extra paper at the top to secure the bag. (4) Spoon the icing into the bag, being careful not to get any icing on the rim of the bag. (5) Before you fold in the top, make sure the seam (the side edge of the paper) is at the back. Squeeze the air out of the bag and fold in the top ends. (6) Cut off the tip with sharp scissors. Remember, the size of the hole determines the thickness of the piped thread.

Left: You can pipe delicate butterflies and flowers that can be decorated with silver balls and candy violets. Hold hands steady while piping. **Right**: The correct consistency for chocolate that is to be piped.

Chocolate

Chocolate comes from the cacao tree. The translation of the botanical name of the tree is "food of the gods," and there are few who would disagree. But chocolate can be difficult to work with and it is important to understand how to use it. Humidity, temperature, and drafts all affect the way chocolate sets. Try to work with it on a day when the humidity is low and the temperature in the kitchen can be controlled at about 65°F. Chocolate should be melted over low heat because it burns easily. The safest way to melt it is in the top of a double boiler set over (not in) simmering water. Remove the top of the double boiler before the chocolate is completely melted and allow it to finish melting off heat. Alternatively, melt only half the chocolate, remove it from the heat, and add the remaining

chocolate. It is of utmost importance that you do not allow any moisture to get into melting chocolate. If even one drop gets into the chocolate, it will stiffen and be impossible to spread. Since moisture collects under a pot cover, this means you must never cover chocolate while it is melting. If the chocolate should stiffen, the problem can be resolved by adding one teaspoon of vegetable shortening for each ounce of chocolate used. But don't add butter as it contains water and it will make the situation worse. Chocolate sold for baking can be unsweetened, semisweet, or sweet. If you do not use the kind of chocolate called for in a recipe, be sure to adjust the sugar accordingly. Whichever kind of chocolate used, remember, the end product will be a direct reflection of the quality of the chocolate.

5 **Spread the chocolate** in a thin layer on a marble slab. Work quickly so the chocolate can be spread evenly before it begins to set. Many decorations must be made before the chocolate is completely hard. (See chocolate rolls, photo 6.)

1 **Chop chocolate** so it will melt quickly in a bowl set over (not in) simmering water. If you have a large piece of chocolate, hold it vertically and cut down the side with a heavy sharp knife. Start by melting only half the chocolate.

3 **Many people prefer** to cool chocolate on a marble slab instead of in the refrigerator. Pour half the melted chocolate onto the marble and work continuously with the palette knife or long spatula until the chocolate is the consistency of thick cream. Return the thickened chocolate to the bowl of warm chocolate.

6 **Make chocolate rolls** when chocolate is only half-set. Hold a wide spatula at a slight angle to the chocolate and push along the top of the chocolate for ½ to 1½ inches to form a thin roll of chocolate.

2 **Add the remaining chocolate.** This will help cool the melted chocolate. Remove the bowl from the water and stir until all the chocolate is completely dissolved. If some chocolate is not dissolved, return the bowl to the warm water and reheat the chocolate slightly.

4 **Reheat chocolate to 90°F over** (not in) a pan of simmering water, stirring constantly. Warm the chocolate slowly. Use a palette knife or spatula to check the chocolate in about 2 to 3 minutes. It should be glossy and firm enough to cut into decorations.

7 **Chocolate fans** are also made with partially set chocolate. Scrape a triangle in the soft chocolate with a wide triangular shaped spatula. Hold one end of the chocolate firmly as you push the spatula and the chocolate will form a fan.

8 **To cut out chocolate shapes,** spread the chocolate on waxed paper in a slightly thicker layer than in photo 5. If available, keep chocolate the correct working temperature in a thermostatically controlled electric pan.

9 **Cut chocolate shapes** with cookie cutters before the chocolate has completely set. It is difficult to cut chocolate once it has set, but can be done by dipping the cutter into warm water. Wipe off the cutter with a damp cloth each time you use it.

In addition to the step-by-step photos, there are several attractive chocolate flower decorations shown on this page. They can be made in advance but they must be stored carefully, protected from dust or potential damage. Use them to decorate cakes and cookies and combine them with other ingredients such as nuts or candied fruit. In these pictures the chocolate has been combined with marzipan and praline, page 146. The marzipan is rolled out before cutting. Hot praline is poured onto an oiled marble slab, rolled out, and cut with oiled cutters or a sharp knife. The chocolate used should not be completely set.

10 **Very thin chocolate flakes** for cake decorating are easy to make. Scrape a block of chocolate with a heavy sharp knife. Keep the chocolate and the knife vertical to the work surface or you may inadvertently cut chunks instead of thin shavings.

11 **To make finely flaked chocolate,** use a cheese grater. These flakes are very thin and fragile and should be grated directly onto the cake. This is a good way to be sure the chocolate flakes will be evenly distributed over the surface of the cake.

Cake Decorations

There is a wide variety of material available for use in cake decorating. What to use and how much decoration is appropriate is a matter of personal preference. Ingredients such as nuts—whole, halved, chopped, or sliced—candied fruit, maraschino cherries, coconut, grated chocolate, and many kinds of fruit can be used. In addition, there is a somewhat motley collection of sugar-based decorations available—gold and silver balls in all sizes, sugar flowers, chocolate sprinkles, chocolate decorations in a variety of shapes, mocha beans coated in sugar or chocolate, and chocolate or sugar leaves. All of them, along with crystallized sugar, are illustrated on this page. However, the collection is by no means complete. All kinds of ready-made decorations are available. You can even buy sugar letters or numbers. Ready-made decorations are used by professional cooks as well as those who cook at home, and there is no reason not to use them, as long as the shape, color, and flavor of the cake harmonizes with the decorations. Since not everyone is artistically inclined, it may be helpful for us to offer a few words of advice, without trying to advocate a particular style of decoration. Use decorations sparingly; it is better to have too few than too many. Cooks must decide for themselves how much decoration they want to use. We cannot make that decision for you. Any decoration you can't make yourself, such as gold and silver balls or mocha beans for a coffee-flavored cake, can be bought ready-made without any sense of guilt. But when it comes to decorations you can make, such as delicate marzipan roses, it is always better to make them yourself than to use ready-made substitutes. Your ultimate goal should be to have a cake with filling, frosting, and decoration that forms an aesthetically pleasing whole.

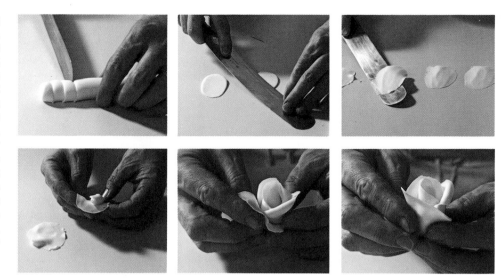

Use gum paste to make roses that are for decoration only. Shape a piece of gum paste into a cylinder (see photo) and cut it into equal-size pieces. Shape the pieces into balls. Flatten the balls, working outward from the center with a small spatula or palette knife, until thin petals have been formed. Make an elongated ball for the bud from a piece of gum. Lift a petal from the work surface with the spatula and place it around the bud, securing it at the base. Repeat with remaining petals. Turn the tops of the petals out with your thumbs. Set aside to dry. Cut a flat edge across the base. Use this method to make full-blown roses or rose buds.

Working with Marzipan

Almond paste, the basis of the marzipan used to cover cakes and to make cake decorations, can be mixed with as much as an equal weight of confectioners' sugar, but the almond flavor is best when it is mixed in the following ratio:

1 pound confectioners' sugar
1 pound 10 ounces almond paste

Sift the confectioners' sugar onto a work surface, marble is ideal. Break the almond paste into small pieces and add it to the confectioners' sugar. Work into a smooth paste quickly. If the marzipan is overworked it will get crumbly, particularly if it has a high sugar content, and will be impossible to roll out or shape properly. If this should happen, add a little beaten egg white. To roll the marzipan, sift the confectioners' sugar lightly onto the work surface and roll the marzipan with a sugar-coated rolling pin. There are two special rolling pins developed specifically for marzipan that make squares or furrows and can be used when appropriate. Use food coloring to color marzipan, if desired. Don't use fruit extracts because they will cause marzipan to ferment if stored.

Piped Decorations

This is an easy-to-learn and inexpensive method of decorating cakes. When piped icing is used, it is essential that the flavor of the decoration harmonize with that of the cake, the filling, and the frosting. Apart from a piping bag and a selection of tips, the only things you need are steady hands and some practice. We advise anyone who has never used a piping bag to practice before trying to decorate a cake. Use a piping icing made with 2 cups confectioners' sugar, sifted, and a little beaten egg white. The icing should not be too thick. Practice by piping onto waxed paper and try to make the patterns shown on the opposite page. The only way you can learn how to pipe is by doing it. Start with a plain tip and try a few lines, making them as straight as possible. When you gain confidence, try a fluted tip, starting with straight lines and progressing to more complicated patterns. You should also learn how to make rosettes

in various sizes. Hold the piping bag in a vertical position and exert a small amount of pressure to make a small swirl. Use additional pressure to make a larger swirl. Pick up the tip quickly to finish the swirl neatly. To pipe a wavy line with a fluted nozzle, hold the piping bag at a slight angle and move it from right to left as you squeeze out the icing.

● Rosettes are made with a fluted tip for a nut-buttercream gâteau. Use a medium-size tip with buttercream.

● When fluted decorations are made with meringue or whipped cream, the size of the tip to use will depend on what is to be piped. Use a small tip with heavy buttercream. Use larger tips with light airy meringues or whipped cream.

● Use a large tip, plain or fluted, with whipped cream.

● A lattice design in buttercream is made with small to medium-size tips, plain or fluted.

● Use small plain or fluted tips with piping icing because piping icing is too sweet to use in large quantities. The English wedding cake is the exception that proves the rule! It is possible to make the most intricate designs with this soft icing—and with chocolate icing as well.

● "Spaghetti icing" can be made with the smallest size plain tip, but the quickest way to make it is with a special tip that has five small holes.

● Use small tips to make these decorations with buttercream. The cream should be quite soft to prevent air bubbles from forming in the bag. Air bubbles will cause breaks in a line as you pipe.

● Special tips are used to make intricate decoration such as those used in England for wedding and Christmas cakes. You can buy tips to make leaves, flowers, bands, swirls, and other special shapes.

To fill a piping bag insert tip into narrow end, fold back top of bag, and fill with icing. Fold top of bag back up, shake icing down, and twist top of bag to close. When using a paper piping bag, cut off tip at narrow end, insert small nozzle, and carefully fill bag with icing or buttercream. Keep rim of bag free of icing so icing will not spill out when top of bag is folded in.

Cakes & Company

We all have taken a delight and pride in producing light sponges and mouthwatering cakes. These have traditionally been achieved either by creaming the butter and sugar then adding the eggs and flour, or by whisking the egg whites and sugar and folding them into the flour and butter.

Whereas in the past this had to be done arduously by hand, these days many cooks have recourse to electric food mixers or whisks that make the task a lot easier. The invention of baking powder (the perfect raising agent) has also helped the home cook a great deal by rendering unnecessary the old-fashioned technique of beating by hand.

Many family recipes for sponge cakes and loaves were and still are surrounded in mystery, especially those mixtures that are more like a heavier traditional sponge than a quick, baking-powder sponge. Such recipes are handed down through the generations from grandmother to mother and from mother to daughter. The strict secrecy that envelops the ingredients is matched only by the strict adherence to the method of preparation. The aim is quite simply to make it impossible for the family recipe to be copied. The serving of a homemade marble cake, for example, can be the highlight of a coffee morning or afternoon tea for a hostess who hopes that her guests will like her baking and even congratulate her on it. The food industry has begun to make inroads in this area, however, and we should not underestimate the proportion of marble or Madeira cake eaten today that comes out of a packet. We should not forget either the excellent sponge cakes sold in small bakeries. This is a logical result of the fact that these cakes go particularly well with coffee and with tea. The traditional English "tea-cake" was first baked and put on public sale in Bath by a lady named Sally Lunn (and there is still a type of tea-cake known as a Sally Lunn). English afternoon tea was until quite recently something that one had in a café or restaurant rather than at home, so it is hardly surprising that this branch of cake making originated in cafés and pastry shops.

One of the most delicious types of sponge is the German "Rehrücken" illustrated opposite. After baking, the cake is stuck all over with almond spikes and covered with chocolate icing. The cake does in fact bear some resemblance to a saddle of venison (the meaning of the word *Rehrücken*) and it is not difficult to guess that this is a modern relic of the old fast days when no meat was eaten.

Sponge Cakes and Leavening Agents

Cakes, except coffee cakes, are usually baked without yeast. However, since a cake that does not rise is not satisfactory, some kind of leavening or rising agent must be used. Whenever possible, professional bakers prefer to use eggs, properly beaten and mixed into the batter, rather than a commercial leavening agent. Baking powder or baking soda are avoided whenever possible because, although most of the chemical aftertaste is destroyed during baking, a slight trace can remain in a delicately flavored cake. Baking powder always contains a small amount of baking soda. But, when baking soda is the only leavening agent used, it must be combined with an acid ingredient. This combination will cause carbon dioxide to be released, and the carbon dioxide will cause the batter to rise. The most popular and easiest leavening agent to use is baking powder, provided it is not used excessively. The taste cannot be detected in a well-flavored heavy batter and the baking powder will improve the texture of the cake considerably. This is particularly true for fruit cake.

Comparison of Two Sponge Cakes

The difference between the cakes pictured above is dramatic. Both cakes were made from the same recipe for Quick Sponge Cake, page 33. The only difference between the cakes is that baking powder was not used to make the cake on the left. Since baking powder was not used, the cake on the left should have been made by the classic method in which butter is creamed with part of the sugar, egg yolks are beaten in gradually, and beaten egg whites are folded into the mixture with flour and cornstarch.

1 **Line pan with parchment paper** to be sure cake will come out of pan easily and will stay moist. Place pan on parchment paper and trace around bottom and sides of pan. (If you prefer, pan can be greased and floured instead of lined with paper.)

2 **Cut paper at four corners** and fold in along lines at ends of pan. Fold at lines along sides of pan.

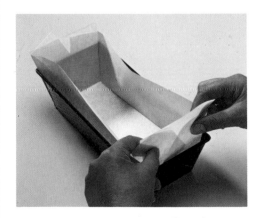

3 **Place folded paper in pan.** Smooth paper against bottom and sides of pan.

4 **Beat eggs,** egg yolks, sugar, salt, and lemon peel in bowl set over pan of barely simmering water. Beat just until mixture leaves trail when beaters are lifted. Gradually fold in sifted flour and cornstarch with wooden spoon.

5 **Gradually stir in** cooled melted butter in slow, steady stream until no streaks remain.

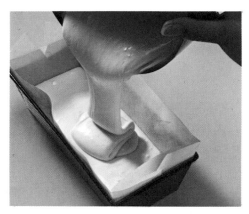

6 **Pour mixture** into lined pan and smooth top with spatula. Make sure there are no air bubbles and mixture is free of lumps.

7 **Bake 15 to 20 minutes**. Slide cake gently out of oven and make shallow cut lengthwise in top of cake with tip of sharp knife dipped in warm water. This will help cake rise evenly. Finish baking.

10- × 4-inch or 9- × 5-inch loaf pan lined with parchment paper (see photos 1–3)

Preheat oven to 350°F

Beat eggs, egg yolks, granulated sugar, salt, and lemon peel in bowl set over (not in) pan of barely simmering water until beaters leave trail when lifted, 3 to 4 minutes. Remove bowl and beat until mixture is cool. Sift flour and cornstarch and gradually fold into egg mixture. Add melted butter in slow, steady stream, stirring just until blended.

Pour mixture into prepared loaf pan.

Bake in preheated oven 15 to 20 minutes or until cake is golden brown. Make shallow cut lengthwise in top of cake with tip of sharp knife dipped in warm water. This will allow cake to rise properly. Bake 30 to 40 minutes longer.

Cool cake in pan on wire rack 15 minutes. Remove from pan and cool completely. Leave paper on cake until ready to serve to keep cake moist. Dust top of cake with sifted confectioners' sugar just before serving.

Light Madeira Cake

This cake is particularly light and airy. It is made in the same way as the Genoise sponge, page 28. This mixture also can be used to make a layer cake in a 10-inch springform pan or cake pan.

3 eggs
2 egg yolks
¾ cup granulated sugar
⅛ teaspoon salt
grated peel of 1 lemon
1 cup cake flour
⅓ cup cornstarch
6 tablespoons melted and clarified butter
confectioners' sugar for dusting

Rum-Raisin Cake

butter and sponge cake crumbs for pan
$\frac{3}{4}$ cup dark raisins
$\frac{1}{4}$ cup chopped candied lemon peel
$1\frac{1}{2}$ tablespoons dark rum
$\frac{1}{2}$ cup (1 stick) butter
1 cup granulated sugar
grated peel of 1 lemon
6 eggs, separated
$1\frac{1}{2}$ cups cake flour
confectioners' sugar for dusting

10- × 4-inch loaf pan

Preheat oven to 350°F

Grease loaf pan with butter and dust with sponge cake crumbs or line pan with parchment paper. Place raisins and candied lemon peel in medium-size bowl. Add rum and stir well. Let stand at room temperature 1 hour. Cream butter in large bowl with $\frac{1}{3}$ cup granulated sugar and grated lemon peel until light and fluffy. Gradually beat in egg yolks, beating until well blended. Add flour to rum-raisin mixture and stir well. Beat egg whites with remaining $\frac{2}{3}$ cup granulated sugar until stiff peaks form. Beat about $\frac{1}{3}$ of beaten egg whites into butter mixture, beating until well blended. Stir in raisin mixture. Fold in remaining beaten egg whites. Pour mixture into prepared pan and smooth top. Bake in preheated oven 60 to 65 minutes or until cake tester inserted in center of cake comes out clean. Cool in pan on wire rack 10 minutes. Remove from pan and cool completely on wire rack. Dust top of cake with confectioners' sugar just before serving. Cake may also be covered with thin coating of Apricot Glaze, page 60, and melted chocolate. Coating will keep cake fresh.

Light Fruit Cake

$\frac{2}{3}$ cup raisins
$\frac{1}{3}$ cup currants
$\frac{1}{4}$ cup chopped candied lemon peel
$\frac{1}{4}$ cup chopped candied orange peel
2 tablespoons chopped preserved stem ginger
2 tablespoons dark rum or arrak
1 cup (2 sticks) butter
1 cup granulated sugar
4 eggs, separated
grated peel of 1 lemon
2 cups cake flour
1 teaspoon baking powder
$\frac{1}{4}$ teaspoon ginger
$\frac{1}{4}$ teaspoon nutmeg
$\frac{1}{4}$ teaspoon ground cloves
$\frac{1}{4}$ teaspoon salt
confectioners' sugar for dusting

12- × 4-inch loaf pan, lined with parchment paper

Preheat oven to 375°F

Place raisins, currants, candied lemon and, orange peels, and stem ginger in bowl. Add rum, stir gently, and let stand at room temperature 1 hour. Cream butter with $\frac{1}{2}$ cup granulated sugar, egg yolks, and lemon peel until light and fluffy. Sift flour, baking powder, spices, and salt, and fold into fruit mixture. Beat egg whites with remaining $\frac{1}{2}$ cup granulated sugar until stiff peaks form. Stir half the beaten egg whites into butter mixture to lighten. Fold in fruit mixture. Fold in remaining beaten egg whites. Spoon into prepared pan and smooth top. Bake in

preheated oven 60 to 65 minutes or until cake tester inserted in center of cake comes out clean. Cool in pan on wire rack 15 minutes. Remove from pan and cool completely. Remove lining paper and dust top of cake with confectioners' sugar before serving.

Walnut Spice Cake

½ cup (1 stick) butter, softened
¾ cup sugar
4 eggs, separated
1 tablespoon brandy
1 tablespoons Curaçao
grated peel of 1 orange
½ cup cake flour
⅓ cup cornstarch
⅓ cup unsweetened cocoa
½ teaspoon cinnamon
¼ teaspoon each ground cloves, allspice, ginger, and salt
¾ cup ground walnuts
10 ounces semisweet chocolate, melted
chopped pistachios for decoration

12-inch fluted loaf pan or 9- × 5-inch loaf pan, greased and floured

Preheat oven to 350°F

Beat butter, sugar, and egg yolks in medium-size bowl until light and fluffy. Add brandy, Curaçao, and orange peel, and beat until blended. Sift flour, cornstarch, cocoa, spices, and salt into bowl, and stir in walnuts. Beat egg whites until stiff. Beat about one third of beaten egg whites into

creamed mixture. Fold in remaining beaten egg whites alternately with flour-spice mixture. Pour into prepared pan. Bake in preheated oven 50 to 60 minutes. Cool in pan on wire rack 10 minutes. Remove from pan and cool completely on rack. Spread melted chocolate over cake and sprinkle with pistachios.

German Rehrücken

6 tablespoons butter, softened
⅔ cup sugar
3 eggs, separated
1 teaspoon vanilla
3 ounces semisweet chocolate, melted
⅓ cup ground almonds
1 cup sponge cake crumbs
Apricot Glaze, page 60
about ½ cup slivered almonds
Boiled Chocolate Icing, page 64, or 16 ounces semisweet chocolate, melted

12-inch fluted loaf pan or 9- × 5-inch loaf pan, greased and floured

Preheat oven to 350°F

Beat butter, sugar, egg yolks, and vanilla in medium-size bowl until light and fluffy. Fold in melted chocolate. Combine ground almonds and sponge cake crumbs. Beat egg whites until stiff. Beat about one third of beaten egg whites into creamed mixture. Fold in remaining beaten egg whites alternately with almond crumb mixture. Spoon into prepared pan and smooth top. Bake in preheated oven 50 to 55 minutes. Cool cake in pan on wire rack 10 minutes. Remove from pan and place on wire rack set over waxed paper. Brush with thin layer of apricot glaze. Let stand until completely cool. Stud cake all over with almond slivers. Spoon chocolate icing over cake, covering cake and almonds completely. (Scrape melted chocolate off waxed paper and save to use another time.)

Almond and Chocolate Cake

4 eggs separated
¾ cup sugar
½ teaspoon vanilla
2 tablespoons Bénédictine
6 tablespoons butter, melted and cooled
1 cup finely ground toasted almonds
3 ounces semisweet chocolate, finely chopped
⅔ cup sifted all-purpose flour
¼ teaspoon cinnamon
¼ teaspoon allspice
¼ teaspoon salt

Apricot Glaze, page 60
10 ounces semisweet chocolate, melted
finely chopped pistachios for decoration

12-inch fluted loaf pan or 9- × 5-inch loaf pan, greased and floured

Preheat oven to 350°F

Beat egg yolks, sugar, vanilla, and Bénédictine in medium-size bowl until thick and lemon-colored. Beat egg whites in separate bowl until stiff. Beat half the beaten egg whites into egg yolk mixture until blended. Gradually fold in melted butter. Combine almonds, chopped chocolate, flour, cinnamon, allspice, and salt, and fold into egg yolk mixture alternately with remaining beaten egg whites. Pour into prepared pan and smooth top. Bake in preheated oven 50 to 60 minutes. Cool in pan on wire rack 10 minutes. Remove from pan and cool on rack. Brush cake with thin layer apricot glaze. Spread melted chocolate over cake, covering completely. Decorate with chopped pistachios. Let stand until chocolate is set.

Basque Cake

Although this cake originated in the Basque region of Spain, it has gained popularity throughout France. In this version, the sponge has a vanilla custard filling. In the Basque area, jam is also used as a filling. Black cherry jam is the most popular.

1¼ cups (2½ sticks) butter, softened
1½ cups granulated sugar
2 teaspoons vanilla
3 eggs
3¼ cups cake flour
2 teaspoons baking powder
½ teaspoon salt
1 tablespoon dark rum
1½ cups Simple Vanilla Custard (Crème Pâtissière), page 50
confectioners' sugar for dusting

Two 7-inch cake pans or one 10-inch springform pan, greased and floured

Preheat oven to 375°F

Grease and flour cake pans or springform pan. Cream butter with sugar and vanilla until light and fluffy. Add eggs, one at a time, beating well after each addition. Sift flour, baking powder, and salt, and gradually fold into butter mixture with wooden spoon. Spoon into large pastry bag fitted with ½-inch plain tip (#10). Pipe mixture in spiral onto bottom of prepared pan(s). Pipe extra ring around inside edge of pan(s) to prevent filling from sticking to sides of pan(s). Stir rum into vanilla custard. Spread evenly over mixture inside of outer ring, using small spatula or palette knife. Pipe remaining mixture in spiral over filling. Bake in preheated oven 40 to 45 minutes or until center of cake(s) spring back when lightly pressed. Cool in pan(s) on wire rack(s) 15 minutes. Remove from pan(s) and cool completely. Dust top with sifted confectioners' sugar just before serving. Alternatively, spread mixture in pan(s) instead of piping it.

French Fig Cake

½ cup snipped dried figs
½ cup snipped pitted dates
¾ cup coarsely chopped walnuts
2 tablespoons brandy or armagnac
1 recipe Cut-in Pastry (Pâté Brisée), page 37
½ cup (1 stick) butter, softened
¾ cup granulated sugar
4 egg yolks
⅔ cup ground almonds
1 teaspoon vanilla
½ teaspoon cinnamon
¼ teaspoon salt
⅛ teaspoon ground cloves
⅓ cup all-purpose flour
3 egg whites
confectioners' sugar for dusting

12- × 4-inch loaf pan

Preheat oven to 350°F

Place figs, dates, and walnuts in bowl. Add brandy, stir gently, and let stand at room temperature 1 hour. Prepare pastry according to directions on page 37. Roll out pastry and use to line loaf pan. Trim pastry edge even with rim of pan. Cream butter with half the granulated sugar until light and fluffy. Beat in egg yolks, one at a time, beating well after each addition. Fold in ground almonds, vanilla, cinnamon, salt, and cloves. Sift flour over fig-date mixture and fold in. Beat egg whites with remaining sugar until stiff peaks form. Stir about half of beaten egg whites into creamed butter-almond mixture to lighten. Fold in fig-nut mixture. Fold in remaining beaten egg whites. Pour into pastry lined pan and smooth top. Bake in preheated oven 50 to 55 minutes or until golden brown. Cool completely in pan on wire rack. Remove from pan and dust with confectioners' sugar. Cake may be glazed with Apricot Glaze, page 60, and covered with melted chocolate, if desired. Fresh figs may be substituted for dried figs.

Traditional British Cakes

Cakes were originally a combination of bread dough and dried fruit, often mixed with spices. A lot of traditional cakes and buns are still based on this history of making use of leftover dough. In Britain many housewives set aside one particular day of the week as a "baking day." Bread and cakes were made to last the week and that is why rich fruit cakes have always been popular in Britain, as they keep so well and are sometimes actually better if eaten a few days after cooking. The fruit cake is a particularly British institution and relies upon the quantity of fruit to flour and eggs to keep it moist. A heavy mixture of fruit to the other ingredients will preserve the cake for many months, not to say years, as in the case of the wedding or Christmas cake for instance.

One of the best-known old recipes for a British cake is that of the pound cake, named after the pound in weight of each ingredient that was incorporated: butter, sugar, eggs, and flour. This quantity does, however, produce an extremely large cake and today the recipe can be adapted to a quarter pound of each ingredient. There are many variations on this basic recipe using different flavorings, or the addition of a varying quantity of fruit.

Another basic recipe that can be adapted is that of the Madeira cake. The name is said to have originated from the eighteenth- and nineteenth-century custom of drinking a glass of the sweet Madeira wine as an accompaniment to the cake. One of the most appealing variations to the Madeira cake is the addition of glacé cherries to turn it into a delicious cherry cake. Alternatively, the addition of carraway seeds will turn it into a traditional seed cake.

One of the most favored occasions to make use of the wide range of cakes that can be made is the traditional British afternoon tea. This custom has been preserved almost unchanged since its conception to the present day. Afternoon tea would normally be taken around four o'clock and is an opportunity for home-baked cakes and pastries to be temptingly displayed. Each person will have their own favorite, be it a fruit cake like the Dundee, or a sponge mixture like the checkered Battenburg covered with marzipan, or the Madeira or cherry cake. These cakes are usually baked at home but there are also a large number of old-fashioned teashops around Britain where the cakes are baked fresh each day and the ritual of afternoon tea is observed.

Tea drinking became a passion in Britain in the eighteenth century. At first only China tea was available and it was very expensive to buy, thus the invention of small tea caddies with locks to prevent anyone taking the precious commodity without permission. Such was the popularity of tea that in the nineteenth-century tea plantations were established in India and Ceylon to supply the growing requirements for more and cheaper tea. Tea drinking became a national pastime and has continued to flourish into the twentieth century.

The Rolls Royce—long a symbol of British quality—is an appropriate setting in which to admire the traditional British glass of sherry and the cakes that accompany it: the Simnel or Easter Cake, the Dundee Cake, and the Madeira Cake.

Dundee Cake

Whether or not it is true that there is a greater variety of cake than whisky in Scotland is a matter of debate, but it is certainly true that Dundee Cake is one of the most popular tea-time cakes served in Scotland and throughout the rest of Great Britain.

4 cups raisins
$\frac{1}{2}$ cup chopped mixed candied fruit
2 tablespoons dark rum
1 cup (2 sticks) butter, softened
$1\frac{1}{4}$ cups firmly packed brown sugar
6 eggs, lightly beaten
1 tablespoon marmalade
$2\frac{1}{3}$ cups all-purpose flour
1 teaspoon baking powder
$\frac{1}{2}$ teaspoon salt
$\frac{2}{3}$ cup ground almonds
about $1\frac{1}{2}$ cups whole blanched almonds, split in half
Apricot Glaze for brushing, page 50

8-inch deep cake pan, greased and lined

Preheat oven to 325°F

Simnel Cake

This is undoubtedly one of the oldest known English cakes, although most people agree its origin actually to be ancient Greece. This cake is often served on special occasions, particularly Easter Sunday or Mother's Day.

1 cup (2 sticks) butter, softened
1 cup sugar
6 eggs, lightly beaten
$2\frac{1}{3}$ cups all-purpose flour
1 teaspoon baking powder
1 teaspoon cinnamon
$\frac{1}{8}$ teaspoon each, allspice, ginger, ground cloves, and salt
$\frac{1}{3}$ cup ground almonds
grated peel of 1 orange and $\frac{1}{2}$ lemon
$2\frac{1}{2}$ cups currants
$\frac{3}{4}$ cup raisins
1 tablespoon orange liqueur
(Cointreau, Grand Marnier, or brandy)
Apricot Glaze, page 60
2 packages (7 ounces each) marzipan
Fondant, page 60
Royal Icing to decorate, page 64

8-inch deep cake pan, greased and lined

Preheat oven to 350°F

Cream butter and sugar in large bowl until light and fluffy. Add beaten eggs to butter-sugar mixture, a little at a time, and continue beating until mixture is light and frothy and has increased in volume. Sift flour, baking powder, spices, and salt together. Stir in almonds and orange and lemon peels. Fold flour mixture carefully into creamed mixture with fruit and liqueur so mixture loses as little volume as possible. Pour mixture into prepared pan and smooth top gently. Bake in preheated oven $1\frac{1}{4}$ to $1\frac{1}{2}$ hours. Cool completely in pan on wire rack. Remove cake from pan and peel off lining paper.

Brush cake with thin layer of hot apricot glaze. Divide marzipan in half and roll out one piece to 8-inch circle. Place on top of cake. Brush marzipan circle with apricot glaze. Cut remaining marzipan into $1\frac{1}{4}$-inch wide circles and arrange around top edge of cake. Place cake under broiler, about 6 inches from source of heat, and broil 2 to 3 minutes or until edges of marzipan circles are lightly browned. Remove from oven and set aside to cool. Warm fondant and spread on top of cake inside marzipan circles. Tint Royal Icing with food coloring and pipe lettering in center of cake.

1 **Place raisins** and candied fruit in bowl. Stir in rum and set aside. Cream butter and brown sugar in large bowl until light and fluffy. Use balloon whisk or heavy duty electric mixer. A mixer, if available, will save time.

2 **Gradually add beaten eggs** to creamed mixture, beating well after each addition.

3 **Continue beating** until mixture has increased in volume. Beat in marmalade until completely incorporated into mixture.

4 **Sift flour**, baking powder, and salt over creamed mixture. Add ground almonds and fruit-rum mixture and fold in with wooden spoon.

Remove cake from oven and brush almonds with apricot glaze. Cool completely in pan on wire rack. Remove cake from pan but leave paper on cake. Wrap tightly in aluminum foil or place in airtight container. Store in cool place until ready to serve. Fruit cakes keep very well and, in fact, improve in flavor during storage.

5 **Spoon mixture** into prepared pan and smooth top. Arrange almond halves on top in concentric circles. Bake in preheated oven 1½ to 2 hours.

Baumkuchen

The Baumkuchen stands at the summit of German baking and has come to be regarded as the symbol of quality baking. It appears in the coat-of-arms of the Society of German Pastry Cooks, and it is a cake that is always mentioned in connection with typical German baking.

The cake is not entirely German in origin however, because it can be traced back to ancient Greece. Just as other cakes have mythological associations, this cake is thought to have been a phallic symbol. The discovery that the cake had been baked on a rotating spit provided a clue to its original texture, which evidently was heavy, probably similar to a bread dough. Over the centuries this kind of cake appeared in various forms in many cultures. The precursors of the modern Baumkuchen had names such as spit cake, makeshift bread, spit loaf, or Prügelkuchen. We know that in early wars, soldiers baked cakes like these on a spit. Even the colonists in America baked similar spit cakes over campfires fueled with buffalo dung. The process of improving the dough from a plain bread dough to the rich mixture of today was undoubtedly a slow one. It can be assumed that, as with most culinary advances, the cooks and confectioners working in the European courts must have played a major role in developing the recipe. With the organization of trade guilds and the growing availability of sugar, regional centers to make Baumkuchen were established in central Germany—Dresden, Cottbus, Salzwedel, etc., and, because sugar was available, it was possible to make changes in the recipe that ultimately brought the Baumkuchen close to the form in which we know it today. It also made it possible to advance from making the cake on a spit to using a wooden roller, still found in the Tirol and known as a "Prügel."

No one seems very sure of the origin of the name Baumkuchen (tree cake). The way the cake is made tends to create a barklike effect. When the cake is cut horizontally, it closely resembles the age rings on a tree. It has been suggested that the name comes from the "Prügel" or wooden roller on which the cake is cooked, but this argument is unconvincing.

This unusual cake certainly merits its lofty position in the culinary world and, despite all the modern kitchen equipment available, it remains a handmade masterpiece. Both the preparation of the mixture and the cooking process require a great deal of experience and skill if the end result is to be successful. But nowadays, when one hears talk of "one-step methods" and "emulsifiers," even this, the masterpiece of the baker's art, seems to be in danger.

Although space does not allow room to provide the method used in the preparation of this cake in detail, there is enough space to give the recipe for a typical Baumkuchen, the Salzwedel Baumkuchen. Beat 25 egg yolks with 1 cup sugar until frothy. Cream $2\frac{1}{2}$ cups (5 sticks) butter with the pith of a vanilla pod until fluffy. Add $\frac{1}{2}$ cup rum. Sift $1\frac{2}{3}$ cups flour and $1\frac{1}{4}$ cups cornstarch and stir into butter mixture just until flour is incorporated. Beat 20 egg whites with 1 cup sugar until very stiff. Stir egg yolks into butter mixture and gently fold in beaten egg whites. After baking the first few layers it may be necessary to thin mixture with a little cream. This recipe will bake a Baumkuchen $23\frac{1}{2}$ to $27\frac{1}{2}$ inches tall.

The wooden roller is wrapped in greaseproof paper and tied with a thread, as with the modern Baumkuchen. The first layer cooks over burning wood. Sensitive rotation is necessary for even browning.

This "Prügelkuchen" from Brannenberg in the Tirol is a home-made Baumkuchen. The method is similar to that of the Baumkuchen but uses a wood fire thus giving the cake a distinctive flavor that is unlike anything produced by a modern gas grill.

Katharina Marksteiner has mastered the art of baking. She uses only beechwood for it burns slowly and gives constant heat. During the two-hour cooking time the fire has to be "mended" and must be kept fully under control.

The Tirolean Prügelkuchen

The fact that this popular cake has survived to the present day is both a piece of good fortune and an example of the historical development of one particular cake and one particular method of preparation. Much credit is due to Katharina Marksteiner of Brannenburg who carries on the traditional method of Prügelkuchen making that she learned from her grandmother: using a hand crank over a wooden fire. Other cooks use a motor-operated roller, but Mrs. Marksteiner is convinced that these produce cakes of inferior quality.

It is a fact that this cake was one of the forerunners of the modern Baumkuchen and that the method used is identical. The "Prügel," a slightly tapering wooden roller, is wrapped in greaseproof paper that is then secured with a cotton thread. This roller is placed over a hand-cranked spit supported by two old-fashioned iron supports. The Prügelkuchen mixture differs from the Baumkuchen recipe although similar ingredients are

used. It is a mixture based on the weight of the eggs; that is, with the weight of butter, sugar, and flour being the same as the weight of the eggs. The eggs are whisked with the sugar and butter until frothy and the flour is folded in last. This makes quite a thick mixture that during baking must always be kept fairly near the fire so that the heat keeps it runny. The end result, however, bears no comparison with the Baumkuchen. This is a long-lasting cake that is baked until relatively dry and that will keep for over six months if properly stored. In this it differs from the German Baumkuchen, which needs to be iced if it is to stay fresh for long. The Prügelkuchen used to be made by the peasants for christenings, special occasions, and weddings when it was decorated with flowers. It is never iced; this is unnecessary because the gleaming brown surface with its many irregularities is attractive enough in itself. They are the result of the hand-cranking whereby it is possible to vary the speed of the roller to give the required effect.

84

Fruit Flans and Tarts

Sponge cakes tend to be dominated by tradition and convention in the basic recipes and in the fillings, whereas fruit flans tend to leave more to the individual's imagination. When considering the range of possible ways that fresh fruit can be used in flans and tarts there would seem to be no recognized classic recipes and no hard-and-fast rules. There are innumerable recipes and every pastry cook will have experimented and come up with his or her own favorite.

Fruit flans, especially simple baking-sheet flans, form part of the standard repertoire of home baking. Originally these forms of patisserie were made in the summer and autumn making use of the abundant fruit that these seasons provide. Each area of Europe has invented its own specialties, which differ not so much in the type of pastry used but more through the choice of fruit. It is up to the individual cook to decide whether he or she would rather bake plums on a shortcrust pastry or on a thin yeast dough, as is customary for example in southern Germany. One of the most popular of the fruit flans throughout Europe is the apple flan or pie, and since apples have always been available all the year round because they store well, numerous apple recipes have been invented. There are shortcrust pies with lids, yeast dough flans, and more unusual recipes such as the French *Tarte Tatin* in which the thin layer of pastry serves only as a container for delicious, caramelized stewed apples.

There is no fruit that seems unsuitable for a fruit flan filling. Cooks have invented a number of ways of using the various qualities of each individual fruit. One of the best known is to fill a prebaked flan case made of shortcrust or flaky pastry. Frequently, a sponge is used as a base, with a layer of jam and custard cream between the fruit and the sponge. Both methods make it unnecessary to cook soft fruit such as raspberries or strawberries.

More robust fruits, such as plums, apples, pears, cherries, and currants, can be cooked with the flan. These two methods both provide a wide range of combinations and adaptations. The "covered" pie has a pastry lid, while in a "sunken" flan the pastry rises to cover the fruit during baking. In Alsace it is customary to take a flan out of the oven half way through the cooking time and to cover it with a "Royale" made with cream, eggs, and flavoring. This sets over the fruit during the remaining baking time and is wonderfully creamy. France has its own light tarts with very thin puff-pastry bases and fruit covered in sparkling jelly. Typical of American and British baking are the flat pies made either with or without lids. For special occasions fruit flans can be covered with meringue and browned under the grill.

The latest development, however, is the use of exotic fruit in our baking. In recent years previously unknown fruit have become commonly available and are now taken for granted just as bananas or oranges are. The most popular is the delicious kiwi fruit with its unpromising exterior but extremely decorative interior, and mangoes, persimmon and lychees all compare well with our native fruits for flavor.

Pear and Custard Flan

5 to 6 small firm Bartlett pears, about 2 pounds
2 tablespoons lemon juice
$\frac{2}{3}$ cup sugar
$\frac{1}{4}$ recipe Sweet Shortcrust Pastry (Pâte Sucrée), page 37
1 cup Simple Vanilla Custard (Crème Pâtissière), page 50
2 ounces almond paste
2 eggs
6 tablespoons heavy cream

$9\frac{1}{2}$-inch tart pan with removable bottom

Preheat oven to 375°F

Peel, halve, and core pears. Place 4 cups water, lemon juice, and $\frac{1}{2}$ cup sugar in large saucepan and bring to a boil. Add pears and poach gently 5 minutes. Remove pears and drain well. Set aside to cool. Roll out pastry and line tart pan. Spread vanilla custard in bottom of pastry-lined pan. Arrange pears, cut side down, over vanilla custard. Beat almond paste, and 1 egg until smooth and creamy. Add remaining egg, heavy cream, and remaining sugar, and beat until well blended. Pour over pears. Bake in preheated oven 55 to 60 minutes or until center is set. Cool completely in pan on wire rack. Serve well chilled.

Virginia Apple Pie

Pastry
$2\frac{1}{2}$ cups sifted all-purpose flour
1 teaspoon salt
$\frac{1}{2}$ cup (1 stick) chilled butter, diced
5 tablespoons vegetable shortening
6 to 7 tablespoons ice water

Filling
7 large tart apples (about $3\frac{1}{4}$ pounds)
2 tablespoons lemon juice
$\frac{1}{3}$ to $\frac{1}{2}$ cup sugar
2 tablespoons cornstarch
2 teaspoons cinnamon
$\frac{1}{8}$ teaspoon allspice
$\frac{1}{8}$ teaspoon ginger
$\frac{1}{8}$ teaspoon nutmeg
1 tablespoon butter
1 egg yolk beaten with 1 tablespoon water for glaze

10-inch pie pan with removable bottom

Preheat oven to 400°F

Stir flour and salt in large bowl. Cut in butter and shortening with pastry blender until mixture resembles fine crumbs. Add ice water, 2 tablespoons at a time, and toss

Use fingertips to press pastry slightly up sides and over rim of pan. Flute edge with tweezers. Prick bottom of pastry lightly with fork. Spread vanilla custard in pastry case and top with pears, cut side down. Pour almond paste mixture over pears. Bake as directed above. Serve cold.

Freshly baked apple pie is usually associated with the very best of home baking. It is also very popular with professional chefs. Serve it warm or cold with sharp Cheddar cheese or topped with your favorite flavor of ice cream.

with fork until mixture binds together. Shape pastry into flattened ball, wrap, and refrigerate 1 hour. Peel, core, and thinly slice apples. Sprinkle apples with lemon juice and toss gently to coat. Combine sugar, cornstarch, cinnamon, allspice, ginger, and nutmeg. Sprinkle over apples and toss to coat. Roll out half the pastry on lightly floured surface and line pie pan. Spoon apples into pastry-lined pan, mounding them in center. Dot apples with butter. Brush pastry edge with egg yolk glaze. Roll out remaining pastry to make top crust and place over apples. Trim edges of pastry to 1 inch beyond rim of pie pan. Press edges together and flute. Cut several vents or small hole in top pastry to allow steam to escape. Brush top of pie with egg yolk glaze. Place on baking sheet and bake 40 to 45 minutes or until pastry is golden brown and apples are tender. Cool in pan on wire rack.

Tart Tatin

Madame Tatin's legendary apple flan is by far the best known of many French regional variations. It is not really a genuine flan, because the thin pastry is only there to hold the caramelized apples in place. As with most apple tarts, this tastes best when served fresh, preferably still warm. Success depends to a large extent on the quality of the apples used. They should soften during baking, but retain their shape.

Pastry:
1 cup all-purpose flour
2 teaspoons confectioners' sugar
½ teaspoon salt
6 tablespoons butter, chilled
3 to 4 tablespoons ice water

Filling:
6 tablespoons butter, softened

¾ cup sugar
8 large tart apples (about 3½ pounds)

9-inch deep pie pan

Preheat oven to 450 F

Prepare pastry according to the directions on page 37 for Cut-in Pastry (Pâte Brisée). Wrap pastry and refrigerate 1 hour. Peel, core, and cut apples into quarters. Prepare caramelized syrup in saucepan. Prepare tart as illustrated below.

Place butter and sugar in pie pan. Place over high heat and cook until butter and sugar are melted. Arrange apples very close together in syrup and cook over high heat about 15 minutes or until sugar is caramelized. Place pie pan in oven a few minutes to soften apples. Remove from oven and cover apples with pastry. Bake 20 to 25 minutes or until pastry is done.

1 **Butter should be very soft** so it can be spread around inside of pan easily. Place sugar in pie pan and tilt pan from side to side to spread sugar evenly over bottom and up sides of pan.

2 **Arrange apples upright in pan**, placing them as close together as possible. Fill pan completely with apples so there are no open spaces.

3 **Place pan on top of stove** and cook over high heat about 15 minutes to caramelize sugar. Roll out pastry and place over apples.

4 **Press pastry edges** to sides of pan to make tight seal. Lightly prick top of pastry.

5 **Bake tart** in preheated oven 20 to 25 minutes or until pastry is golden brown. Place on wire rack and let stand 5 to 8 minutes but no longer, because caramel syrup will begin to harden and stick to pan.

6 **Invert tart onto serving plate**. Apples should be covered with thin layer of caramel and should hold their shape, but be soft enough to melt in the mouth. Cortland, Golden Delicious, Northern Spy, or Granny Smith apples are the best kinds of apples to use.

Swiss Apple Flan

As with many baked fruit flans in Germany and Alsace, Swiss flans are part of the tradition of country baking. They are seasonal dishes, served only when a particular fruit is in season. While the season is short for plums, apricots, and berries, apples, with their relatively long shelf life, are the exception and are used more or less continuously throughout the year.

Pastry:
2 cups all-purpose flour
2 tablespoons sugar
$\frac{1}{2}$ teaspoon salt
$\frac{1}{2}$ cup (1 stick) butter, chilled and diced
$\frac{1}{4}$ cup vegetable shortening
1 egg
3 to 4 tablespoons ice water

Filling:
9 large tart cooking apples (about $3\frac{1}{2}$ pounds)
$\frac{2}{3}$ cup sugar
grated peel and juice of 1 lemon
1 teaspoon cinnamon
$\frac{1}{2}$ cup ground almonds
$\frac{1}{2}$ cup sponge cake crumbs
2 eggs
1 cup heavy cream
2 tablespoons dark rum

Apricot Glaze, page 60

12-inch tart pan with removable bottom

Preheat oven to 400°F

Stir flour, sugar, and salt together in medium-size bowl. Cut in butter and shortening until mixture resembles coarse crumbs. Add egg and ice water and toss with fork until mixture binds together. Shape pastry into flattened ball. Wrap and refrigerate 1 hour. Roll out pastry on lightly floured surface to 14-inch circle and line tart pan, pressing pastry well into sides of pan. Trim pastry edge even with rim of pan. Prick bottom of pastry with fork.

Peel, core, and cut apples into $\frac{1}{4}$-inch thick slices. Place apples in large bowl, sprinkle with $\frac{1}{3}$ cup sugar, lemon peel, lemon juice, and cinnamon, and toss gently to coat. Combine almonds and sponge cake crumbs and sprinkle over bottom of pastry-lined pan. Arrange apple slices over crumb mixture. Bake 20 minutes. Beat eggs, cream, remaining $\frac{1}{3}$ cup sugar, and rum until well blended. Remove tart from oven and pour egg-cream mixture carefully over apples. Return to oven and bake 25 to 30 minutes or until apples are golden brown and filling is set. Brush apples with thin layer of apricot glaze.

Apple Currant Flan

Dough:
about 1¾ cups all-purpose flour
1 package active dry yeast or 1 cake (0.6
ounce) fresh yeast
2 tablespoons sugar
⅓ cup warm milk (105° to 115°F)
3 tablespoons butter, melted
½ teaspoon salt
grated peel of ½ lemon
¼ teaspoon allspice
1 egg

Filling:
1½ cups dairy sour cream
¼ cup sugar
3 tablespoons cornstarch
2 egg yolks
grated peel of ½ lemon
3 to 4 medium-size tart apples, peeled
and cored

¾ pound red currants or raspberries,
stewed
confectioners' sugar for dusting

15- × 10-inch jelly roll pan, greased

Preheat oven to 400°F

To make dough, sift flour into bowl and make well in center. Place yeast and 1 tablespoon sugar in well. Add milk and stir to dissolve yeast. Sprinkle a little flour over yeast mixture. Cover bowl and let stand 10 minutes. Beat butter, remaining sugar, salt, lemon peel, allspice, and egg until blended. Stir butter mixture into yeast-flour mixture to make soft dough. Turn out dough onto lightly floured surface and knead until smooth and elastic. Place in greased bowl and turn to coat. Cover and let rise 1 to 1½ hours. Punch dough down. Roll or pat out dough to fit prepared pan. Prick dough all over with fork. Cover and let rise 30 minutes.

To make filling, place sour cream, sugar, cornstarch, egg yolks, and lemon peel in saucepan, and stir well. Place saucepan over low heat and cook, stirring constantly, until mixture is thickened (do not let mixture come to a boil). Remove from heat and cool slightly. Spread filling over dough to within ¼ inch of edges. Cut apples into ¼-inch thick rings. Arrange apple rings over filling in slightly overlapping rows. Fill each apple center with 1 teaspoon red currants. Bake in preheated oven 30 minutes. Remove from oven and dust top with sifted confectioners' sugar. Return to oven and bake 5 minutes or until sugar is melted.

Variation: Apricot and plum flans can be made in the same way. Add ⅓ cup ground almonds to sour cream filling and omit currants.

Cherry Crumb Flan

Dough:
about 1¾ cups all-purpose flour
1 package active dry yeast or 1 cake (0.6 ounce) fresh yeast
2 tablespoons sugar
⅓ cup warm milk (105° to 115°F)
3 tablespoons butter, melted
½ teaspoon salt
grated peel of ½ lemon
¼ teaspoon allspice · 1 egg

Cherry filling:
4 teaspoons cornstarch
1 cup milk · 3 egg yolks
½ vanilla bean
2 ounces marzipan
confectioners' sugar
about 2 pounds dark sweet cherries, pitted

Crumb topping:
1¼ cups all-purpose flour
½ cup sugar
½ cup (1 stick) plus 2 tablespoons butter

15- × 10-inch jelly-roll pan, greased

Preheat oven to 400°F

To make dough, sift flour into bowl and make well in center. Place yeast and 1 tablespoon sugar in well. Add milk and stir to dissolve yeast. Sprinkle a little flour over yeast mixture. Cover bowl and let stand 10 minutes. Beat butter, remaining sugar, salt, lemon peel, allspice, and egg until blended. Stir butter mixture into yeast-flour mixture to make soft dough. Turn out dough onto lightly floured surface and knead until smooth and elastic. Place in greased bowl and turn to coat. Cover and let rise 1 to 1½ hours. Punch dough down. Roll or pat out dough to fit prepared pan. Prick dough all over with fork. Cover and let rise 30 minutes.

To make cherry filling, blend cornstarch, 2 tablespoons milk, and egg yolks in bowl. Place remaining milk and vanilla bean in saucepan and bring to a boil. Remove vanilla bean. Stir a little hot milk into cornstarch mixture. Pour into saucepan and cook, stirring constantly, until thickened. Cut marzipan into small pieces and beat into custard mixture until smooth. Remove from heat and sprinkle with a little confectioners' sugar to prevent skin from forming. Let cool. Spread custard over dough and top with cherries.

To make crumb topping, stir flour and sugar in bowl. Cut in butter until mixture resembles coarse crumbs. Sprinkle topping over cherries. Bake in preheated oven 35 to 40 minutes. Cool in pan on wire rack 10 minutes. Remove from pan and cool

completely on rack or cut into slices and serve warm.

Apricot Crumb Flan

Dough:
about 1¾ cups all-purpose flour
1 package active dry yeast or 1 cake (0.6 ounce) fresh yeast
2 tablespoons sugar
⅓ cup warm milk (105° to 115°F)
3 tablespoons butter, melted
½ teaspoon salt
grated peel of ½ lemon
¼ teaspoon allspice
1 egg

Apricot cheese filling:
2 to 2¼ pounds apricots
2 packages (8 ounces each) cream cheese, softened
3 eggs
⅔ cup granulated sugar
grated peel of 1 lemon
4 tablespoons cornstarch

Crumb topping:
1¼ cups all-purpose flour
½ cup sugar
½ teaspoon cinnamon
½ cup (1 stick) plus 2 tablespoons butter
confectioners' sugar for dusting

12-inch tart flan pan, greased

Preheat oven to 400°F

To make dough, prepare according to recipe for Cherry Crumb Flan, this page. While dough is rising, drop apricots, a few at a time, into boiling water and blanch 1 to 2 minutes. Peel apricots, cut in half, and remove pits. Roll or pat out dough to fit prepared pan. Prick all over with fork. Cover and let rise 30 minutes. Beat cream cheese, eggs, sugar, lemon peel, and cornstarch until blended. Spread over dough. Arrange apricots, cut side up, over cheese filling.

To make crumb topping, stir flour, sugar, and cinnamon in bowl. Cut in butter until mixture resembles coarse crumbs. Sprinkle crumbs over apricots. Let rise 15 minutes. Bake in preheated oven 45 to 55 minutes. Cool in pan on wire rack. Dust top with confectioners' sugar.

Plum Crumb Flan

not illustrated

There are many ways to make a plum flan: The base can be made from shortcrust pastry or yeast dough; the pastry base can be covered with vanilla custard, sprinkled with ground almonds, or covered directly with fruit; the fruit can be covered with a streusel topping or sliced almonds. The following recipe is a basic recipe for a simple plum flan with a fruit filling and a streusel topping.

Dough:
1¾ cups all-purpose flour
1 package active dry yeast or 1 cake (0.6 ounce) fresh yeast
2 tablespoons sugar
⅓ cup warm milk (105° to 115°F)
3 tablespoons butter, melted
½ teaspoon salt
grated peel of ½ lemon
¼ teaspoon allspice
1 egg
about 3¼ pounds small purple plums

Crumb topping:
1¼ cups all-purpose flour
½ cup sugar
½ teaspoon cinnamon
½ cup (1 stick) plus 2 tablespoons butter

15- × 10-inch jelly-roll pan, greased

Preheat oven to 400°F

Prepare dough according to recipe for Cherry Crumb Flan, this page. Cut plums into quarters and remove pits. Arrange plums over dough in slightly overlapping rows.

To make crumb topping, stir flour, sugar, and cinnamon in bowl. Cut in butter until mixture resembles coarse crumbs. Sprinkle crumbs over plums. Let rise 15 minutes. Bake in preheated oven 30 to 35 minutes.

Flat Flans with Fruit Toppings

These recipes are for large flat flans with fruit toppings, baked on rectangular baking sheets, and cut into slices or squares. One of the oldest methods of using fruit in baking is to make fruit flans. In the Near East and Mediterranean countries figs, sweet grapes, cherries, and apricots have been used as toppings for years. In the colder climate of central and northern Europe less exotic fruits such as apples, pears, plums, and wild berries were used. Although they were not as exotic as the fruit used in warmer climates, their flavor was just as good, and therefore chefs and home bakers were able to develop excellent recipes with them.

The combinations and variations possible are almost endless. Yeast dough, shortcrust pastries, or even a firm cake mixture can be used as a base. Cake can also be used for a middle layer. It is important to select the correct fruit for each base so the baking time required for the base and the fruit will be compatible. Apples, plums, apricots, cherries, blueberries, gooseberries, and rhubarb, which require a relatively long cooking time, are the best choice to combine with yeast pastry. Raspberries, strawberries, and blackberries should be covered with meringue and browned very quickly so they retain their shape and flavor.

Additional variations are possible by adding a middle layer between the fruit and the pastry. This layer can be made with cookie crumbs, nuts, or a flavored cream filling that will complement the flavor of the fruit. The recipes provided on the right should be viewed as guidelines only. You can create your own variations easily.

Blueberry Flan

Line 15- × 10-inch jelly-roll pan with yeast dough, page 89. Prick dough all over with fork. Wash and pick over 4 cups fresh blueberries. Scatter blueberries over dough and sprinkle with sugar to taste. Stir 2 cups all-purpose flour, $\frac{3}{4}$ cup firmly packed light brown sugar, and 1 teaspoon cinnamon in bowl. Cut in 1 cup butter until mixture resembles coarse crumbs. Sprinkle crumbs over blueberries. Let rise 20 minutes. Bake in preheated 400°F oven 35 to 40 minutes.

Red Currant Meringue Flan; Chocolate Cherry Flan; Apricot Flan. These flans should be eaten fresh from the oven or at least on the same day on which they are baked. They cannot be kept for a long time. Don't cut the flan until you are ready to serve it.

Tart Red Cherry Flan

Wash and pit $2\frac{1}{2}$ to 3 pounds tart red cherries. Place in bowl, sprinkle with sugar to taste, and let stand 1 to 2 hours. Line 15- × 10-inch jelly-roll pan with yeast dough, page 89. Prick dough all over with fork. Combine $\frac{2}{3}$ cup toasted ground hazelnuts with $\frac{1}{3}$ cup cookie crumbs. Sprinkle crumbs over dough. Drain cherries well, reserving juice. Arrange over dough. Let rise 20 minutes. Bake in preheated 400°F oven 35 to 40 minutes. Place reserved cherry liquid, $\frac{1}{2}$ cup water, $\frac{1}{2}$ teaspoon cinnamon, 1 tablespoon lemon juice, and 1 tablespoon cornstarch in saucepan. Stir until blended and smooth. Place saucepan over low heat and cook, stirring constantly, until mixture thickens and comes to a boil. Remove from heat and pour over warm cherry flan immediately.

Rhubarb Flan

Line 15- × 10-inch jelly-roll pan with ½ recipe Sweet Shortcrust Pastry (Pâte Sucrée), page 37. Prick pastry all over with fork. Bake in preheated 400°F oven 10 minutes. Let cool. Combine 1 cup ground almonds and ⅔ cup cookie crumbs and sprinkle over pastry. Wash 4 pounds rhubarb and cut into 2-inch pieces. Arrange rhubarb over pastry. Sprinkle with ¾ cup sugar and ½ teaspoon cinnamon. Return to 400°F oven and bake 35 to 40 minutes or until golden brown. Cool slightly. Beat 4 egg whites with 1 cup sugar until stiff. Spoon into pastry bag fitted with ½-inch star tip (#9) and pipe meringue in lattice pattern over rhubarb. Brown meringue in preheated 425°F oven 10 minutes.

Chocolate Cherry Flan

Line 15- × 10-inch jelly-roll pan with ½ recipe Sweet Shortcrust Pastry (Pâte Sucrée), page 37. Prick pastry all over with fork. Bake in preheated 400°F oven 10 minutes. Let cool. Cream 1 cup butter and ⅔ cup sugar until light and fluffy. Add 6 egg yolks, one at a time, and beat until well blended. Add ¼ teaspoon salt, grated peel of 1 lemon, and 1 teaspoon cinnamon. Beat until blended. Fold in 1¼ cups ground almonds and 1 cup all-purpose flour. Beat 6 egg whites until stiff. Add ½ cup sugar and beat until stiff and glossy. Fold beaten egg whites into creamed mixture. Fold in 8 ounces grated semisweet chocolate. Spread half of chocolate mixture over pastry. Arrange 1½ pounds pitted dark sweet cherries over chocolate mixture. Cover cherries with remaining chocolate mixture. Bake in preheated 400°F oven 50 to 60 minutes. Dust cooled flan with confectioners' sugar.

Red Currant Meringue Flan

Line 15- × 10-inch jelly-roll pan with ½ recipe Sweet Shortcrust Pastry (Pâte Sucrée), page 37. Prick pastry all over with fork. Bake in preheated 400°F oven 15 minutes. Let cool. Beat 8 egg whites until stiff. Gradually add 1 cup sugar and beat until stiff and glossy. Fold in ½ pound red currants. Spread meringue mixture over pastry. Bake in preheated 450°F oven 10 to 12 minutes or until meringue is golden brown.

Apricot Flan

Line 15- × 10-inch jelly-roll pan with yeast dough, page 89. Prick dough all over with fork. Prepare Simple Vanilla Custard, page 50. Cut 7 ounces almond paste into small pieces and stir into hot custard until smooth. Cool slightly. Spread almond custard over dough. Blanch 2 pounds apricots in boiling water 1 to 2 minutes. Remove apricots with slotted spoon and peel. Cut apricots in half and remove pits. Arrange, cut side down, over custard filling. Let rise 20 minutes. Bake in preheated 400°F oven 35 to 40 minutes. Brush with Apricot Glaze, page 60, and sprinkle with toasted sliced almonds.

Gooseberry Flan

Line 15- × 10-inch jelly-roll pan with ½ recipe Sweet Shortcrust Pastry (Pâte Sucrée), page 37. Prick pastry all over with fork. Bake in preheated 400°F oven 15 minutes. Let cool. Spread ¾ cup red currant jelly over pastry. Top with Sponge Roll, page 30. Beat 8 egg whites until stiff. Gradually add 1 cup sugar and beat until stiff and glossy. Fold in 1 cup ground almonds. Spread half meringue mixture over Sponge Roll. Arrange 1¾ pounds drained, stewed gooseberries over meringue mixture. Spread remaining meringue mixture over gooseberries. Brown meringue in preheated 425°F oven 12 to 15 minutes or until meringue is golden brown.

Plum Flan

Line 15- × 10-inch jelly-roll pan with yeast dough, page 89. Prick dough all over with fork. Wash 3¼ pounds small purple plums. Cut plums into quarters and remove pits. Arrange cut plums over dough in slightly overlapping pattern. Stir 1¼ cups all-purpose flour, ½ cup sugar, and ¼ teaspoon cinnamon in bowl. Cut in ½ cup (1 stick) plus 2 tablespoons butter until mixture resembles coarse crumbs. Sprinkle crumbs over plums. Sprinkle ⅔ cup sliced almonds on top. Let rise 20 minutes. Bake in preheated 400°F oven 35 to 40 minutes. Dust cooled flan with confectioners' sugar.

Lemon Meringue Flan

The French *tarte au citron* is usually made with a rich egg cream and lots of butter. This is a lighter recipe and an unusually good one.

Pastry:
½ cup (1 stick) butter, softened
¼ cup confectioners' sugar
¼ teaspoon salt
½ teaspoon vanilla
1 egg yolk

1½ cups all-purpose flour
1 tablespoon ice water

Lemon filling:
⅓ cup granulated sugar
3 tablespoons cornstarch
3 egg yolks
1 cup milk
grated peel and juice of 1 lemon

Meringue:
1 cup granulated sugar
5 egg whites
confectioners' sugar for dusting

10-inch fluted tart/flan pan

Preheat oven to 375°F

To make pastry, prepare according to mixer method on page 37. Wrap dough and refrigerate 1 hour. Roll out pastry on lightly floured surface and line tart pan. Prick pastry all over with fork. Line with waxed paper or aluminum foil and weigh down with dried beans or pie weights. Bake in preheated oven 15 minutes. Remove foil and beans and bake 10 to 15 minutes or until pastry is golden brown. Cool on wire rack.

To make lemon filling, stir sugar, cornstarch, egg yolks, and milk in saucepan until blended and smooth (see Simple Vanilla Custard, page 50). Place saucepan over low heat and cook, stirring, until thickened (do not allow mixture to boil). Remove from heat and stir in lemon peel and juice. Set aside to cool.

To make meringue, bring sugar and ½ cup water to a boil in saucepan over moderate heat. Boil until temperature registers 240°F on candy thermometer. Beat egg whites until stiff. Beat in sugar syrup in slow, steady stream, beating constantly. Fold half the meringue into cooled lemon custard. Spread lemon mixture in pastry-lined pan. Increase oven temperature to 450°F. Spoon remaining meringue into pastry bag fitted with ½-inch open star tip and pipe decoratively on top of flan (see photo). Place in preheated oven and bake 6 to 8 minutes or until meringue is lightly browned. Cool completely on wire rack. Dust top of flan with sifted confectioners' sugar.

Apple Cake with Calvados Cream

2 11-inch Quick Puff Pastry bases, page 44
about 2 pounds tart apples, peeled, cored, and cut into ½-inch thick slices
2 tablespoons Calvados
¼ cup sugar
⅓ cup currants

Cream filling:
1 envelope unflavored gelatin
3 egg yolks
⅓ cup sugar
1 cup milk
½ teaspoon vanilla
2 to 3 tablespoons Calvados
1 cup heavy cream, whipped

Glaze:
1 cup dry white wine
¼ cup sugar
1½ tablespoons cornstarch
⅓ cup toasted sliced almonds

Preheat oven to 425°F

Line two baking sheets with parchment paper. Prepare pastry bases according to directions on page 44. Place bases on lined baking sheets and let stand 15 minutes. Prick all over with fork and bake in preheated oven 18 to 20 minutes or until golden brown. If bases lose their shape during baking, place flan ring over baked pastry bases and cut around inside edge of flan ring with sharp knife. Place apple slices in simmering water and cook 3 to 4 minutes or until almost soft. Drain well and let cool. Place apples in bowl and sprinkle with 1 tablespoon Calvados and ¼ cup sugar. Toss to coat and set aside. Place currants in small bowl and sprinkle with 1 tablespoon Calvados. Set aside.

To make filling, sprinkle gelatin over ¼ cup water and let stand 5 minutes. Place over low heat and cook, stirring, until gelatin is dissolved. Remove from heat and cool. Beat egg yolks and sugar until thick and creamy. Heat milk to just below boiling point. Remove from heat and stir 4 tablespoons hot milk into beaten egg yolk mixture. Return mixture to saucepan and cook, stirring constantly, until mixture thickens and coats back of spoon. Remove from heat and stir in vanilla and cooled gelatin. Set aside to cool. When cool, fold in 3 tablespoons Calvados and whipped cream. Refrigerate 30 minutes. Place 1 pastry base on serving plate and spread with half the cream. Top with second pastry base and spread remaining cream over top and around sides of cake. Drain apples and arrange in concentric circles on top.

To make glaze, place wine and sugar in saucepan and bring to a boil. Blend cornstarch and 2 tablespoons water until smooth. Stir into wine-sugar mixture and cook, stirring, until mixture thickens and comes to a boil. Remove from heat and let cool slightly. Brush over apples. Press almonds around sides of cake. Drain currants and sprinkle over apples.

Black Currants with Vanilla Custard

Prepare Simple Vanilla Custard according to directions on page 50, using ¼ cup sugar, 2 tablespoons cornstarch, 2 egg yolks, 1 cup milk, and ¼ teaspoon vanilla. Cool slightly and stir until smooth. Spoon custard into 6 baked 4-inch tart shells. Bring ½ cup sugar and 2 tablespoons water to a boil over low heat. Add 3 tablespoons crème de cassis, 2 tablespoons lemon juice, and 1 pound black or red currants. Return to a boil, lower heat, and simmer 3 minutes. Remove from heat and cool. Spoon over custard-filled tarts. Decorate with split pistachios.

Plums on Almond Custard

Prepare Simple Vanilla Custard according to directions on page 50, using ¼ cup sugar, 2 tablespoons cornstarch, 2 egg yolks, 1 cup milk, and ¼ teaspoon vanilla. Cool slightly. Stir in 1 tablespoon Amaretto liqueur and ⅔ cup finely ground almonds. Spoon almond custard into 6 baked 4-inch tart shells. Cut 1 pound small purple plums into quarters and remove pits. Bring 2 cups water, juice of 1 lemon, and ½ cup sugar to a boil. Add plums and cook 1 to 2 minutes. Remove plums with slotted spoon, reserving ½ cup syrup, and arrange plums on top of custard-filled tarts. Blend 4 teaspoons cornstarch with ¼ cup white wine in small saucepan. Add reserved syrup and cook, stirring constantly, until mixture is thickened. Remove from heat and spoon over plums.

Caramelized Raspberry Tarts

Prepare Simple Vanilla Custard according to directions on page 50, using ¼ cup sugar, 2 tablespoons cornstarch, 2 egg yolks, 1 cup milk, and ¼ teaspoon vanilla. Cool slightly. Stir in 2 tablespoons raspberry-flavored liqueur and ¼ cup crushed Amaretto biscuits. Beat 1 egg white with 2 tablespoons sugar until stiff and fold into cooled custard. Spoon custard into 6 baked 4-inch tart shells. Arrange fresh raspberries over custard, covering custard completely. Sprinkle raspberries with confectioners' sugar. Place tarts under broiler about 4 inches from source of heat and broil just until sugar is melted and begins to caramelize. Watch carefully. Remove immediately and cool completely.

Kiwis with Lime Cream

Soak 1½ teaspoons unflavored gelatin in 2 tablespoons cold water 5 minutes. Bring ½ cup dry white wine, juice and grated peel of 2 limes, and ⅓ cup sugar to a boil. Add gelatin and cook, stirring, until gelatin is dissolved. Remove from heat and cool. Stir in ½ cup plain yogurt. Let cool. Beat ½ cup heavy cream until firm and fold into yogurt mixture. Brush insides of 4 baked 4-inch meringue shells with melted semisweet chocolate and let stand until chocolate is set. Spoon lime-cream mixture into meringue shells and let stand until set. Peel and thinly slice 6 to 8 kiwis and arrange on top. Decorate with thin slices of lime and cranberry conserve.

Sugared Berry Tart

Brush insides of 6 baked 4-inch tart shells with melted semisweet chocolate and let stand until chocolate is set. Combine 1 cup sponge cake crumbs and 1½ tablespoons brandy and let stand 30 minutes. Beat 1 cup heavy cream with 3 tablespoons confectioners' sugar until firm. Fold in 1 cup crushed berries (strawberries, blackberries, or raspberries). Fold in cake crumbs. Spoon cream mixture in tart shells. Roll ½ cup fresh berries in superfine sugar until heavily coated and arrange on top of tarts.

Apples on Wine Cream

Peel, core, and thinly slice 4 to 5 Golden Delicious or Pippin apples. Bring 1 cup white wine and ⅓ cup sugar to a boil. Add apple slices and cook 2 minutes. Remove apple slices with slotted spoon and set aside. Reserve ¼ cup syrup. Soak 1 envelope unflavored gelatin in ¼ cup water 5 minutes. Blend 2 egg yolks, grated peel and juice of 1 lime, 2 tablespoons Calvados, and 1 teaspoon cornstarch until smooth. Stir in reserved syrup until blended. Return to saucepan and bring to a boil, stirring constantly. Add gelatin, stirring until dissolved. Remove from heat and let cool. Beat 1 cup heavy cream with 2 tablespoons confectioners' sugar until firm. Fold whipped cream into cooled gelatin mixture. Spoon into 6 baked 4-inch tart shells. Refrigerate until set. Arrange apple slices in circular pattern on top of filled tarts. Sprinkle with currants or raisins. Brush with Apricot Glaze, page 60.

Gooseberry Meringues

Blend 3 tablespoons sugar syrup, 1 tablespoon Amaretto liqueur, and 3 tablespoons ground almonds. Brush mixture inside 6 meringue shells. Bring ¼ cup dry white wine, ¼ cup sugar, and 1 tablespoon lemon juice to a boil. Add 1 pound fresh gooseberries and cook 2 to 3 minutes or until gooseberries are transparent. Drain gooseberries, reserving syrup, and spoon gooseberries into meringue shells. Blend 2 teaspoons cornstarch, 1 tablespoon water, and reserved syrup in small saucepan. Place saucepan over low heat and cook, stirring, until mixture thickens and comes to a boil. Brush over gooseberries and edge of meringue shells. Sprinkle edge of shells with toasted sliced almonds.

Blackberry Tarts

Bring ¼ cup red wine, ¼ cup sugar, and 1 tablespoon lemon juice to a boil. Boil rapidly until reduced by one third. Remove from heat, add 1 pound fresh blackberries and 1 tablespoon dark rum, and stir well. Pour into bowl, cover, and let stand 1 hour. Beat 3 egg whites until stiff. Gradually beat in ¼ cup sugar and beat until stiff and glossy. Spoon one-third meringue mixture into pastry bag fitted with open star tip and set aside. Fold ¼ cup ground almonds into remaining meringue mixture. Spoon almond-meringue mixture into 6 baked 4-inch tart shells. Spoon blackberries and their juice on top of almond-meringue mixture. Pipe reserved meringue in swirl on top of each tart. Place tarts under broiler, about 4 inches from source of heat, and broil until meringue is lightly browned, 2 to 4 minutes.

Cherries in Burgundy

Bring 1 cup Burgundy wine and ¼ cup sugar to a boil. Boil rapidly 5 minutes. Add 1 pound pitted tart or sweet cherries and cook 2 to 3 minutes. Remove from heat and drain cherries, reserving syrup. Set cherries aside. Blend 2 teaspoons cornstarch with 2 tablespoons water. Stir into reserved syrup until blended. Cook, stirring constantly, until mixture thickens and comes to a boil. Return cherries to saucepan and simmer 1 minute. Spoon cherries into 6 baked 4-inch tart shells. Decorate with toasted sliced almonds.

Wild Strawberry Tarts

Stir 1½ cups dairy sour cream, ¼ cup sugar, juice of 1 orange, 1 egg yolk, and 2 teaspoons cornstarch in small saucepan until blended. Place saucepan over low heat and cook, stirring, just until thickened. (Do not allow mixture to come to a boil.) Remove from heat and cool. Spoon into 6 baked 4-inch tart shells. Bring 1 cup dry white wine and ¼ cup sugar to a boil. Boil until reduced by half. Stir in grated peel of ½ orange and 1 pound small wild strawberries. Remove from heat and spoon strawberries over cream-filled tarts.

Figs in Sauterne

Soak 1½ teaspoons unflavored gelatin in 2 tablespoons water 5 minutes. Place ¼ cup Sauterne wine and 3 tablespoons sugar in saucepan and bring just to boiling point. Lower heat, add gelatin, and cook, stirring, just until dissolved. Remove from heat and cool completely. Beat ⅔ cup heavy cream until firm. Fold whipped cream into cooled Sauterne mixture. Spoon cream mixture into 6 baked 4-inch tart shells. Refrigerate until set. Peel and slice 10 to 12 fresh ripe figs. Arrange figs on top of filled tarts. Decorate center of each tart with seedless grapes. Brush with apricot glaze, page 60. Sprinkle edge of tarts with toasted sliced almonds.

Red Currant Tarts

Prepare ½ recipe Simple Vanilla Custard according to directions on page 50. Let cool. Add 2 tablespoons kirsch and 3 ounces marzipan and blend until smooth. Add a little heavy cream if mixture is too thick to spread. Spoon into 6 baked 4-inch tart shells. Bring ¼ cup white wine and ⅓ cup sugar to a boil. Boil rapidly until mixture is syrupy. Add 1 pound fresh red currants and simmer 2 to 3 minutes. Remove from heat and cool slightly. Spoon red currants on top of cream-filled tarts. For variety, substitute cranberries for red currants and increase cooking time to 5 to 6 minutes.

Cheesecakes

The Romans loved cheese and had at least thirteen different types. Although they were not responsible for creating cheesecake, they did develop it into a fine delicacy. To combine cheese with sweet ingredients in a cake was directly in line with the rather exotic tastes of the period. The combination of savory and sweet things of which the Romans were so fond was best exemplified in the *savillum*, the ancient version of the cheesecake, which developed over the centuries into the versions we know today. The recipe was extremely simple: "Work together half a pound of flour, two and a half pounds of curds, a quarter of a pound of honey, and one egg. Cook the mixture in a buttered clay pot with a close-fitting lid. When the cake is cooked pour honey over it and sprinkle it with poppy seeds."

Cheesecakes are still eaten in modern-day Italy, with ricotta often used as the main ingredient for the cheese filling. Ricotta is a type of curd cheese prepared from sheep's milk. Wonderful cheesecakes are still made in Italy, of which the crustless *crostata di ricotta* is just one example. It is not generally appreciated that the famous *cassata Siciliana* really belongs in this chapter as it should not properly be filled with ice cream but with curd cheese! The confusion arises from the fact that the *cassata* is chilled to make it firm. There is an excellent phrase to describe this delicacy decorated with the finest candied fruit or any other of the excellent cheesecakes: 'Tout est beaute, tout est charme en elle"—it contains everything of beauty and charm.

Cheesecakes were popular in seventeenth- and eighteenth-century Britain and have always been popular in this country where they were called curd cakes and originally brought over from Europe by Russian and Polish immigrants.

Yogurt originated in Eastern Europe and is still very popular there. It is claimed to be the secret of the longevity of the people in the Balkans and is claimed to have other health-giving properties. The first man in Western Europe to realize its beneficial effects on stomach disorders is reputed to be Francis I of France.

Yogurt has been produced commercially in the second half of this century. Natural yogurt is popular both for sweet and savory dishes especially because of its low fat content. Fruit, nuts, or honey can be added to natural yogurt as it goes well with any flavoring. Yogurt can be used in place of cream for many dishes but care should be taken to keep natural "live" yogurt in the refrigerator otherwise the live bacteria in it will become active again in the warmth and the yogurt will separate.

Cheese and Raisin Tart

Cheesecakes are hardly a modern invention. There is a recipe for cheesecake in the world's oldest known cookbook. Although cheesecakes can be made with cream cheese, Neufchâtel, cottage cheese, ricotta cheese, farmer cheese, or a combination of two of these cheeses, it is the invention of cream cheese in America in 1872 that revolutionized the quality of modern cheesecakes. When cream cheese is used, the texture of the cake is velvety smooth. The recipe that follows uses a combination of ricotta cheese and farmer cheese. They are combined with beaten egg whites to make the texture of this cheese tart, light and airy.

Pastry:

1½ cups all-purpose flour
2 tablespoons sugar
½ teaspoon salt
½ cup (1 stick) chilled butter, diced
1 egg yolk
2 to 3 tablespoons ice water

Filling:

1 tablespoon dark rum
⅓ cup raisins
1 cup (8 ounces) ricotta cheese
1 cup (8 ounces) farmer cheese
2 eggs
⅔ cup granulated sugar
grated peel of 1 lemon
4 tablespoons melted and clarified butter
⅓ cup all-purpose flour
confectioners' sugar for dusting

11-inch tart pan with removable bottom

Preheat oven to 375°F

Stir flour, sugar, and salt in medium-size bowl. Cut in butter with pastry blender until mixture resembles coarse crumbs. Add egg yolk and ice water, and toss with fork until mixture begins to bind together. Gather dough and shape into flattened ball. Wrap and refrigerate 1 hour. Roll out pastry on lightly floured surface and line tart pan.

Press pastry into sides of pan. Trim pastry edge even with rim of pan. Line pastry with aluminum foil or parchment paper and fill with pie weights or dried beans. Bake blind according to directions on page 39. Remove lining paper and pie weights and finish baking. Cool pastry before filling.

Pour rum over raisins and set aside. Prepare cheese mixture as illustrated in step-by-step photos on opposite page. Be sure to reduce oven temperature to 325°F after crust has been baked. If tart is baked in oven hotter than 325°F it may rise too much and split open. If oven temperature is too low, tart may not rise enough. Bake 60 to 70 minutes or until top is golden. Cool completely in pan on wire rack. Dust top of tart with sifted confectioners' sugar. Score top with heated wire mesh rack or long metal skewer for decorative effect. If desired, raisins may be omitted without spoiling recipe. They can be replaced with firm, ripe fruit such as cherries or apricots. If fresh fruit is used, increase baking time by about 10 minutes.

1 **Press ricotta cheese** and farmer cheese through fine mesh sieve. This will lighten cheese so it can be beaten easily.

2 **Place cheese in medium-size bowl**. Separate eggs carefully and add egg yolks to cheese mixture with ⅓ cup sugar. Place egg whites in separate bowl and set aside.

3 **Beat cheese mixture** until light and fluffy with wire whisk or hand-held electric mixer set at medium speed.

4 **Wash lemon** and pat dry with paper towel. Grate lemon peel into cheese mixture. Scrape off any peel that sticks to grater

5 **Add warm butter** in thin, steady stream, beating constantly until well blended. Sift flour over cheese mixture and fold in.

6 **Add rum soaked raisins**. Stir until raisins are blended into cheese mixture. Reduce oven temperature to 325°F.

7 **Beat egg whites** with remaining ⅓ cup sugar until stiff peaks form. Stir about half of beaten egg whites into cheese mixture to lighten. Fold in remaining beaten egg whites carefully.

8 **Pour cheese filling** into cooled pastry-lined pan.

9 **Smooth cheese mixture** with long flat spatula. Bake in preheated oven 60 to 70 minutes or until top is golden and is set. Cool in pan on wire rack. Refrigerate until ready to serve.

Cheese and Cream Cake

Pastry bases:
10 tablespoons (1¼ sticks) butter
¾ cup confectioners' sugar
2 egg yolks
1¾ cup all-purpose flour

Filling:
4 egg yolks
1 cup granulated sugar
grated peel of 1 lemon
1 cup milk
7 gelatin leaves or 2 envelopes unflavored gelatin
1 package (8 ounces) cream cheese, softened
1 cup small curd cottage cheese
2 cups heavy cream
confectioners' sugar for dusting

3 **Soak gelatin leaves** in cold water 10 minutes. Squeeze out as much liquid as possible. Stir leaves into hot custard until dissolved. Alternatively, soak powdered gelatin in ¼ cup cold water 5 minutes. Add to hot custard, stirring, until gelatin is completely dissolved. Remove from heat and cool slightly.

5 **Beat mixture thoroughly** until smooth and creamy. Let cool to room temperature.

1 **To prepare cream filling,** place egg yolks, granulated sugar, lemon peel, and milk in saucepan and stir until blended and smooth.

4 **Beat cream cheese** and cottage cheese in bowl until smooth. Gradually add warm gelatin mixture, beating constantly.

two 10-inch springform pans

Preheat oven to 400°F

To make pastry, beat butter, confectioners' sugar, and egg yolks until creamy. Fold in flour to make soft dough. Divide in half. Wrap each piece separately and refrigerate 1 hour. Roll out dough to two 10-inch circles. Place one circle in each prepared pan. Bake in preheated oven 12 to 15 minutes. Remove side of one pan and cut pastry into twelve to fourteen wedges. Don't separate wedges or remove lining paper. Cool completely on wire rack on base of pan. When cool remove from pan, peel off paper and return to base.

2 **Place saucepan over low heat** and cook, stirring constantly, until mixture is thickened. Mixture should coat back of spoon.

6 **Beat cream until firm**. Fold whipped cream into cheese mixture with wire whisk.

7 **Pour cheese mixture** over pastry base in pan and smooth top.

8 **Slide cut pastry wedges** on top of cheese mixture. Refrigerate 2 to 3 hours or until set. Run tip of knife around inside edge of pan and remove sides of pan. Dust top with confectioners' sugar.

Cool remaining pastry in pan on wire rack. Follow step-by-step photos to prepare cheese and cream filling.

When fruit is added to a Cheese and Cream Cake the amount of the cheese mixture used can be reduced as follows:

2 pastry bases (opposite page)

Cherry or apricot filling (below)

4 egg yolks
$\frac{3}{4}$ cup granulated sugar
grated peel of $\frac{1}{2}$ lemon
1 cup milk
7 gelatin leaves of 2 envelopes unflavored gelatin
2 packages (8 ounces each) cream cheese or 2 cups small curd cottage cheese or ricotta cheese
$1\frac{1}{4}$ cups heavy cream
confectioners' sugar for dusting

Prepare fruit before making cheese mixture. Prepare cheese filling according to step-by-step photos. Spread thin layer of cheese filling over pastry base in springform pan. Arrange fruit on top. Spoon remaining cheese mixture over fruit and smooth top. Slide pastry wedges on top of cheese filling. Refrigerate 2 to 3 hours. Run tip of knife around inside edge of pan and remove sides of pan. Dust top with confectioners' sugar.

Cherry filling:
1 pound dark sweet cherries, stewed
$\frac{1}{2}$ cup reserved cherry cooking liquid
2 tablespoons sugar
2 teaspoons cornstarch
1 stick cinnamon

Place cherry cooking liquid, sugar, and cornstarch in pan, and stir until well blended. Add cinnamon stick. Place saucepan over low heat and cook, stirring, until mixture comes to a boil and thickens. Discard cinnamon stick. Add cherries and stir gently. Cool 1 minute. Remove from heat and cool completely.

Apricot filling:
$1\frac{1}{2}$ pounds apricots
1 cup dry white wine
$\frac{3}{4}$ cup sugar
3 tablespoons apricot-flavored liqueur

Blanch apricots in boiling water 1 to 2 minutes. Remove with slotted spoon and peel. Cut apricots in half and remove pits. Place wine and sugar in saucepan and bring to a boil. Boil rapidly 3 minutes. Add apricots and return to a boil. Remove from heat and cool slightly. Stir in liqueur. Cool completely. Drain apricots well before using.

Tamarillo Yogurt Flan

Pastry:
½ cup (1 stick) butter, softened
¼ cup confectioners' sugar
¼ teaspoon salt · ½ teaspoon vanilla
1 egg yolk · 1½ cups all-purpose flour
1 tablespoon ice water

Yogurt filling:
¾ pound tamarillos 2 envelopes unflavored
gelatin · ¾ cup sugar
3 egg yolks · juice of 2 limes
1 cup plain yogurt
1 cup heavy cream, whipped

To decorate:
1 cup heavy cream, sweetened and
whipped
chocolate shavings

9- or 10-inch fluted tart/flan pan

Preheat oven to 375°F

Prepare pastry according to mixer method on page 37. Wrap and refrigerate 1 hour. Roll out and line pan. Prick pastry all over with fork. Line with waxed paper or aluminum foil and weigh down with dried beans or pie weights. Bake 15 minutes. Remove foil and beans and bake 10 minutes or until pastry is golden brown. Cool on wire rack.

To make yogurt filling, peel and puree tamarillos. Strain to remove seeds. Soak gelatin in ¼ cup cold water 5 minutes. Stir pureed fruit, sugar, egg yolks, and lime juice in saucepan. Place saucepan over low heat and cook, stirring, just until thickened. Add gelatin and stir until completely dissolved. Remove from heat and cool Stir in yogurt and cool completely. Fold in whipped cream. Pour mixture in pastry-lined pan and smooth top. Refrigerate 2 to 3 hours or until set.

To decorate, spoon sweetened whipped cream into pastry bag fitted with open star tip and pipe decoratively on top of flan. Sprinkle with chocolate shavings.

Orange-Yogurt Ring

Pastry:
½ cup (1 stick) butter, softened
½ cup sifted confectioners' sugar
1 teaspoon vanilla · 1 egg yolk
½ cup finely ground almonds
1 cup all-purpose flour, sifted
⅓ cup strained marmalade

Yogurt cream:
2 envelopes plus 1 teaspoon unflavored
gelatin
½ cup orange juice · juice of ½ lemon
½ cup granulated sugar · 4 egg yolks
grated peel of 1 orange
1 cup plain or lemon-flavored yogurt
2 cups heavy cream
¼ cup sifted confectioners' sugar
toasted sliced almonds for decoration

6½- cup ring mold (9½-inches in diameter)

Preheat oven to 400°F

Beat butter, confectioners' sugar, vanilla, and egg yolk until thick and creamy. Combine almonds and flour and work into mixture to make soft dough. Divide in half. Wrap separately and refrigerate 2 hours. Roll out dough to two 9½-inch circles . Place on ungreased baking sheet and prick with fork. Bake 12–15 minutes or until golden brown. Cool on wire rack. Spread marmalade over one pastry circle, reserving small amount, and top with second circle.

To make yogurt cream, soak gelatin in ¼ cup orange juice 5 minutes. Stir remaining orange juice, lemon juice, sugar, egg yolks, and orange peel in saucepan. Place over low heat, add gelatin, and cook, stirring constantly, until gelatin is dissolved. Remove from heat and cool slightly. Stir in yogurt. Refrigerate until mixture is consistency of egg whites. Beat cream and confectioners' sugar until firm. Fold into yogurt mixture. Pour into mold and top with pastry circles. Refrigerate 4–5 hours. Brush pastry edge with reserved marmalade and sprinkle with almonds.

Raspberry-Yogurt Cake

Sponge:
4 eggs · ½ cup sugar
¾ cup cake flour
3 tablespoons cornstarch
¼ cup (½ stick) butter, melted

Filling:
1 cup milk · ¾ cup sugar · 4 egg yolks
2 packages unflavored gelatin or 8 gelatin
leaves
2 cups vanilla yogurt
½ pound fresh raspberries
1 tablespoon raspberry-flavored liqueur
1 cup heavy cream
2 tablespoons confectioners' sugar
juice of 1 lemon

To decorate:
1½ cups heavy cream
2 tablespoons confectioners' sugar
⅓ cup toasted sliced almonds
10-inch deep flan ring or springform pan

Preheat oven to 375°F

Prepare sponge according to photos on page 27 for Genoise Mixture. Cut sponge into two layers. Place one layer on flat plate and place 10-inch flan ring around it. Set both layers aside.

To make filling, place milk, sugar, and egg yolks in saucepan. Cook over moderate heat until thick enough to coat back of spoon. Soak gelatin in ¼ cup warm water and stir into custard until gelatin is dissolved. Fold in yogurt. Divide mixture between two bowls. Set 16 raspberries aside for decoration. Puree remaining raspberries. Stir into one bowl of yogurt mixture. Add raspberry liqueur. Whip cream with confectioners' sugar until stiff. Stir half of whipped cream into raspberry-yogurt mixture and spread over sponge layer in flan ring. Refrigerate until set. Stir lemon juice into remaining yogurt mixture and fold in remaining whipped cream. Spread over set raspberry-cream mixture. Top with second sponge layer. Refrigerate 2–3 hours.

To decorate, remove flan ring from cake. Whip cream with sugar until firm. Spoon 1 cup whipped cream into pastry bag fitted with open star tip. Spread remaining cream over top and around sides of cake. Sprinkle almonds around sides and over top of cake. Decorate with piped whipped cream and reserved raspberries.

Fruit-Yogurt Flan

Pastry:
½ cup (1 stick) butter, softened
¼ cup confectioners' sugar
½ teaspoon vanilla · 1 egg yolk
1½ cups all-purpose flour
1 tablespoon ice water

Chocolate yogurt filling:
1 envelope plus 1 teaspoon gelatin
½ cup milk · ⅓ cup granulated sugar
2 egg yolks
¼ cup unsweetened cocoa
1 tablespoon dark rum
¾ cup plain yogurt
1 cup heavy cream
2 tablespoons confectioners' sugar
6 canned peach halves

Strawberry-cream topping:
1 pint strawberries
1 teaspoon unflavored gelatin
1½ cups heavy cream
¼ cup confectioners' sugar

chocolate shavings for decoration

10-inch fluted tart/flan pan with removable bottom

Preheat oven to 375°F

To prepare pastry, cream butter, confectioners' sugar, vanilla, and egg yolk in bowl. Add flour and beat at low speed until mixture resembles coarse crumbs. Add ice water and toss with fork until dough binds together. Wrap and refrigerate 1 hour. Roll out pastry to ¼-inch thickness and line tart pan. Prick pastry all over with fork. Line with waxed paper or aluminium foil and fill with dried beans or pie weights. Bake 10 minutes. Remove paper and pie weights and bake 5 more minutes or until golden brown. Cool on wire rack.

Sprinkle gelatin over ¼ cup milk and let stand 5 minutes. Bring remaining milk, granulated sugar, egg yolks, and cocoa to a boil, stirring until mixture is thick enough to coat back of spoon. Add gelatin and cook, stirring, until gelatin is dissolved. Remove from heat and stir in rum and yogurt. Let cool. Beat cream with confectioners' sugar until firm. Fold into yogurt mixture. Pour mixture into pastry shell and refrigerate until set. Thinly slice peach halves and arrange in concentric circles over chocolate mixture.

Reserve half the strawberries for decoration and puree remainder. Sprinkle gelatin over ¼ cup cream and let stand 5 minutes. Place over low heat and cook, stirring, until gelatin is dissolved. Remove from heat and cool. Beat remaining cream with confectioners' sugar until soft peaks form. Add gelatin and beat until firm. Fold strawberry puree into two-thirds of the whipped cream. Spoon strawberry cream over peaches. Sprinkle with grated chocolate.

Spoon reserved whipped cream into pastry bag fitted with small open star tip. Pipe decoratively on top of grated chocolate. Decorate with reserved strawberries.

Baking with Yeast

Bread is a staple product all over the world and the making of bread dates back to the Stone Age. There are various types of bread that are made without the use of yeast—such as Irish soda bread or Indian chapati—but since the discovery of yeast in the sixteenth century we have become used to leavened breads made with wheat flour.

As well as being baked in a loaf pan, yeast dough is very adaptable and lends itself well to shaping. At harvest time, for example, it is traditional to have a loaf baked in the shape of a wheatsheaf. Plaited loaves have always looked appealing and remain very popular.

The Gugelhupf, one of the best known German cakes, was once a symbol of middle-class status and wealth. It was, and in many places still is, an essential feature of the middle-class family breakfast or the Sunday afternoon tea shop. The Gugelhupf is as much a feature of Sunday in Germany as an outing or visit to relatives. This can probably be explained by the time involved in making the cake, so that the job was left for the weekend, and the fact that all yeast cakes are best eaten fresh, preferably warm from the oven.

The strange etymology of the wonderful name *gugelhupf* is extremely interesting, and the spelling alone poses insoluble problems. Whether the word should begin with a *k* or a *g*, whether the first syllable should be *gugel* or *gogel*, whether it should be *hupf* or *hopf* are all matters of debate. Apparently the word *gugel* refers to the shape of the cake as, according to Zenker's *Kochkunst* (*The Art of Cookery*) it should be tall. The word *kugel* has similar connotations; in the Alps a high cone-shaped mountain is referred to as a *kogel*, and in many areas peasant women still wear the spherical headdresses known as *gugel*, which first became popular in the twelfth century. The syllable *hupf* or *hopf* on the other hand refers to the amazing way in which yeast dough rises thus bringing to mind the term *hupfen* (to jump, leap).

These cakes were popular as long ago as Roman times. The excavations at Herculaneum produced tall, straight-sided bakeware, and museums in Speyer and Berne include finds of bakeware with amazing similarities to the later Gugelhupf. Experts claim that the shape originally represented the "rotating sun." Admittedly, the medieval version lacked the characteristic "chimney" placed in the center of the cake to ensure more even heat distribution. At that time the Gugelhupf was baked in a mortar, as a Viennese manuscript reveals. From the eighteenth century onward richly decorated copper molds began to appear and the range of recipes that could be cooked in them was widened. The "ordinary" Gugelhupf was joined by sponge, almond, or Malaga versions, the Waltersdorf Gugelhupf, and even the Kaiser-Gugelhupf (the Emperor Franz Joseph was reputedly fond of what he referred to as this "old German dish").

Whether for emperor or peasant these cakes, topped with almonds or glistening sugar, covered in chocolate or icing, with their light golden bases and juicy raisins, undoubtedly create a festive atmosphere of well being.

Braided Yeast Breads

It is an ancient custom to make breads and cakes in the shape of braid (plait). The dough should be elastic and pliable in order to make a neatly braided bread, but it should not be too rich because an excessive amount of eggs and butter will cause the braid to loose its shape during baking. Braided loaves do not have to be multistranded masterpieces. They can be made with three simple strands. The following recipe will make enough dough for two large loaves.

about 7½ cups all-purpose flour
2 packages active dry yeast or 2 cakes
(0.6 ounce each) fresh yeast
⅓ cup sugar
2 cups warm milk (105° to 115°F)
½ cup (1 stick) butter, melted
2 teaspoons salt
1 egg yolk beaten with 1 tablespoon
water for glaze

Preheat oven to 400°F

Prepare dough according to photos for Basic Yeast Dough, page 46. Punch dough down, shape, and braid as desired. Brush tops with egg yolk mixture and sprinkle with coarse salt if desired. Place on greased baking sheets and bake 25 to 30 minutes or until loaves sound hollow when tapped on bottom.

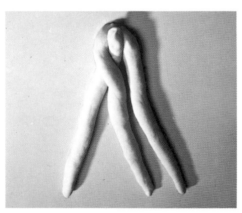

1 **Three-stranded plait**. This is the easiest braid to make. Divide dough into three equal pieces. Shape each piece into 18- to 22-inch-long strand. Place strands on flat work surface fairly close together.

2 **Press and pinch** top ends of strands together. Place left strand over center strand so it is now the center strand. Place right strand over center strand.

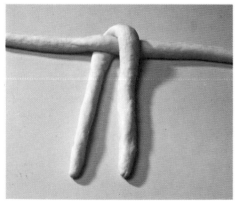

1 **A four-strand braided loaf** is made from two strands of dough. Divide dough in half. Shape each piece into 32-inch-long strand. Place first strand on work surface. Loop center of second strand over center of first so centers of each are together and ends of second strand are at right angle to first and slightly apart.

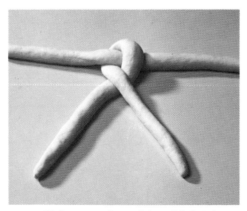

2 **Pick up second strand** from left in left hand. Pick up second strand from right in right hand. Cross strands over each other.

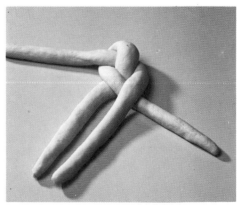

3 **Pick up right side** of horizontal strand in right hand and place it over strand next to it.

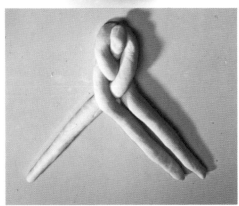

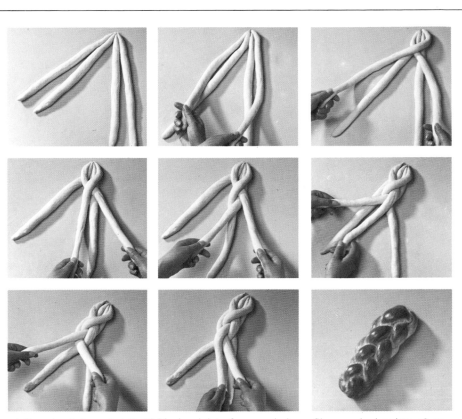

A four-stranded round plait. Divide dough into four equal pieces. Shape each piece into 18- to 20-inch-long strand. Place two strands together on each side. Pinch all top ends together and braid, following step-by-step photos above. Pinch and tuck bottom ends under. As you braid, keep strands spread apart, two on each side. This is the easiest way to keep track of which strand should be braided after each step.

3 **Place left strand** over center strand again. Repeat, placing outer strands over center strands alternately (left over center, then right over center) until strands are completely braided. Press and pinch ends together, tucking ends under slightly to prevent them from coming apart on baking sheet.

Prepare dough according to step-by-step photos for Basic Yeast Dough, page 46. Add lemon peel, chopped almonds, candied lemon peel, and raisins with flour and beaten egg-butter mixture (step 3). Punch dough down, shape, and braid as desired. Brush top with egg yolk mixture and sprinkle with almonds and crystal sugar. Place on greased baking sheet and bake in preheated oven 25 minutes or until loaf sounds hollow when tapped on bottom.

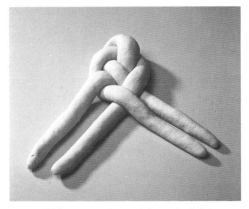

4 **Pick up second strand** from the left in right hand. Pick up strand to the left of it in left hand. Bring the strand you are holding in your left hand under the strand you are holding in your right hand and over the strand next to it. Repeat last two steps until strands are completely braided.

Poppy Seed Stollen

Pastry:
about 3 cups all-purpose flour
1 package active dry yeast or 1 cake (0.6 ounce) fresh yeast
4 tablespoons sugar
$\frac{1}{2}$ cup warm milk (105° to 115°F)
5 tablespoons butter, melted and cooled
2 eggs
$\frac{1}{2}$ teaspoon salt
grated rind of 1 lemon
2 tablespoons ground almonds

Poppy seed filling:
$1\frac{3}{4}$ cup milk
1 cup poppy seeds, ground
5 tablespoons cornstarch
1 egg yolk, beaten
$\frac{1}{3}$ cup sugar
2 tablespoons butter

Apricot Glaze, page 60
Fondant, page 60
toasted sliced almonds

Preheat oven to 375°F

To make pastry, sift flour into bowl and make well in center. Place yeast and 1 tablespoon sugar in well. Add warm milk and stir to dissolve yeast. Sprinkle with flour. Cover and set aside 10 minutes. Beat remaining sugar, butter, eggs, salt, lemon peel, and ground almonds until blended. Add to flour and beat vigorously with wooden spoon to make soft dough. Knead dough until smooth and elastic. Place in greased bowl and turn to coat. Cover and let rise 1 to $1\frac{1}{2}$ hours.

To make filling, bring $1\frac{1}{4}$ cups milk and poppy seed to a boil over moderate heat in medium-size saucepan. Lower heat and simmer 10 minutes. Blend cornstarch with remaining $\frac{1}{2}$ cup milk until smooth. Stir into poppy seed mixture with beaten egg yolk, sugar, and melted butter. Cook, stirring, until mixture is thickened. Remove from heat and cool.

Grease baking sheet. Punch dough down. Roll out dough on lightly floured surface to 16- by 12-inch rectangle. Spread poppy seed filling over dough to within $\frac{1}{4}$ inch of edges. Starting at one long end, roll dough, jelly-roll style, in toward center. Roll opposite long end in toward center until rolls meet. Place on prepared baking sheet. Cover and let rise 30 to 35 minutes or until almost doubled in volume.

Bake in preheated oven 30 to 35 minutes or until golden brown. Remove from baking sheet and cool on wire rack. Brush with apricot glaze while still warm. Cover with fondant and sprinkle with almonds. Let stand until fondant is set.

Almond-Raisin Plait

Dough:
$2\frac{1}{2}$ cups all-purpose flour
1 package active dry yeast or 1 cake (0.6 ounce) fresh yeast
3 tablespoons sugar
$\frac{1}{2}$ cup warm milk (105° to 115°F)
3 tablespoons butter, melted and cooled
1 egg
1 teaspoon salt

Filling:
$\frac{1}{4}$ cup apricot jam, warmed
2 ounces almond paste
$\frac{1}{3}$ cup raisins, finely chopped
$\frac{1}{4}$ cup finely chopped almonds
1 tablespoon beaten egg white
1 egg yolk beaten with 1 tablespoon water for glaze

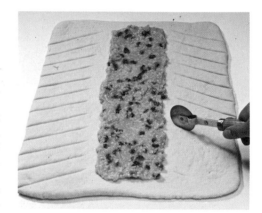

1 **Roll out dough** to 16- by 12-inch rectangle. Spread filling down center in 3-inch-wide strip. Use pastry wheel or knife to make diagonal cuts about 1 inch apart down each side of dough.

2 **Beginning at top**, fold alternate left and right strips over filling. Pinch and tuck ends under. Place on greased baking sheet. Cover and let rise, brush with egg glaze, and bake as directed above.

Apricot Glaze, page 60
Fondant, page 60
toasted sliced almonds for decoration

Preheat oven to 375°F

Prepare dough according to step-by-step photos on page 46 for Basic Yeast Dough. Cover and let rise 1 to 1½ hours. Beat apricot jam and almond paste until smooth. Fold in raisins and chopped almonds. Stir in beaten egg white. Prepare and fill plait as illustrated below. Place on greased baking sheet. Cover and let rise 45 minutes. Brush with egg glaze. Bake in preheated oven 30 to 35 minutes or until golden brown. Brush with apricot glaze while still warm. Let cool. Spread fondant over top and sprinkle with almonds.

Nut Twist

Pastry:
about 3 cups all-purpose flour
1 package active dry yeast or 1 cake (0.6 ounce) fresh yeast
3 tablespoons sugar
½ cup warm milk (105° to 115°F)
¼ cup (½ stick) butter, melted and cooled
2 eggs
1 teaspoon salt
grated peel of ½ lemon

Filling:
4 ounces almond paste
2 egg whites · ¼ cup sugar
½ teaspoon cinnamon
¾ cup finely ground hazelnuts or almonds
1 egg yolk beaten with 1 tablespoon milk for glaze
Apricot Glaze, page 60
Fondant, page 60

Preheat oven to 375°F

Prepare dough according to step-by-step photos for Basic Yeast Dough, page 46. Cover and let rise 1 to 1½ hours. Beat almond paste, egg whites, ¼ cup sugar, and cinnamon until smooth. Fold in ground hazelnuts. Punch dough down. Roll out dough on lightly floured surface to 16- by 14-inch rectangle. Spread nut filling over dough to within ½ inch of edges. Brush with egg yolk mixture. Grease baking sheet. Starting at long end, roll up dough jelly-roll style. Cut and twist dough as illustrated below. Place on prepared baking sheet. Cover and let rise 30 to 40 minutes or until almost doubled in bulk. Bake in preheated oven 30 to 35 minutes or until golden brown. Remove from baking sheet and cool on wire rack. Brush with apricot glaze and cover with fondant while still warm.

1 **Roll out dough** on lightly floured surface to 16- by 14-inch rectangle. Spread nut filling over dough to within ½ inch of edges. Brush edges with beaten egg yolk mixture. Starting at long end, roll up jelly-roll style.

2 **Place roll**, seam side down, on clean work surface. Cut roll in half lengthwise with sharp knife, cutting down center of roll to make two strands.

3 **Place strands**, side by side, and pinch top ends together. Twist strands together. Pinch and tuck ends under. Place twisted loaf on greased baking sheet. Proceed as directed above.

Gugelhupf

This is a basic Gugelhupf recipe that can be varied by adding extra raisins, candied lemon peel, almonds, etc.

1 tablespoon dark rum
$\frac{2}{3}$ cup raisins
$3\frac{1}{2}$ cups all-purpose flour
1 package active dry yeast or 1 cake (0.6 ounce) fresh yeast
$\frac{1}{2}$ cup granulated sugar
$\frac{3}{4}$ cup warm milk (105° to 115°F)
$\frac{3}{4}$ cup (1$\frac{1}{2}$ sticks) butter, softened
1 teaspoon salt
$\frac{1}{8}$ teaspoon nutmeg
grated peel of 1 lemon
3 eggs
butter and cake crumbs for pan
16 whole blanched almonds
confectioners' sugar for dusting

8$\frac{1}{2}$-inch traditional gugelhupf pan

Preheat oven to 375°F

Pour rum over raisins and set aside. Sift flour into large bowl and make well in center. Add yeast and 1 tablespoon granulated sugar. Stir in milk to dissolve yeast. Cover bowl with clean towel and let rise 10 minutes. Add creamed butter-egg mixture

to bowl and beat vigorously with wooden spoon. Fold in raisins. Cover and let rise. Place dough in greased Gugelhupf pan and pack down with back of wooden spoon. Cover pan and let rise again. Bake in a preheated oven 40 to 45 minutes or until cake tester or long metal skewer inserted into cake comes out clean. Remove from pan and cool on wire rack. Dust top of cake with sifted confectioners' sugar.

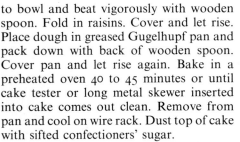

2 **Beat butter mixture** with balloon whisk or electric mixer until doubled in volume. If butter mixture starts to curdle, beat in 2 to 3 tablespoons of flour.

1 **Soak raisins in rum**. Cut butter into cubes and place in bowl. Add remaining granulated sugar, salt, nutmeg, and lemon peel, and beat until creamy. Beat in eggs, one at a time.

3 **Stir butter mixture** into yeast-flour mixture and stir with wooden spoon until well blended and dough comes away from sides of bowl. Cover bowl with clean towel and set aside in warm, draft-free place to rise until doubled in bulk, 1 to 1$\frac{1}{2}$ hours.

4 **Grease gugelhupf pan** with butter. Place pan in refrigerator to harden butter. Remove pan from refrigerator and grease again. Place almonds in bottom of pan and sprinkle inside of pan with sponge cake crumbs or flour.

5 **Stir soaked raisins** into risen yeast dough with wooden spoon.

6 **Transfer dough** to prepared pan, packing dough in pan with back of wooden spoon. Smooth top of dough. Cover pan with clean towel and let rise 1¼ hours or until dough has risen to 1½ inches from rim of pan. Bake as directed above.

Chocolate-covered Gugelhupf

3½ cups all-purpose flour
½ cup sugar
1 package active dry yeast or 1 cake (0.6 ounce) fresh yeast
¾ cup warm milk (105° to 115°F)
1 cup (2 sticks) butter, softened
2 whole eggs · 3 egg yolks
1 teaspoon vanilla
1 teaspoon salt
⅛ teaspoon allspice
⅛ teaspoon ginger
3 tablespoons light cream
¼ cup currants · ⅓ cup raisins
3 tablespoons chopped candied lemon peel
2 tablespoons chopped candied orange peel
1 tablespoon dark rum
½ cup chopped blanched almonds
2 ounces semisweet chocolate, chopped
Apricot Glaze, page 60
melted semisweet chocolate
toasted sliced almonds

8½-inch traditional gugelphupf pan, greased and floured

Preheat oven to 375°F

Prepare yeast dough as directed in Gugelhupf recipe on opposite page. Prepare butter mixture adding eggs, egg yolks one at a time, vanilla, salt, allspice, ginger, and cream. Beat butter mixture into yeast dough until dough comes away from sides of bowl. Cover bowl with clean towel and set aside in warm, draft-free place to rise until doubled in bulk, 1 to 1½ hours.

While dough is rising, place currants, raisins, lemon peel, and orange peel in bowl. Add rum and stir well. Let stand 30 minutes. Add chopped almonds and chopped chocolate. Stir fruit-nut mixture into risen dough. Transfer dough to prepared pan, cover, and let rise about 1¼ hours. Bake 40 to 45 minutes or until cake tester inserted in cake comes out clean.

Remove Gugelhupf from pan and place on wire rack. While Gugelhupf is still warm, spread thin layer of apricot glaze over cake and let stand until cool. Cover cake with melted chocolate and decorate edge with toasted sliced almonds. Let stand until chocolate is set.

Baking for the Morning

"It is the variety and ornamental complexity of our baking that reveals the long history of our culinary culture." This is a quotation from Otto Stradal's book *Wiener Stadt, Wiener Leut* (*The City and People of Vienna*). Vienna does indeed seem to merit its reputation as the foremost city in the world for patisserie and for breakfast baking in particular. In Gdansk there are small rolls known as "Vienna rolls," in Prague there are "Vienna butter croissants," in Silesia there are "Vienna horns," in Saxony "Vienna knots," and in Copenhagen pastries in croissant dough are known as "Vienna bread" (though the Viennese themselves call these same pastries "Danish pastries").

The crescent-shaped kipferl, one of the best known of the croissant-dough pastries, reputedly has close links with the history of Vienna. A master baker called Peter Wendler is said to have baked them after the Turkish siege of the city in mockery of the Islamic crescent moon, which the defeated Turks had set up in front of the cathedral of St. Stephan. There can however be no truth in the story for Peter Wendler had already been dead for three years in 1683 (the year of the siege), and the kipferl is in fact much older than this. The Viennese Annals of 1670 mention "knupfl" cakes; in the Baroque period Abraham a Santa Clara describes "long, short, curved and straight kupfel,"; while as early as 1227 a Viennese baker presented Duke Leopold the Glorious with a "basket of Chipfen" at Christmas. Even earlier, the kipferl featured among Germanic Easter cakes and is thought to have represented the fertility symbol of the goat's horn.

It seems likely that the kipferl spread from Germany not only to Vienna but also westward toward France—where the crescent-shaped pastries were developed into the croissant. What better way could there be to start the day than to drink your breakfast coffee with fresh croissants, warm from the oven and smelling of butter! The same could also be said of brioches, a fine French roll of delicate yeast dough. These extremely light creations come in a variety of forms, as small individual rolls or as loaves known as nanterre and Brioche mousseline—all famous for the characteristic flavor of fresh butter.

Another traditional breakfast roll in Germany is the pretzel. Medieval monks called these pastries "brachitum" and the diminutive form "brachitellum" from the Latin *brachium* (arm) because their shape resembles two linked arms. In the baking of small pastries in dough, the baker has always been able to give free rein to his imagination when it came to twisting and plaiting them into a multitude of different shapes. It would be impossible to try to list the wide variety of shapes and the richness of invention that pastry cooks have brought to breakfast baking. The Viennese, for example, make a very precise distinction between kipfel and kipferl. The latter is often subdivided into separate types such as butter kipferl, brioche kipferl, or the flaky "splitterkipferl." The first group on the other hand includes such items as hearth kipfel, radetzky kipfel, ham kipfel, and baking sheet kipfel, which is said to have been the favorite of Mozart's wife Konstanze. To sum up in the words of Otto Stradal, "The specialty of the Viennese baker's basket could form the subject of a thesis."

Brioche

These buttery French yeast rolls can be made in a variety of shapes and sizes. The most popular version is the small individual brioche, baked in a small fluted mold. Brioches should be eaten fresh and are considered to be one of the lightest and most delicious yeast dough delicacies that can be made.

Brioche dough should be made the day before it is to be baked. It can be frozen if desired.

about 4¼ cups all-purpose flour
1 package active dry yeast or 1 cake (0.6 ounce) fresh yeast
½ cup warm water (105° to 115°F)
6 eggs
1½ teaspoons salt
⅓ cup sugar
1 cup (2 sticks) butter, softened
all-purpose flour for kneading
1 egg yolk beaten with 1 tablespoon water for brushing

Preheat oven to 450°F

When dough has been made, place in greased bowl. Cover with plastic wrap or aluminum foil and place in refrigerator to rise 2 to 2½ hours. Dough will not rise very much at this temperature. Stir dough down and knead a few minutes. Return to greased bowl, re-cover, and refrigerate overnight. Grease brioche pans lightly with butter. Just before baking, brush brioche with beaten egg yolk mixture.

1 **Sift flour onto work surface** and make well in center. Add yeast and warm water to well and stir with fingers. Sprinkle a little flour over yeast mixture and let stand 10 minutes.

2 **Break eggs into well**. Add salt and sugar. Mix ingredients with hands, working out from center. Bring flour in from edge with dough scraper, mixing until dough is soft.

4 **Cream butter**. Squeeze butter into dough with finger tips and knead dough with heel of hand.

5 **Lift dough** and slam it back onto work surface several times. Continue lifting and slamming until dough is smooth and shiny. Place in greased bowl and cover with plastic wrap or aluminum foil. Refrigerate 2 to 2½ hours. Stir dough down with wooden spoon. Knead a few minutes. Return to bowl, re-cover, and refrigerate overnight.

7 **Grease small brioche molds**. Roll ball of dough with side of hand. Make indentation in ball one third of way in from end. Place dough in greased molds, large end in bottom of mold.

8 **Alternatively**, roll ball of dough with side of hand. Divide ball into two pieces, one piece two thirds of ball. Place large piece of dough in mold and press hole in center with fingertip. Taper end of small piece of dough and insert tapered end into hole.

9 **Press tops down** to prevent balls from separating during rising or baking. Turn mold with one hand and press dough down around outer edge with index finger of opposite hand. Small ball of dough should sit deep in base.

3 **Knead dough vigorously** about 15 minutes. Lift dough off work surface and drop it back onto work surface several times. Loosen dough that sticks to work surface with dough scraper.

Brioches Nanterre. This kind of brioche is baked in a loaf pan. Grease two 8- × 4-inch loaf pans. Divide dough in half. Cut each half into four equal-size pieces and shape each piece into ball (see photo 6). Place balls in greased pan and let rise 1 to 1½ hours or until doubled. Brush with beaten egg yolk mixture. Dip scissors in cold water and cut tops of brioches. Bake in preheated oven 30 to 35 minutes or until golden brown. Remove from pan and cool on wire rack.

6 **Remove dough from bowl** and knead a few minutes. To make individual brioches, divide dough into small balls. Flour hands and work surface. Roll balls back and forth to shape evenly.

10 **Let brioches rise** about 45 minutes or until doubled. Brush lightly with beaten egg yolk mixture. Bake in preheated oven 12 to 15 minutes.

A selection of brioches made from the recipe on the opposite page: small brioches; large brioches made in the same shape with four cuts in outer edge; Brioche Nanterre made in four sections; and tall Brioche Mousseline baked in 4-inch conical mold. The main characteristic of this dough—lightness and lovely buttery flavor—come from the high egg and butter content.

Rich Breakfast Rolls

about 5½ cups all-purpose flour
2 packages active dry yeast or 1 cake (2 ounces) fresh yeast
¼ cup sugar
1½ cups warm milk (105° to 115°F)
¼ cup (½ stick) butter, melted and cooled
2 eggs
1 teaspoon salt
¼ teaspoon grated nutmeg
1 egg yolk beaten with 1 tablespoon cream for glaze
crystal sugar for decoration

Preheat oven to 400°F

Sift 4 cups flour into bowl and make well in center. Place yeast and 1 tablespoon sugar in well. Add milk and stir to dissolve yeast. Sprinkle yeast mixture with flour. Cover bowl with clean towel and let stand 10 minutes or until cracks appear in flour layer over yeast mixture. Beat remaining sugar, butter, eggs, salt, and nutmeg until blended. Add to bowl with 1 cup flour. Beat vigorously with wooden spoon until smooth. Stir in enough remaining flour to make smooth dough that comes away from sides of bowl. Knead dough until smooth and elastic. Place dough in greased bowl and turn to coat. Cover and let rise 40 minutes. Grease baking sheets. Punch dough down and divide in half. Cut each half into twelve equal-size pieces. Shape pieces into 18- to 20-inch-long strands. Shape strands into any of rolls illustrated alongside. Place rolls on prepared baking sheets. Cover and let rise 20 minutes. Brush rolls with beaten egg yolk mixture and sprinkle with crystal sugar if desired. Bake in preheated oven about 20 minutes or until golden brown. (Makes 18 to 24 rolls.)

Cheese Crumb Coffeecake

about 3 cups all-purpose flour
1 package active dry yeast or 1 cake (0.6
ounce) fresh yeast
3 tablespoons sugar
½ cup warm milk (105° to 115°F)
6 tablespoons butter, melted and cooled
2 eggs · 1 teaspoon salt
⅛ teaspoon allspice
grated peel of 1 lemon

Cheese filling:
1 cup milk · ½ cup sugar
3 tablespoons cornstarch
1 cup creamy cottage cheese
grated peel and juice of ½ lemon
1 tablespoon dark rum

Crumb topping:
1¼ cups all-purpose flour
½ cup sugar · ¼ teaspoon cinnamon
6 tablespoons butter

16- × 12-inch jelly-roll pan, greased

Preheat oven to 400°F

Sift flour into bowl and make well in center.
Place yeast and 1 tablespoon sugar in well.
Add milk and stir to dissolve yeast. Cover
and set aside 10 minutes. Beat remaining
sugar, butter, eggs, salt, allspice, and lemon
peel until blended. Add to flour and beat
vigorously with wooden spoon to make soft
dough. Knead until smooth and elastic.
Place in greased bowl and turn to coat.
Cover and let rise 1 to 1½ hours. Punch
dough down. Roll or pat dough out to fit
pan. Prick dough all over with fork.

To make filling, stir milk, sugar, and
cornstarch in saucepan until blended. Place
pan over low heat and cook, stirring, until
thickened. Remove from heat and stir in
cottage cheese, lemon peel, lemon juice, and
rum. Cool slightly and spread over dough.

To make topping, stir flour, sugar, and
cinnamon in bowl. Cut in butter until
mixture resembles coarse crumbs. Sprinkle
crumbs over cheese filling. Let rise 30
minutes. Bake 25 to 30 minutes.

Almond and Custard Slices

about 3 cups all-purpose flour
1 package active dry yeast or 1 cake (0.6
ounce) fresh yeast
2 tablespoons sugar
½ cup warm milk (105° to 115°F)
6 tablespoons butter, melted and cooled
2 eggs · 1 teaspoon salt

Almond topping:
10 tablespoons butter
1 cup sugar · 1 tablespoon honey
3 tablespoons heavy cream
¾ cup sliced almonds

Custard filling:
⅔ cup sugar
4 tablespoons cornstarch
4 egg yolks · 2 cups milk
1 teaspoon vanilla
1 envelope plus 1 teaspoon unflavored
gelatin
2 cups heavy cream

16- × 12-inch jelly-roll pan, greased

Preheat oven to 400°F

Prepare dough according to photos for
Basic Yeast Dough, page 46. Cover and let
rise 1 to 1½ hours. Roll out or pat dough to
fit pan. Prick dough all over with fork.

Bring butter, sugar, honey, and cream to
a boil in saucepan. Remove from heat and
stir in almonds. Set aside to cool. When
cool, spread over dough. Bake 20 to 25
minutes or until brown and crisp.

Make vanilla custard with sugar, cornstarch, egg yolks, milk, and vanilla as
directed on page 50. Soak gelatin in ¼ cup
warm water 5 minutes. Add gelatin to hot
custard and stir until dissolved. Set aside to
cool. Whip cream and fold into cooled
custard. Cut cake in half to make two layers.
Spread custard mixture over bottom layer.
Refrigerate 1 to 2 hours or until custard
mixture is firm. Cut top layer into twenty
slices. Place slices over custard. Cut through
to bottom layer using cut slices as cutting
guide.

Dresden Slices

about 3 cups all-purpose flour
1 package active dry yeast or 1 cake (0.6
ounce) fresh yeast
3 tablespoons sugar
½ cup warm milk (105° to 115°F)
4 tablespoons butter, melted and cooled
2 eggs
1 teaspoon salt
grated peel of ½ lemon

Cheese filling:
2 eggs
½ cup sugar
¼ teaspoon salt
grated peel of 1 lemon
2 packages (8 ounces each) cream cheese,
softened

Butter-egg mixture:
¾ cup (1½ sticks) butter
⅔ cup sugar
½ teaspoon vanilla
4 eggs
⅓ cup all-purpose flour
⅓ cup sliced almonds

16- × 12-inch jelly roll-pan, greased

Preheat oven to 400°F

To make dough, prepare according to step-
by-step photos for Basic Yeast Dough, page
46. Cover and let rise 1 to 1½ hours. Punch
dough down. Roll out or pat dough to fit
prepared pan, bringing sides of dough up
slightly. Prick all over with fork.

To make cheese filling, beat eggs and
sugar until creamy. Add salt, lemon peel,
and cream cheese, and beat until light and
fluffy. Spread cheese mixture over dough.
Let rise 20 minutes.

To prepare butter-egg mixture, beat
butter and sugar until fluffy. Add vanilla
and 1 egg. Add flour and beat in remaining
eggs, one at a time. Spread over cheese layer
and sprinkle with almonds. Bake in preheated oven 25 to 30 minutes. Slice in pan.

Butter Kuchen

Dough:
about 3 cups all-purpose flour
1 package active dry yeast or 1 cake
(0.6 ounce) fresh yeast
2 tablespoons sugar
$\frac{1}{2}$ cup warm milk (105° to 115°F)
6 tablespoons butter, melted and
cooled
2 eggs
1 teaspoon salt

Topping:
$1\frac{1}{4}$ cups ($2\frac{1}{2}$ sticks) butter, softened
1 cup sliced almonds
$\frac{3}{4}$ cup sugar
$\frac{1}{2}$ teaspoon cinnamon

1 **Let dough rise** 20 minutes in prepared pan. Make indentations all over dough with tips of two fingers. Press all the way through dough to prevent holes from closing when dough rises again.

16- × 12-inch jelly-roll pan, greased

Preheat oven to 400°F

Prepare dough according to step-by-step photos for Basic Yeast Dough, page 46. Cover and let rise 1 to $1\frac{1}{2}$ hours. Punch dough down. Roll out or pat dough to fit prepared pan. Cover and let rise 20 minutes. Prepare cake according to photos alongside. Bake in preheated oven 20 to 25 minutes. Cake should be brown and crisp on top, but still nice and soft inside. Cut into rectangles to serve.

2 **Cream butter** until light and fluffy. Spoon into pastry bag fitted with plain tip (#6) and pipe small swirls of butter all over cake. (Butter does not have to be piped directly into holes because it will melt during baking.) Alternatively, drop small dots of butter over cake with demitasse spoon.

3 **Sprinkle almonds** evenly over cake. Combine sugar and cinnamon and sprinkle over almonds. Bake in preheated oven 20 to 25 minutes or until top is lightly browned and crisp. Cool in pan on wire rack.

Poppy Seed and Nut Crescents

Dough:
about 3¾ cups all-purpose flour
1 package active dry yeast or 1 cake (0.6 ounce) fresh yeast
⅔ cup sugar
1 cup warm milk (105° to 115°F)
½ cup (1 stick) butter, melted and cooled
3 egg yolks, beaten
1 teaspoon salt
grated peel of 1 lemon

Nut filling:
6 tablespoons ground walnuts
⅔ cup sponge cake crumbs
1 teaspoon lemon peel
2 tablespoons finely chopped raisins
¼ cup hot sugar syrup

Poppy seed filling:
⅓ cup poppy seed, ground
½ cup sponge cake crumbs
3 tablespoons sugar
2 tablespoons finely chopped raisins
3 tablespoons milk
1 tablespoon dark rum

3 egg yolks, beaten for glazing

Preheat oven to 400°F

To make dough, prepare according to step-by-step photos for Basic Yeast Dough, page 46, or make pastry by method shown on page 38. Shape dough into ball. Place in greased bowl and turn to coat. Cover and let rise 1 hour.

To make nut filling, combine ground walnuts, cake crumbs, grated lemon peel, and raisins. Stir in boiling syrup. Mixture should be firm and pliable.

To make poppy seed filling, combine poppy seed, cake crumbs, sugar, and raisins. Bring milk to a boil in medium-size saucepan. Add poppy seed mixture and cook, stirring, until most of milk has evaporated. Remove from heat and stir in rum.

Grease baking sheets. Punch dough down. Divide dough in half. Shape each piece into long roll about 24 inches long and 1¼ inches thick. Cut rolls into 1-inch pieces. Shape each piece into ball. Spoon teaspoonfuls of both fillings onto waxed paper and shape into small thick ovals. Roll out balls of dough with rolling pin into small flat ovals. Place one ball of filling on each oval and roll up. Pinch ends of dough together to prevent any filling from seeping out during baking. Roll each filled oval back and forth on work surfaces until thick at center but tapered at ends. Shape into "V" shapes or crescents. Place on prepared baking sheets. Brush with beaten egg yolks. Set aside in a cool dry place 30 minutes. Brush with beaten egg yolks again and set aside to dry 30 minutes. Bake in preheated oven 18 to 20 minutes or until golden brown. (Makes 4 dozen filled crescents.)

Poppy Seed–Cheese Pastries

Dough:
$4\frac{1}{4}$ cups all-purpose flour
1 package active dry yeast or 1 cake (0.6 ounce) fresh yeast
$\frac{1}{4}$ cup sugar
1 cup warm milk (105° to 115°F)
$\frac{1}{4}$ cup ($\frac{1}{2}$ stick) butter, softened
1 teaspoon salt
2 eggs
grated peel of 1 lemon
1 egg yolk beaten with 1 tablespoon water for glaze

Topping:
12 ounces cream cheese, softened
$\frac{1}{4}$ cup ($\frac{1}{2}$ stick) butter
1 cup sugar
2 eggs, separated
3 tablespoons cornstarch
1 tablespoon dark rum
1 cup milk
$1\frac{1}{2}$ cups poppy seed, ground
2 tablespoons dry bread crumbs
Apricot Glaze, page 60
toasted sliced almonds

Preheat oven to 400°F

To make dough, sift flour into large bowl and make well in center. Place yeast and 1 tablespoon sugar in well. Add milk and stir to dissolve yeast. Cover bowl and let stand 10 minutes. Melt butter and beat in sugar, salt, eggs, and lemon peel. Add to yeast mixture and stir with wooden spoon. Knead dough until smooth and elastic. Place dough in greased bowl and turn to coat. Cover and let rise 1 to $1\frac{1}{2}$ hours. Lightly grease baking sheets. Divide dough into twenty equal-size pieces. Shape each piece into ball. Press balls into flat rounds 4 to 5 inches in diameter with raised rims. Prick several times with fork to prevent air bubbles from forming during baking. Place on prepared baking sheets and brush rims with egg yolk glaze.

To make topping, beat cream cheese, butter, and $\frac{1}{2}$ cup sugar until smooth. Beat in egg yolks, cornstarch, and rum. Beat egg whites until stiff and fold into cream cheese mixture. Bring milk to a boil. Stir in poppy seed, remaining $\frac{1}{2}$ cup sugar, and bread crumbs. Cook until most of milk has evaporated. Remove from heat. Spoon alternating teaspoonfuls of cream cheese and poppy seed mixtures around top of pastries. Spoon small teaspoonful of poppy seed mixture in center. Cover and let rise 30 minutes. Bake in preheated oven 20 to 25 minutes. Remove from baking sheets and cool on wire racks. Brush with apricot glaze and sprinkle with almonds while still warm.

Almond Bows

Pastry:
about $3\frac{1}{2}$ cups all-purpose flour
2 packages active dry yeast
$\frac{1}{4}$ cup sugar
1 cup warm milk (105° to 115°F)
$\frac{1}{4}$ cup ($\frac{1}{2}$ stick) butter, melted
$\frac{1}{2}$ teaspoon salt
2 egg yolks
1 cup (2 sticks) butter, softened
5 tablespoons all-purpose flour

Filling:
6 ounces marzipan
$\frac{2}{3}$ cup toasted ground almonds
$\frac{1}{2}$ teaspoon cinnamon
grated peel of 2 oranges
1 tablespoon dark rum
4 egg whites, lightly beaten
1 egg yolk beaten with 1 tablespoon water for brushing
Apricot Glaze, page 60
Fondant, page 60

Preheat oven to 425°F

Sift 2½ cups flour into bowl and make well in center. Add yeast and 1 tablespoon sugar to well. Add milk and stir to dissolve yeast. Sprinkle a little flour over yeast mixture. Cover bowl and let stand 10 minutes. Blend melted butter, remaining sugar, salt, and egg yolks. Add to yeast-flour mixture and beat with wooden spoon until well blended. Stir in enough remaining flour to make soft dough that comes away from sides of bowl. Turn dough out onto lightly floured surface and knead until smooth and elastic. Cover dough with bowl and let rise 30 minutes.

Work 1 cup softened butter and 5 tablespoons flour together until well blended. Place between two sheets of waxed paper. Roll out butter-flour mixture to 12- by 8-inch rectangle. Refrigerate 20 minutes. Roll out dough on lightly floured surface to 18- by 9-inch rectangle. Remove butter-flour mixture from refrigerator and peel off one sheet of waxed paper. Invert butter onto two thirds of dough, leaving 1 inch of dough on three sides. Peel off top sheet of waxed paper. Fold dough into thirds to make 9- by 6-inch rectangle, folding unbuttered side of dough in first. Press edges of dough to seal in butter. Roll out dough to 18- by 9-inch rectangle and fold into thirds. Wrap and refrigerate 30

minutes. Repeat rolling and folding twice.

Blend marzipan, ground almonds, cinnamon, orange peel, rum, and egg whites in bowl until throughly combined. Divide dough in half. Roll out each piece of dough to 21- by 14-inch rectangle. Spread half the filling over two thirds of one piece of dough, leaving 4-inch strip on one side and 1-inch strip on opposite side of filling. Brush dough with beaten egg yolk mixture. Fold over filling in thirds, folding wide strip over first. Pinch edges to seal. Repeat with remaining dough and filling. Cut each roll into slices, 1½ inches wide. Cut slit lengthwise down each slice with pastry wheel to within ¼ inch of each end. Tuck ends into slit. Place on ungreased baking sheets about 2 inches apart. Cover and let rise 30 to 40 minutes. Brush with beaten egg yolk mixture. Bake in preheated oven 15 to 18 minutes or until golden brown. Remove from baking sheets and cool on wire racks. Brush with apricot glaze and spread fondant over top. (Makes 28 bows.)

Hazelnut Snails

2 cups ground, toasted hazelnuts
¼ teaspoon allspice
⅛ teaspoon salt
⅔ cup sugar
3 egg whites, lightly beaten
1 tablespoon milk
Apricot Glaze, page 60
Fondant, page 60
½ recipe Croissant pastry, page 124

Preheat oven to 425°F

Blend all ingredients except croissant dough until mixture is of spreading consistency. Grease baking sheets. Roll out dough on lightly floured surface to 30- by 14-inch rectangle. Spread filling over dough to within ¼ inch of edges. Draw line lengthwise down center of dough with back of knife. Starting at one long side, roll dough in toward center line jelly-roll style. Roll opposite side in toward center line so rolls meet. Trim ends. Cut into ¾-inch slices. Place slices on prepared baking sheets. Cover and let rise 30 minutes. Bake in preheated oven 15 to 18 minutes. Remove from baking sheets and cool on wire racks. Brush with apricot glaze and cover with fondant. (Makes 40 snails.)

Croissants

Croissants, plain or filled with chocolate, are specialties of France eaten with coffee, particularly at breakfast. They should be eaten when freshly baked and still warm in order to appreciate their crisp and crumbly texture and the full flavor of fresh butter. Croissants have an unusual amount of salt, and it is the ratio of salt to sugar that contributes to their individual flavor. If salt butter is used in this recipe, reduce the amount of salt called for.

2 packages of active dry yeast
$\frac{2}{3}$ cup sugar
$2\frac{1}{2}$ cups warm milk (105° to 115°F)
about $7\frac{1}{2}$ cups all-purpose flour
2 teaspoons salt
1 pound block unsalted butter
all-purpose flour for rolling
2 egg yolks beaten with 2 tablespoons water for brushing

Preheat oven to 425°F

Sprinkle yeast and 1 tablespoon sugar over $\frac{1}{2}$ cup milk. Stir to dissolve yeast and let stand 10 minutes. Sift 4 cups flour into large bowl and make well in center. Add salt and remaining sugar to well. Stir in yeast mixture and remaining 2 cups milk. Stir in remaining flour, 1 cup at a time, to make soft dough that comes away from sides of bowl. Turn dough out onto lightly floured surface and knead until smooth and elastic. Place dough in greased bowl and turn to coat. Cover and let rise 1 to 1$\frac{1}{2}$ hours.

Cream butter. Roll butter between two sheets of waxed paper to 12- by 9-inch rectangle. Refrigerate 15 minutes. Roll out dough on lightly floured surface to 20- by 11-inch rectangle. Remove butter from refrigerator and peel off one sheet of waxed paper. Invert butter onto two thirds of dough leaving 1 inch of dough on three sides. Peel off top sheet of waxed paper. Fold dough into thirds to make 11- by 8-inch rectangle, folding unbuttered side of dough in first. Press edges of dough to seal in butter. Roll out dough to 20- by 11-inch rectangle and fold into thirds. Wrap and refrigerate 30 minutes. Repeat rolling and folding three more times. (See Puff Pastry, page 42.) Proceed, following step-by-step photos alongside. Place crossants on ungreased baking sheets, and let rise 40 to 50 minutes. Brush lightly with beaten egg yolk mixture. Bake in preheated oven 12 to 15 minutes or until golden brown. (Makes 24 croissants.)

1 **Divide dough in half**. Roll out one piece of dough at a time to 24- by 6-inch rectangle. Cut into triangles, 4 inches wide at base with sharp knife. Repeat with remaining piece of dough.

2 **Cut 1-inch slit** in toward center in base of triangle (see photo). Cut out all triangles before shaping any.

3 **Roll up croissants**, starting at base and rolling toward point.

4 **Press thumb on point of triangle**. Roll croissant back slightly with opposite hand to make point long and thin.

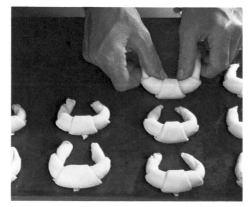

5 **Place croissants**, pointed end down, on ungreased baking sheets about 2 inches apart. Curve ends of croissants in to make crescent shapes. Set aside to rise until almost doubled.

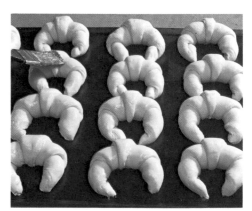

6 **Brush lightly** with beaten egg yolk mixture. If desired add 1 teaspoon confectioners' sugar to beaten egg yolk mixture before brushing to darken croissants. Bake according to directions above.

Croissants taste best when eaten warm and fresh from the oven. Both croissant pastry dough and baked croissants freeze well.

Roll out dough to ¼ inch thickness and cut into 5- by 3½-inch rectangles. Place chocolate stick or pieces of bar chocolate along one short end, about ½ inch in from edge of dough. Brush edge with beaten egg yolk mixture. Roll up and place on ungreased baking sheet. Let rise until doubled. Bake in 425°F oven 15 minutes.

Pains au chocolat, French chocolate rolls, have a wonderful combination of flavors. The chocolate flavor provides a delicious contrast to the salty pastry and taste of butter. If the sticks of chocolate with which they are usually made are not available, use a few pieces of semisweet or sweet bar chocolate. Melted chocolate can also be used. Flavor melted chocolate with a few drops of rum. Cool and spoon into pastry bag fitted with small plain writing tip. Pipe chocolate in strip on each piece of pastry.

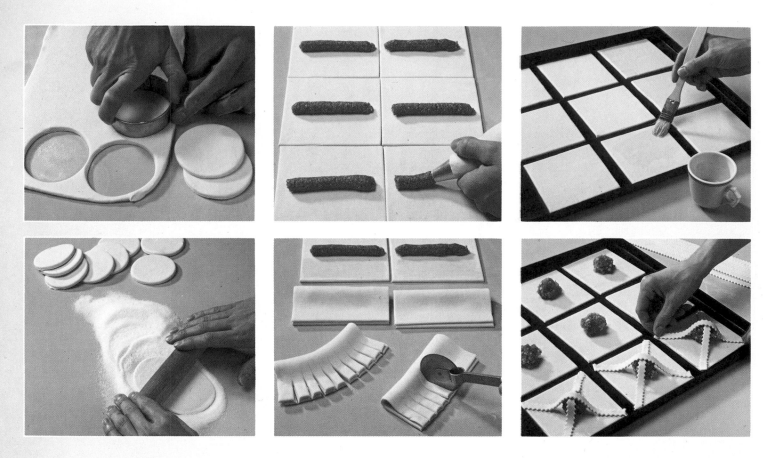

Shoe Soles

Roll out 1 pound Puff Pastry, page 42, to ⅜-inch thickness. Cut with 2½ to 3-inch biscuit cutter. Sprinkle work surface with sugar. Roll out pastry rounds on sugared surface to long ovals. Roll on both sides to coat with sugar. Arrange on ungreased baking sheets. Bake in preheated 425°F oven 4 to 5 minutes or until browned and crisp on top. Turn pastries over and bake until browned and crisp on second side.

Nut Combs

Roll out 1 pound Puff Pastry, page 42, to ⅛-inch thickness. Cut into 4½-inch squares. Stir 1 cup toasted ground hazelnuts, 1 egg white, ⅓ cup sugar, and 1 tablespoon dark rum until blended. Spoon mixture into pastry bag fitted with ½-inch plain tip. Pipe nut mixture in strip down centers of pastry squares. Brush pastry edges with beaten egg yolk and fold over. Cut slashes along pastry edge with pastry wheel or sharp knife to make "teeth." Brush with beaten egg yolk. Let stand 30 minutes. Bake in preheated 425°F oven 12 to 15 minutes. Brush with Apricot Glaze, page 60, and cover with fondant, page 60. (Enough filling for 12 to 16 Nut Combs.)

Cherry Puffs

Roll out 1 pound Puff Pastry, page 42, to ¼-inch thickness. Cut into 4-inch squares and brush with beaten egg yolk. Mix 4 ounces almond paste, ⅓ cup chopped glacé cherries, ¼ cup finely chopped walnuts, and 1 tablespoon kirsch. Place 1 tablespoonful in center of each pastry square. Thinly roll out leftover pastry and cut into strips ⅜-inch wide with fluted pastry wheel. Arrange strips in cross over filling. Brush strips with beaten egg yolk. Let stand 15 minutes. Bake in preheated 425°F oven 15 to 18 minutes or until golden brown. Brush with Apricot Glaze, page 60, and spread with Fondant, page 60.

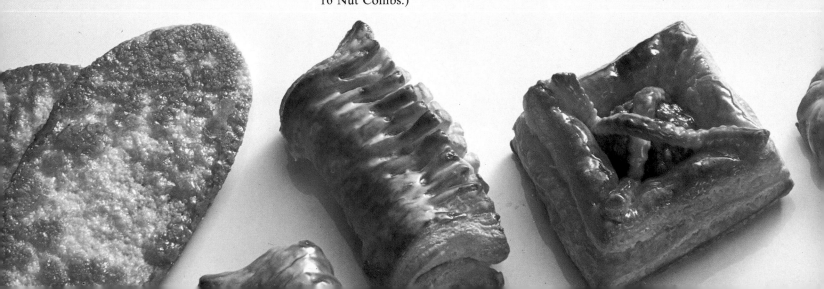

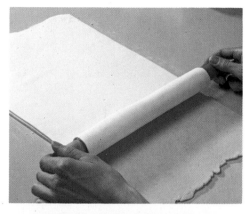

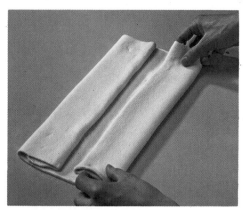

Pastry Pretzels

Roll out 1 pound Puff Pastry, page 42, to 20- by 12-inch rectangle. Roll out Cut-in Pastry (Pâté Brisée), page 37, to same size rectangle and brush with beaten egg yolk. Roll puff pastry over rolling pin and place over Pâté Brisée. Cut into ½-inch wide strips. Twist strips into spirals. Shape into pretzels and brush with beaten egg yolk. Bake in preheated 425°F oven 12 to 15 minutes. Brush with Apricot Glaze, page 60, and dip in Fondant, page 60.

Pinwheels

Roll out 1 pound Puff Pastry, page 42, to ¼-inch thickness. Cut into 4½-inch squares and brush with beaten egg yolk. Place stewed apricot halves, cut side down, in center of each square. Cut pastry in toward center from each corner. Fold alternate points over apricot halves and pinch ends together. Brush with beaten egg yolk. Thinly roll out leftover pastry and cut into 2-inch fluted circles. Place one circle over each filled pastry square. Let stand 30 minutes. Bake in preheated 425°F oven about 15 minutes. Brush with Apricot Glaze, page 60, and spread Fondant, page 60, over top.

Palmiers

Sprinkle work surface with 1 cup sugar. Roll out 1 pound Puff Pastry, page 42, to 18- by 12-inch rectangle. Turn pastry over frequently during rolling so both sides are covered with sugar. Fold short sides of pastry over twice to meet in center. Fold pastry in half lengthwise. Cut into twenty-four ½-inch slices. Place on ungreased baking sheets, cut side up. Let stand 15 minutes. Bake in preheated 425°F oven about 10 minutes. Turn Palmiers over. Bake 8 to 10 minutes or until sugar is caramelized on both sides.

1 **Divide dough** into sixteen equal-size pieces. Roll out each piece to 4-inch circle. Place 1 teaspoonful jam in center of each circle. Brush edges with water.

2 **Hold filled doughnut** in palm of hand and bring edges of dough up over jam, pinching edges to seal. Gently roll filled doughnuts between palms to flatten slightly. Place on floured cloth.

Yeast Doughnuts

about 3 cups all-purpose flour
1 package active dry yeast
5 tablespoons sugar
$\frac{2}{3}$ cup warm milk (105° to 115°F)
$\frac{1}{4}$ cup ($\frac{1}{2}$ stick) butter, melted and cooled
$\frac{1}{2}$ teaspoon salt
3 eggs
plum jam for filling
confectioners' sugar for dusting
vegetable oil for deep frying

Prepare dough with ingredients above, according to step-by-step photos on page 46. Cover and let rise 1 to 1$\frac{1}{2}$ hours. Punch dough down and divide in half. Cut each piece into eight pieces and roll into sixteen flattened rounds. Place teaspoonful of jam in center of each round. Brush edges of dough with water. Bring edges of dough up and over jam, pinching ends to seal (see photo). Place filled doughnuts, seam side down, on lightly floured dish towel about 2 inches apart. Cover and let rise until doubled.

Heat 3 to 4 inches oil in deep-fat fryer until temperature registers 350°F on deep-fat thermometer. Slide wide spatula under doughnuts and place, a few at a time, in hot oil. Cover pan and deep fry 2 to 3 minutes. Turn doughnuts over and deep fry, uncovered, 2 to 3 minutes or until well browned. Remove doughnuts with slotted spoon and drain on paper towels. Repeat with remaining doughnuts. Dust with sifted confectioners' sugar.

Alternative methods: (1) Punch dough down. Roll out dough on lightly floured surface to $\frac{1}{4}$-inch thickness. Cut dough with floured 3-inch plain biscuit cutter. Place 1 teaspoonful jam in center of half the rounds. Brush edges with water and place remaining rounds on top, pinching edges to seal. Deep fry as directed above. (2) Roll out dough to $\frac{1}{2}$-inch thickness. Cut dough with floured 3-inch plain biscuit cutter. Place doughnuts on floured cloth, cover, and let rise until doubled. Deep fry as directed above. Remove and drain on paper towels. Cut small slit on side of each doughnut and pipe jam into slit with pastry bag. Although this last method is the quickest, the results are not as satisfactory as they are when filling is cooked inside doughnuts.

The narrow strip of white around the center of each doughnut is a sign the doughnuts have been fried properly. Cover pan and deep fry on one side. The steam will cause doughnuts to swell nicely. Turn doughnuts over and deep fry, uncovered. It is important to use fresh oil. Oil used previously may bubble too much, in which case there will not be a white rim around the center. Brush off any excess flour that may adhere to doughnuts before frying.

French Crullers

1 cup milk
½ cup (1 stick) butter
pinch of salt
1 teaspoon sugar
1½ cups sifted all-purpose flour
5 to 6 eggs
vegetable oil for deep frying
confectioners' sugar for dusting or
Apricot Glaze, page 60, and Fondant,
page 60

Bring milk, butter, salt, and sugar to a boil. Add flour all at once and beat vigorously with wooden spoon until mixture forms ball and comes away from sides of pan. Transfer mixture to bowl and let cool slightly. Beat in 1 egg. When egg is fully incorporated into mixture, add second egg. Beat in remaining eggs, one at a time. Choux paste for piping should be soft, but firm enough to hold its shape. The number of eggs required will vary according to size of eggs used and degree to which choux paste dries out over heat.

Pipe mixture onto greased parchment paper and deep fry immediately before skin forms on surface of dough, which would prevent crullers from swelling and cause them to crack open. Crullers are deep fried in a covered pan in the same way doughnuts are fried. Turn over after 2 to 3 minutes and fry, uncovered, 2 to 3 minutes. Lift crullers out of oil with slotted spoon and drain on paper towels. Let cool before dusting with confectioners' sugar.

Crullers are delicious frosted with brandy-flavored fondant. Brush tops of warm crullers with thin layer of apricot glaze and let cool. Dip tops of crullers in fondant. (Makes 12 crullers.)

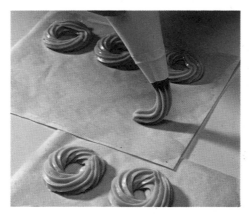

1 **Grease parchment paper lightly** with butter. Use pastry bag fitted with open star tip (#8A) to pipe rings of choux paste onto paper. Leave space between rings.

2 **Hold paper in both hands** and turn upside down over hot oil. Crullers will cling to underside of paper. Lower crullers into oil and peel paper back slowly. Heat from oil will melt butter on paper and crullers will fall off easily into hot oil.

Top quality fresh oil is essential for successful deep-fat frying. The oil should have relatively little flavor and must have a high smoking point. Liquid oils such as corn oil, safflower and cottonseed oil are appropriate to use. Soybean oil should not be used because it will foam. Nut oils cannot be used because they break down when heated. Butter and margarine have very low smoking points. Bring oil to 350°F before frying crullers. Check temperature of oil with deep-fat thermometer constantly to maintain correct temperature.

129

Famous Cakes and Pies

All over the world cakes and pastries have been made for symbolic reasons or for festive occasions such as birthdays, weddings, or for Christmas. Cakes baked for symbolic purposes have a tradition that dates back centuries: disk-shaped cakes were baked in northern Europe for the festival of midsummer. Their shape was derived from that of the sun whose image was worshiped as the symbol of life and fertility. After the advent of Christianity, cakes were made that celebrated great events in the Christian calendar. In monasteries, for example, cakes and pies were created to mark the most important religious festivals. A Twelfth Night cake is still made in some parts of Europe, especially in predominantly Catholic countries such as France or Italy, to symbolize the great feast of Epiphany on January 6.

It was from these ancient traditions of a celebratory cake that the modern gâteau was born. The gâteau is based on the basic sponge or pastry mixtures, which are then combined with creams and custards or buttercream, marzipan, chocolate, fondant, or royal icing. This delectable confection is often further enhanced by being sprinkled with almonds, pistachios, or other nuts that have been flaked, grated, toasted, or made into praline; or decorated with caramel, chocolate shapes, marzipan flowers, or candied fruit.

The choice of what to do is enormous and it is left to the individual to decide what combination best suits his or her need and taste. There is almost no limit to what can be achieved with a little patience, creativity, and imagination. In order to stir the imagination, this chapter contains a good variety of different combinations that have proven to be very popular, and it is worth trying out a few of these first before embarking on your own experiments.

The choice can be between a heavier cake or a lighter one such as the French Gâteau Saint-Honoré or Mille-feuille, which are truly melt-in-the mouth concoctions and should be eaten as soon as possible after being made and filled—a requirement that should not pose too many problems as they look and taste so good! Each country produces its own specialties but Germany and Austria are particularly renowned for the variety of gâteau that they have invented. One of the most famous of these must surely be the Black Forest Gâteau, which is traditionally eaten with morning or afternoon coffee in German *Konditorei*. This is a rich but light confection of chocolate sponge soaked in kirsch and layered with cherries and cream. The equally famous Austrian specialty, the Sachertorte, is discussed in detail at the conclusion of this chapter because its history is so interesting.

Almond and Chocolate Gâteau

1 10-inch pastry base, page 102
8 ounces marzipan

8 egg yolks
1 teaspoon vanilla
½ cup sugar
4 egg whites
½ cup cake flour
5 tablespoons unsweetened cocoa

⅓ cup finely ground almonds
¼ cup red currant jelly
2 tablespoons Amaretto liqueur
1 recipe German Buttercream, page 54
4½ ounces semisweet chocolate, melted and cooled

16 small macaroons to decorate

16- × 12-inch jelly-roll pan, greased and lined

Preheat oven to 450°F

Prepare and bake pastry base. Beat 2 ounces marzipan and 2 egg yolks in large bowl until thick and creamy. Add remaining 6 egg yolks, vanilla, and sugar. Beat until well blended. Beat egg whites until stiff. Stir flour, cocoa, and ground almonds until blended. Beat one-third beaten egg whites into egg yolk mixture. Fold in remaining egg whites alternately with flour mixture. Spread mixture in prepared pan. Bake in preheated oven 10 to 12 minutes or until center springs back when lightly pressed. Sprinkle towel with confectioners' sugar. Invert cake onto towel and peel off paper. Let cool completely. Spread jelly over pastry base. Stir Amaretto into buttercream. Spread half of buttercream over cooled cake. Cut cake into strips and roll up on pastry base (see photo). Spoon 1 cup buttercream into pastry bag fitted with open star tip and set aside. Spread remaining buttercream over top and sides of cake. Roll out remaining 6 ounces marzipan to 10-inch circle and cover with melted chocolate. Score lattice pattern on chocolate with blunt side of knife. Let stand until chocolate is set. Cut into sixteen equal-size wedges and place on top of cake. Decorate with rosettes of buttercream and small macaroons.

1 **Prepare one pastry base** according to directions on page 102, using half the ingredients. Spread red currant jelly over baked pastry.

2 **Spread sponge mixture** in prepared pan and bake as directed above. Invert cake onto sugared towel and let cool. Spread about half the buttercream over cake.

3 **Cut cake lengthwise** into eight 1½-inch wide strips. Use a ruler to measure correctly so no cake is wasted.

4 **Roll up first strip** in spiral and place, upright, in center of jelly-covered pastry base. Wind remaining strips around spiral. Push ends of strips as close together as possible (see photo).

5 **Place 10-inch deep flan ring** or side of springform pan around cake. Spread half the remaining buttercream over top of cake. Carefully remove flan ring and finish cake as directed above.

Pistachio Cake

¼ cup plus 1 tablespoon maraschino
liqueur
Egg Buttercream, page 54
2 ounces semisweet chocolate, melted
2 tablespoons finely chopped preserved
stem ginger
⅔ cup ground pistachios
1 Genoise sponge, page 28
10-inch baked pastry base, page 102
¼ cup seedless raspberry jam
1 tablespoon sugar syrup
1 tablespoon lemon juice
toasted sliced almonds
16 small chocolate flowers

Stir ¼ cup maraschino liqueur into butter-cream until blended. Divide buttercream in half. Set half aside and divide remainder in half again. Add melted chocolate and chopped ginger to one small portion. Sift pistachios over second small portion and stir. (Reserve any large pieces of pistachios for decoration.) Leave reserved large portion plain.

Cut cake into three layers. Place pastry base on serving plate and spread with raspberry jam. Place one sponge layer over jam. Blend sugar syrup, lemon juice, and remaining tablespoon maraschino liqueur. Sprinkle 1 tablespoon over layer. Spread with chocolate-ginger buttercream. Top with second sponge layer, sprinkle with 1 tablespoon sugar syrup mixture, and spread with pistachio buttercream. Top with remaining sponge layer and sprinkle with remaining 1 tablespoon sugar syrup mixture. Spread thin layer plain buttercream over top and around sides of cake. Refrigerate 30 minutes. Spoon about ⅔ cup remaining plain buttercream into pastry

bag fitted with small plain writing tip and set aside. Spread remaining plain buttercream over cake. Press almonds into side of cake. Divide cake into sixteen wedges. Pipe small

dab reserved buttercream onto each wedge. Sprinkle cake with reserved pistachios and decorate with chocolate flowers.

1 **Spread thin layer plain buttercream** over top and around sides of cake with long flat icing spatula. Spread buttercream as evenly as possible. Refrigerate 30 minutes.

2 **Spread remaining plain buttercream** around sides and over top of cake. When sides of cake are covered, smooth buttercream by turning cake with one hand and smoothing buttercream with icing spatula held in other hand.

3 **Smooth sides of cake** with pastry scraper. Hold scraper vertical to cake and turn cake in slow continuous motion. Don't lift scraper off cake until buttercream has been completely smoothed.

4 **Smooth top edge** of cake with icing spatula by pushing excess buttercream in toward center of cake. Wipe blade of spatula after each stroke to prevent excess buttercream from being put back on edge of cake.

5 **Tilt cake slightly** off table and lightly press almonds onto sides of cake.

Spanish Vanilla Cake

butter and sponge cake crumbs for pan
3 ounces unsweetened chocolate
¼ cup diced, candied lemon peel
½ cup chopped blanched almonds
¾ cup all-purpose flour
¼ cup (½ stick) butter
5 ounces almond paste
¾ cup granulated sugar
2 teaspoons vanilla
6 egg yolks
5 egg whites

To decorate:
Apricot Glaze, page 60
6 ounces almond paste
¾ cup sifted confectioners' sugar
10 ounces semisweet chocolate, melted
12 marzipan flowers

9-inch cake pan with sloping sides (moule a manqué pan)

Preheat oven to 375°F

Grease pan and sprinkle with cake crumbs. Coarsely chop chocolate. Combine chopped chocolate, lemon peel, chopped almonds, and flour in small bowl and set aside. Beat butter and almond paste in medium-size bowl until well blended and smooth. Add ¼ cup granulated sugar, vanilla, and 1 egg yolk, and beat until light and fluffy. Beat in remaining egg yolks, one at a time. Beat egg whites until soft peaks form. Gradually add remaining ½ cup granulated sugar and beat until stiff peaks form. Fold beaten egg whites into butter mixture with wooden spatula. Fold in reserved flour-chocolate mixture. Pour into

prepared pan and smooth top.

Bake in preheated oven 40 to 45 minutes. Cool in pan on wire rack 10 minutes. Remove from pan and cool completely on wire rack.

Brush top and sides of cake with apricot glaze. Work almond paste and confectioners' sugar together until smooth and pliable. Roll out to thin circle between two sheets of waxed paper and place over top and sides of cake. Place cake on wire rack and spread melted chocolate over top and sides. While chocolate is still warm, score top of cake into twelve portions with knife dipped in hot water. (This will prevent chocolate from cracking when cake is cut.) Decorate each portion with marzipan flower. Let stand until chocolate is completely set.

An alternative to the method shown for icing a cake on page 133 is shown in the photographs to the right. Although this method can be used to ice any size cake, it is particularly effective for icing an 8- or 9-inch cake.

Place the cake on a firm base either the same size as the cake or slightly smaller. The bottom part of a loose-bottomed pan is ideal.

1 **Place the cake on a firm base.** Hold the cake in one hand and spread the buttercream over the sides of the cake with the other hand in long continuous strokes.

2 **Place a flan ring,** smaller than the cake, on a large piece of waxed paper. Place the cake, with the base still in place, on the flan ring and spread the buttercream over the top of the cake. Cover buttercream with chocolate.

Marzipan Tart

Pastry:
½ cup (1 stick) butter, softened
¼ cup confectioners' sugar
¼ teaspoon salt
½ teaspoon vanilla
1 egg yolk
1½ cups all-purpose flour
1 tablespoon ice water

Filling:
10 tablespoons (1¼ sticks) butter
1¼ cups confectioners' sugar
grated peel of 1 lemon
½ teaspoon almond extract
2 eggs
1 cup finely ground almonds
¼ cup sifted all-purpose flour

9- or 10-inch fluted tart/flan pan

Preheat oven to 375°F

To make pastry, cream butter, confectioners' sugar, salt, vanilla, and egg yolk in medium-size bowl. Add flour and beat at low speed just until mixture resembles coarse crumbs. Add ice water and toss with fork until dough binds together. Wrap dough and refrigerate 1 hour. Roll out pastry on lightly floured surface to ¼-inch thickness and line tart pan. Prick pastry all over with fork. Line with waxed paper or aluminum foil and fill with dried beans or pie weights. Bake in preheated oven 10 minutes. Remove foil and pie weights and bake 5 minutes. Cool on wire rack.

To make filling, beat butter, confectioners' sugar, lemon peel, and almond extract until light and fluffy. Add eggs, one at a time, beating well after each addition. Stir in ground almonds and flour. Spoon into pastry-lined pan and smooth top. Bake in preheated oven 40 to 45 minutes or until center is set and top is golden brown. Dust top with confectioners' sugar or cover with Fondant, page 60.

Macaroon Cake

Sponge:
8 eggs, separated
¾ cup granulated sugar
¼ cup finely ground almonds
1 teaspoon vanilla
5 tablespoons butter, melted
½ cup sifted all-purpose flour
1 cup sponge cake crumbs

Filling and decoration:
1 cup (12 ounces) seedless raspberry jam
1 tablespoon raspberry-flavored liqueur
sugar syrup
¾ cup confectioners' sugar, sifted
14 ounces almond paste
4 to 5 egg yolks
toasted sliced almonds for decoration

10-inch springform pan, bottom lined only

Preheat oven to 375°F

Prepare and bake Chocolate Genoise, page 30. Cool cake completely. Wrap and store overnight. Cut cake into three layers.

To make filling, press jam through fine mesh sieve and set aside ⅓ cup. Add liqueur and 1 tablespoon sugar syrup to remaining jam and stir until well blended. Spread all three cake layers with jam mixture and stack them. Work confectioners' sugar into almond paste and beat in egg yolks, one at a time, until thoroughly blended and of piping consistency. Spoon about ⅔ mixture into pastry bag fitted with medium-size star tip. Set aside. Add enough sugar syrup to remaining almond mixture to make it spreading consistency. Spread over top and sides of cake. Press sliced almonds gently into sides. Make thin lines in top of cake, dividing it into fourteen equal portions. Pipe reserved almond mixture along lines and in center of cake. Place cake under broiler until top is lightly browned. Pipe reserved raspberry jam into center of each outlined portion.

Hazelnut Sandwich Cake

Pastry:
1 cup (2 sticks) butter, softened
1¾ cups confectioners' sugar
1 teaspoon vanilla
¼ teaspoon salt
4 ounces semisweet chocolate, finely chopped
2 eggs, beaten
1½ cups toasted ground hazelnuts
3 cups all-purpose flour, sifted

Filling and icing:
Apricot Glaze, page 60
1 tablespoon kirsch
Fondant, page 60
1 cup (12 ounces) pineapple jam
6 glacé cherries, halved
1 candied pineapple ring, cut into 12 pieces

Preheat oven to 350°F

Cream butter, sugar, vanilla, and salt. Fold in chocolate and eggs. Stir hazelnuts and flour together and fold into butter mixture until blended. Divide pastry into four equal-size pieces. Wrap each piece separately and refrigerate 2 hours. Grease baking sheets. Roll out pastry to four 10-inch circles. Place on prepared baking sheets. Bake in preheated oven 20 to 25 minutes. Remove from baking sheets and cool completely on wire racks.

Select nicest looking pastry round for top of cake. Spread with thin layer of apricot glaze. Stir kirsch into fondant until blended. Spread fondant over apricot glaze. Let stand 10 to 15 minutes. Score top into twelve portions. Sandwich remaining pastry rounds with pineapple jam. Place fondant covered pastry on top. Decorate with glacé cherries and candied pineapple.

For variation, fill layers with orange marmalade and flavor icing with rum. Decorate with slices of candied orange.

Mille-feuille

A specialty of France, this pastry should be eaten soon after it has been made because the custard filling will make the pastry soggy.

1½ pounds Quick Puff Pastry, page 44
Simple Vanilla Custard, page 50
Apricot Glaze, page 60
Fondant, page 60
1 tablespoon kirsch
1 cup toasted blanched chopped almonds
12 sugar mimosa balls to decorate

Preheat oven to 425°F

Divide pastry into three equal-size pieces. Roll out each piece to 10-inch circle. Roll pastry in both directions to be sure it will rise evenly. Refrigerate 1 hour. Place on parchment-lined baking sheets and prick all over with fork. Bake in preheated oven 15 to 18 minutes or until crisp and golden. Remove from baking sheets and cool completely on wire racks. Assemble and fill cake. Brush top with apricot glaze. Warm fondant and stir in kirsch. If fondant is too thick, thin with a little sugar syrup. Spread over top of cake and sprinkle almonds around sides. When fondant is almost set, decorate with mimosa balls.

Pithiviers

Despite the limited number of ingredients in this pie, fairly precise work is necessary to make it a success. The combination of almond cream filling and the buttery flavor of puff pastry is particularly good.

1⅓ pounds Puff pastry, page 42
2 cups Almond Cream, page 56
1 egg yolk beaten with 1 tablespoon milk for brushing
confectioners' sugar for dusting

Preheat oven to 450°F

It is important to allow puff pastry adequate resting time following each step of preparation so it will not lose its shape during baking. Bake in preheated oven 15 minutes. Lower oven temperature to 400°F and bake 20 to 25 minutes.

1 **Spread vanilla custard** over two baked pastry bases. Place filled bases on top of each other and plain base on top. Press down lightly and spread custard that will squeeze out around sides of cake.

2 **Brush top of cake** with apricot glaze and cover with kirsch-flavored fondant. Sprinkle almonds around sides of cake and decorate top with mimosa balls.

1 **Divide pastry in half.** Roll out each piece to ¼-inch thickness. Place bottom of 10-inch springform pan upside down over pastry and cut around outside edge with sharp knife to make neat circle. Repeat with second piece of pastry. Alternatively, roll out whole piece of pastry and cut in same manner. Place one pastry circle on ungreased baking sheet.

3 **Place second pastry circle** over filling and press edges together firmly to seal. Refrigerate 30 minutes.

The top of the Pithiviers should have a good shine and be golden brown and crisp. Dust top with sifted confectioners' sugar 10 minutes before baking is finished. The sugar will caramelize quickly. Caramel coating adds to the flavor of the pie because the pie is not very sweet.

2 **Spread almond cream** over pastry circle on baking sheet to within 1 inch of edge. Brush edge with beaten egg yolk mixture. (Do not allow egg yolk mixture to run over edge.)

4 **Press pastry edge down** with middle fingers and flute edge with blunt side of knife held at an angle.

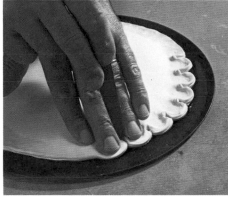

5 **Alternatively,** press pastry edge down firmly with middle and ring fingers. Hold knife vertical to edge of pastry and draw blade in slightly between fingers.

6 **Lightly brush top of pie** with beaten egg yolk mixture. Cut curved lines close together from center of pie to outside edge with tip of very sharp knife. Be careful not to make cuts too deep or filling will run out during baking. Refrigerate 15 minutes.

137

Rich Poppy Seed Cake

Poppy seed is popular in Austria and there are many recipes for poppy seed cakes and pastries.

½ cup (1 stick) plus 2 tablespoons butter
2½ cups sifted confectioners' sugar
grated peel of ½ lemon
1 tablespoon dark rum
½ teaspoon salt
6 eggs, separated
1½ cups poppy seed, ground
¼ cup all-purpose flour
¼ cup raisins, finely chopped

To decorate:
½ cup Apricot Glaze, page 60
6 ounces almond paste
¾ cup sifted confectioners' sugar
10 ounces semisweet chocolate, melted

9-inch springform pan

Preheat oven to 375°F

Grease springform pan and line bottom with parchment paper. Cream butter with 1¼ cups sugar. Add grated lemon peel, rum, and salt, and beat until blended. Beat in egg yolks, one at a time. Beat egg whites with remaining 1¼ cups sugar until stiff peaks form. Stir about one third of beaten egg whites into creamed butter mixture. Fold in remaining beaten egg whites. Combine poppy seed with flour and raisins. Sprinkle poppy seed mixture on top and fold in carefully. Pour into prepared pan.

Bake in preheated oven 40 to 45 minutes. Cool in pan on wire rack 20 minutes. Remove from pan and cool completely on wire rack. Wrap cake and let stand overnight.

Brush top and sides of cake with apricot glaze. Work almond paste and confectioners' sugar together until smooth and pliable. Roll out to thin circle between two sheets of waxed paper and place over top and sides of cake. Place cake on wire rack and spread melted chocolate over top and sides. While chocolate is still warm, score top of cake into fourteen portions with knife dipped in hot water. (This will prevent chocolate from cracking which cake is cut.) Serve with Zabaglione if desired. The distinct flavor of poppy seed goes well with the Marsala in Zabaglione.

Swiss Carrot Cake

This cake has long been a favorite of home-bakers, but now is available in many European bakeries as well. The finely grated carrots add a distinctive flavor and make the cake nice and moist.

2 cups finely ground almonds
¾ cup all-purpose flour
1½ cups finely grated carrots (about 3 medium-size carrots)
1¼ cups sugar
½ teaspoon salt
grated peel of 1 lemon
6 eggs, separated
Apricot Glaze, page 60
Fondant, page 60
toasted sliced almonds
14 marzipan carrots for decoration

10-inch springform pan

Preheat oven to 375°F

Grease springform pan and line bottom with parchment paper. Combine ground almonds, flour, and grated carrot. Beat sugar, salt, lemon peel, and egg yolks until thick and well blended. Beat egg whites until stiff. Beat one third of beaten egg whites into egg yolk mixture. Fold in remaining beaten egg whites alternately with flour-carrot mixture. Pour into prepared pan. Bake in preheated oven 60 to 65 minutes. Cool in pan on wire rack 15 minutes. Remove from pan and cool completely on rack. When cool, spread top and sides of cake with apricot glaze. Cover top of cake with fondant. Press almonds into sides of cake. Let stand 1 to 2 hours. Decorate top with marzipan carrots.

Nut Pie Engadine

"Tuorta da nusch a la veglia," as this pie is known in Europe, is a fine example of the baking of the Engadine region of Switzerland, an area known for its excellent bakers.

Pastry:
¾ cup (1½ sticks) butter
1 cup confectioners' sugar
¼ teaspoon salt
1 egg
2½ cups all-purpose flour

Walnut filling:
1½ cups sugar
3 tablespoons liquid glucose or 3 tablespoons light corn syrup diluted with 1 tablespoon water
2 tablespoons lemon juice
½ cup heavy cream
2 tablespoons butter
3 tablespoons honey
2½ cups coarsely chopped walnuts

1 egg yolk beaten with 1 tablespoon milk for glaze

10-inch pie pan with removable bottom or 10-inch springform pan.

Preheat oven to 400°F

Prepare pastry according to mixer method on page 37. Wrap pastry and refrigerate 1 hour. Bring ¾ cup sugar, liquid glucose, and lemon juice to a boil, and cook until light caramel in color. Bring cream, remaining ¾ cup sugar, butter, and honey to a boil in separate saucepan. Stir into caramel syrup. Return mixture to a boil and stir in chopped walnuts. Remove from heat and cool. Roll out about two thirds of pastry to ⅛-inch thickness and line pie pan. Trim pastry slightly above rim of pan. Spread walnut filling in pastry-lined pan. Fold edge of pastry over filling. Brush pastry edge with beaten egg yolk mixture. Roll out remaining pastry and place over filling. Press pastry edge down and trim off excess pastry. Brush top with glaze and score pattern over pastry with fork (see photo). Bake in preheated oven 35 to 40 minutes or until golden brown. Cool completely in pan on wire rack. This pie keeps well and can be stored several weeks in a cool place. It is often given as a present in Europe because it can be made in advance.

Gâteau Saint-Honoré

This French specialty is a well-known favorite inside and outside of France. The filling is usually made with crème pâtissière mixed with Italian meringue to make crème chiboust. Alternatively the meringue can be mixed with cold custard and set with gelatin, as illustrated below.

The pastry used for the base can also be varied. It can be made with Pâte Brisée, Quick Puff Pastry, or leftover puff pastry.

1 10-inch Quick Puff Pastry base, page 44
½ recipe Choux Paste, page 36
1 egg yolk beaten with 1 tablespoon milk
for glaze
1¾ cups sugar
1 teaspoon unflavored powdered gelatin
dissolved in 2 tablespoons water

2 cups Simple Vanilla Custard, page 50
3 egg whites

Preheat oven to 425°F

Place puff pastry base on baking sheet or bottom of large springform pan and prick with fork. Spoon choux paste into pastry bag fitted with ½-inch plain tip. Pipe as illustrated below. Pipe remaining choux paste into seventeen small balls on separate baking sheet. Brush balls with beaten egg yolk mixture. Bake ring and balls in preheated oven 20 minutes or until golden brown.

Bring 1 cup sugar and 6 tablespoons water to a boil over moderate heat and cook, stirring, until light caramel in color. Remove from heat. Dip top half of balls in caramel syrup. Attach balls to ring with dab of caramel syrup. Stir dissolved gelatin into custard. Beat egg whites until stiff. Bring remaining ¾ cup sugar and 6 tablespoons water to a boil and boil until temperature registers 234°F on candy thermometer. Add to beaten egg whites in slow steady stream, beating constantly. Fold into custard mixture. Spread layer of custard cream over spiral. Spoon remaining custard cream into pastry bag fitted with open leaf tip and pipe decoratively in center of gâteau. Refrigerate until ready to serve.

1 **Spoon choux paste** into pastry bag fitted with ½-inch plain tip and pipe around outside edge of pastry base. Pipe spiral in center of base.

2 **Bring 1 cup sugar** and 6 tablespoons water to a boil and cook until light caramel in color. Dip top half of balls in caramel to coat. Attach balls to ring with dab of caramel syrup.

3 **Stir dissolved gelatin** into custard. Prepare meringue as directed above and fold lightly into custard.

4 **Spread layer of custard cream** over spiral. Spoon remaining custard cream into pastry bag fitted with open leaf tip and pipe decoratively in center of gâteau.

Zuger Kirsch Cake

This Swiss specialty has a wonderful combination of flavors that is hard to beat. It is agreed that it is essential to use a good quality kirsch, although opinions vary about the quantity to use.

Sponge:
4 eggs
½ cup sugar
¾ cup cake flour
3 tablespoons cornstarch
¼ cup butter, melted
½ recipe French Buttercream, page 55
5 tablespoons kirsch
2 10-inch Japonais Layers (made entirely with almonds), page 35
3 tablespoons sugar syrup
toasted sliced almonds
confectioners' sugar for dusting
6 glacé cherries, halved

Preheat oven to 375°F

Make the sponge according to step-by-step photos for Genoise Mixture, page 28. Bake in preheated oven 25 to 30 minutes. Flavor buttercream with 2 tablespoons kirsch.

Spread one Japonais Layer with kirsch-flavored buttercream. Combine 3 tablespoons kirsch with sugar syrup. Remove top crust from sponge layer and brush layer with kirsch mixture. Place on top of Japonais Layer and spread with thin layer of buttercream. Top with second Japonais Layer. Cover cake with remaining buttercream. Press almonds into sides of cake. Chill 1 to 2 hours. Sprinkle top with confectioners' sugar and score top with back of knife in lattice pattern. Decorate with cherries.

Dobos Torte

Many recipes for this Austro-Hungarian specialty use a heavy buttercream made with egg yolks and chocolate. This recipe has a lighter filling.

Buttercream:
1¼ cups butter · 2 cups milk
3 egg yolks
5 tablespoons cornstarch
1 cup sugar · 1 teaspoon vanilla
½ cup unsweetened cocoa
4 ounces semisweet chocolate, melted

8 Dobos layers, page 29

Caramel topping:
1 teaspoon butter · ¾ cup sugar
few drops lemon juice

To make buttercream, place butter in medium-size bowl and cream until light and fluffy. Set aside. Blend 4 tablespoons milk with egg yolks and cornstarch and stir until smooth. Bring remaining milk, sugar, vanilla, and cocoa to a boil in medium-size saucepan. Stir in cornstarch mixture and bring back to a boil, stirring constantly. Simmer 2 minutes. Remove from heat and set aside to cool. Beat chocolate custard into butter gradually. Beat in melted chocolate. Sandwich Dobos layers together with buttercream. Cover top and sides of torte with buttercream as illustrated in photos alongside.

To make caramel topping, melt butter in saucepan Add sugar and a few drops of lemon juice. Bring to a boil. Cook, stirring, until sugar syrup is caramel in color. Spread hot caramel over last Dobos layer immediately.

Prince Regent Cake

7 eggs · ½ cup sugar
¾ cup cake flour
6 tablespoons cornstarch
¼ cup butter, melted
1 recipe buttercream (see Dobos Torte above)
12 ounces semisweet chocolate, melted

Prepare cake according to directions for Genoise Mixture, page 28. Spread cake mixture on eight sheets of parchment paper and bake according to directions for Dobos layers, page 29. These layers will be crisper than Dobos layers and therefore more fragile. Sandwich layers together with buttercream. Spread chocolate over top and around sides of cake. Score chocolate into sixteen equal-size wedges with blade of warm knife to prevent chocolate from breaking when it is set.

1 **Set aside best looking Dobos layer** for top of cake. Place one layer, paper side up, on flat foil covered cake board. Peel off paper and spread with thin layer of chocolate buttercream. Do not allow any buttercream to drip over edge of layer.

2 **Place second layer**, paper side up, directly over bottom layer, lining up layers exactly. Run hand gently over layer to press into place.

6 **Trim reserved layer** and place on lightly greased flat work surface. Remove paper from layer. Grease icing spatula and spread hot caramel over layer.

7 **Cut layer** into fourteen equal-size wedges while caramel is still warm. Cut with well-greased long, sharp knife, greasing knife after each cut to prevent caramel from sticking to blade. Work rapidly because caramel sets quickly.

3 **Pick up corner of paper** on layer in one hand and peel back, holding layer in place with other hand to prevent it from lifting off buttercream. Spread second layer with buttercream. Repeat with four more layers. Add one more layer, but do not cover with buttercream.

4 **Hold 10-inch flan ring** directly over layers as guide and cut down inside flan ring with long sharp knife to trim edge of layers.

5 **Cover top and sides** of cake completely with thin layer of buttercream. Place cake in refrigerator until buttercream is firm. Spread second layer of buttercream over top and sides of cake and refrigerate again.

8 **Loosen caramel wedges** from work surface and place on top of cake.

Sandwiched Lemon Cream Cake

3 lemons
about ⅓ cup (24) sugar cubes
1½ cups (3 sticks) unsalted butter, softened
¾ cup granulated sugar
4 egg yolks, lightly beaten
6 Dobos layers, page 29
12 ounces semisweet chocolate, melted and cooled
16 marzipan flowers
lemon curd (about 1 cup)

Scrub lemons under hot running water and pat dry with paper towels. Rub sugar cubes firmly over lemons. Place sugar cubes, ½ cup butter, juice of 3 lemons, granulated sugar, and egg yolks in medium-size saucepan. Place saucepan over low heat and cook, stirring constantly, until mixture is smooth and has thickened. (Do not allow mixture to boil.) Remove from heat and cool. Beat remaining 1 cup butter until light and fluffy. Fold butter into lemon mixture. Sandwich Dobos layers with lemon mixture. Refrigerate cake 30 minutes. Spread melted chocolate over top and around sides of cake. Divide cake into sixteen wedges with back of knife. Decorate with marzipan flowers. Fill center of flowers with lemon curd. Let stand until chocolate is set.

Coffee Gâteau with Cherries

1 jar (17 ounces) light sweet cherries
1 tablespoon cornstarch
$\frac{1}{8}$ teaspoon cinnamon
2 tablespoons powdered instant coffee
1 tablespoon confectioners' sugar
2 tablespoons boiling water
1 recipe German Buttercream, page 54
1 Genoise Mixture, page 28
3 tablespoons sugar syrup
1 tablespoon kirsch · 7 ounces marzipan
4 ounces semisweet chocolate, melted and
cooled

Drain cherries, reserving juice. Blend cornstarch with 2 tablespoons cherry juice and set aside. Bring remaining cherry juice and cinnamon to a boil. Add cornstarch mixture and cook, stirring, until thickened. Stir in cherries and simmer 1 minute. Remove from heat and set aside. Dissolve coffee and confectioners' sugar in boiling water and allow to cool. Add to buttercream and beat until well blended. Spoon about $1\frac{1}{4}$ cups buttercream into pastry bag fitted with small open star tip and set aside.

Cut cake into three layers. Set aside about $\frac{2}{3}$ cup buttercream in small bowl. Place one cake layer on serving plate and spread with buttercream. Spread cherries over butter-cream. Top with second layer and press down firmly. Blend sugar syrup with kirsch and sprinkle 2 tablespoons over cake layer. Spread with buttercream and top with remaining cake layer. Sprinkle remaining kirsch mixture over top of cake. Spread thin layer of buttercream over top and around sides of cake. Refrigerate 30 minutes. Spread reserved buttercream in thin layer over cake. Divide top of cake into sixteen wedges. Pipe buttercream on top of cake in sixteen spirals starting from edge of cake.

Remove bottom of 10-inch springform pan and sprinkle bottom with confectioners' sugar. Roll out marzipan to 10-inch circle and place on bottom of pan. Spread melted chocolate over marzipan and score with icing comb. Cut into sixteen wedges. Let stand until chocolate is completely set. Arrange chocolate wedges at slight angle on top of cake between spirals.

Prince Puckler Cake

1 10-inch sponge layer, page 141
1 10-inch chocolate sponge ($\frac{1}{2}$ recipe Classic Chocolate Mixture, page 30)
French Buttercream, page 55
14 ounces semisweet chocolate, melted and cooled
$\frac{1}{4}$ cup strawberry jam
2 tablespoons sugar syrup
1 tablespoon dark rum
glacé cherries · chopped pistachios

Cut cakes into two layers. The four layers can be sandwiched together alternately or made into a checkerboard cake. To make checkerboard cake, cut each layer into five rings, using a stencil as a guide. Separate rings and reassemble layers with alternate rings of plain and chocolate cake.

Divide buttercream into four portions. Stir 2 ounces melted chocolate into one portion. Stir strawberry jam into second portion. Stir sugar syrup and rum into third portion. Leave remaining buttercream plain. Spread one cake layer with chocolate-flavored buttercream. Top with second layer. Spread with rum-flavored butter-cream. Place third layer on top and spread with strawberry-flavored butter-cream. Top with remaining layer. Spoon about $\frac{2}{3}$ cup plain buttercream into pastry bag fitted with $\frac{1}{2}$-inch open star tip and set aside. Spread remaining plain buttercream over top and around sides of cake in thin layer. Refrigerate 30 minutes. Spread remaining chocolate over top and around sides of cake. Score cake into fourteen wedges with warm knife. Pipe buttercream rosettes on top of cake and decorate with glacé cherries and chopped pistachios. Let stand until chocolate is set.

Hunyadi Gâteau

6 eggs, separated
2 cups confectioners' sugar
1½ cups toasted ground hazelnuts
4 ounces semisweet chocolate, finely
chopped
1 recipe Simple Vanilla Custard, page 50
1 envelope unflavored gelatin
1 cup heavy cream
Apricot Glaze, page 60
14 ounces semisweet chocolate, melted
1 cup chocolate-flavored Egg
Buttercream, page 54

3 10-inch springform pans, greased and
bottoms lined

Preheat oven to 400°F

Beat egg whites until stiff. Gradually add sugar and beat until stiff and glossy. Lightly beat egg yolks and fold into beaten egg whites. Combine hazelnuts and chocolate and fold into egg white mixture. Divide mixture in prepared pans. Bake in preheated oven 20 to 25 minutes. Remove from pans immediately and cool on wire racks.

Strain custard. Sprinkle gelatin over ¼ cup cold water in small saucepan and let stand 5 minutes. Place saucepan over low heat and cook, stirring, until gelatin is dissolved. Remove from heat and cool. Stir gelatin into custard. Beat cream until firm and fold into custard. Place one layer on serving plate and spread with remaining custard cream. Refrigerate 1 hour. Brush cake all over with apricot glaze. Spread 12 ounces melted chocolate over top and around sides of cake. Score top of cake into sixteen wedges with warm knife. Let stand until set. Spoon remaining 2 ounces melted chocolate into pastry bag fitted with plain writing tip and pipe sixteen small circles of chocolate onto foil-lined baking sheet. Tap baking sheet on work surface to spread chocolate into flat buttons. Let stand until set. Spoon chocolate buttercream into pastry bag fitted with medium-size open star tip. Pipe buttercream into small rosettes on each wedge of cake and top rosettes with chocolate buttons.

Hazelnut and Nougat Cake

7 egg whites
3 cups confectioners' sugar, sifted
1¼ cups toasted, ground hazelnuts
⅔ cup all-purpose flour, sifted
½ teaspoon cinnamon
½ teaspoon vanilla
2 ounces nut nougat
1 tablespoon brandy
½ recipe French Buttercream, page 55
⅔ cup seedless raspberry jam
3 ounces semisweet chocolate, melted
½ cup toasted flaked nuts or almonds

Preheat oven to 400°F

Draw three 10-inch circles on parchment-lined baking sheets. Beat egg whites until stiff. Gradually add sugar and beat until stiff and glossy. Fold in hazelnuts, flour, cinnamon, and vanilla. Spoon mixture into pastry bag fitted with ½-inch open star tip. Pipe into spirals, filling two circles. To make top layer, pipe mixture in ring around edge of remaining circle. Pipe center of ring in lattice pattern. Bake layers in preheated oven 15 minutes. Remove from baking sheets and cool on paper on wire racks. Peel off paper when cool.

Beat nougat and brandy until smooth. Fold into buttercream. Heat jam and brush half of jam over lattice layer. Let stand until set. Spread melted chocolate thinly over jam. Sprinkle with half the almonds. Place one spiral layer on serving plate and spread with remaining jam. Top with second spiral layer and spread with half the buttercream. Top with lattice layer. Spread remaining buttercream around sides of cake and sprinkle with remaining almonds.

Marron Gâteau

1 can (15½ ounces) chestnut puree
8 egg yolks
1 teaspoon vanilla
1 teaspoon cinnamon
6 egg whites
2½ cups confectioners' sugar
1 cup cake flour, sifted
1 tablespoon dark rum
1½ teaspoons unflavored gelatin

1 cup heavy cream
Apricot Glaze, page 60
14 ounces semisweet chocolate, melted
and cooled
4 ounces marzipan
2 tablespoons chopped pistachios

10-inch springform pan, greased and lined

Preheat oven 350°F

Divide chestnut puree in half. Reserve half for filling. Beat half of puree, egg yolks, ½ cup sugar, vanilla, and cinnamon until smooth. Beat egg whites until stiff peaks form. Gradually add 1½ cups sugar and beat until stiff and glossy. Fold into egg yolk mixture. Fold in flour. Pour mixture into prepared pan. Bake in preheated oven 60 to 65 minutes. Cool in pan on wire rack 10 minutes. Remove from pan and cool completely on rack. Wrap cake in foil and let stand overnight.

To make chestnut cream, blend reserved chestnut puree with rum and remaining ½ cup sugar. Place 2 tablespoons water in saucepan and sprinkle gelatin over. Let stand 5 minutes. Place over low heat and cook, stirring, until gelatin is dissolved. Remove from heat and stir into chestnut mixture. Beat cream until firm and fold into chestnut mixture. Split cake into three layers. Spread chestnut cream between layers. Press down lightly on cake and smooth edges. Refrigerate 30 minutes. Brush cake all over with apricot glaze. Spread 12 ounces melted chocolate over top and around sides of cake. Shape marzipan into 16 chestnuts. Dip marzipan chestnuts into remaining chocolate leaving tops uncoated. Dip bottom of coated chestnuts in chopped pistachios. Cut top of cake into sixteen wedges with warm knife. Decorate with marzipan chestnuts.

Fresh Coconut Cake

2 fresh coconuts
1 cup sugar
2 tablespoons dark rum
2⅓ cups milk
6 tablespoons cornstarch
3 eggs, separated
1 teaspoon vanilla
10-inch Genoise Mixture, page 28
16 glacé cherries

Preheat oven to 350°F

Pierce "eye" of coconut with ice pick. Pour off liquid and reserve 2 tablespoons. Bake coconuts in preheated oven about 20 minutes. Tap all over with hammer to break open. Separate coconut meat from skin. Finely grate meat and set aside. Bring 2 tablespoons reserved coconut liquid and ¼ cup sugar to a boil in small saucepan, stirring until sugar is dissolved. Remove from heat and stir in rum. Set aside.

Combine ½ cup milk, cornstarch, and egg yolks, and stir until smooth. Bring remaining milk, ¾ cup sugar, and vanilla to a boil in medium-size saucepan over moderate heat. Stir about ¼ cup hot milk into cornstarch mixture until blended. Return to saucepan and cook, stirring, until mixture thickens. (Do not allow mixture to boil.) Beat egg whites until stiff and beat into hot custard mixture. Remove from heat immediately. Cut cake into three layers. Place one layer on serving plate and spread with custard. Top with second layer. Sprinkle with half reserved coconut-sugar mixture and spread with layer of custard. Top with third layer and sprinkle with remaining coconut-sugar mixture. Spread remaining custard over top and around sides of cake. Refrigerate 30 minutes. Sprinkle grated coconut over cake and press lightly into custard. Decorate top of cake with glacé cherries.

Mocha Meringue Cake

Meringue:
1 cup egg whites (about 8 egg whites)
1 cup superfine sugar
2 cups sifted confectioners' sugar

Mocha buttercream:
4 eggs
2 egg yolks
1 cup sugar
1½ cups (3 sticks) unsalted butter, softened
1 tablespoon powdered instant espresso
2 tablespoons boiling water

toasted sliced almonds
candied coffee beans

Preheat oven to 225°F

Prepare meringue according to directions on page 54. Spoon into large pastry bag fitted with plain writing tip (#8 or #9) and pipe four 9-inch bases onto parchment-lined baking sheets. Bake in preheated oven 3 hours. Turn oven off and dry in oven overnight. Remove from baking sheet and peel off lining paper.

Prepare buttercream according to directions for Egg Buttercream on page 54. Dissolve espresso in boiling water and beat into buttercream until well blended. Spoon about ¾ cup buttercream into pastry bag fitted with small star tip and set aside. Set aside 1 cup buttercream in small bowl. Place one meringue layer on serving plate and spread with thin layer of remaining buttercream. Repeat with remaining layers, spreading thin layer buttercream over top and around sides of cake. Refrigerate 1 hour. Spread reserved cup buttercream over cake. Sprinkle almonds around sides of cake and press lightly into buttercream. Pipe reserved buttercream into fourteen small rosettes on top of cake. Decorate rosettes with candied coffee beans.

Black Forest Gâteau

1 10-inch chocolate sponge (Classic Chocolate Mixture, page 30)
1 pound dark sweet cherries, pitted and poached
1 cup cherry cooking liquid
3 tablespoons sugar
4 teaspoons cornstarch
1 stick cinnamon

Filling:
3 cups heavy cream
5 tablespoons confectioners' sugar
4 tablespoons kirsch
4 tablespoons sugar syrup
chocolate rolls, page 66
confectioners' sugar

Cut cake into three layers and set aside. Set aside 16 cherries for decoration. Stir cherry cooking liquid, 3 tablespoons sugar, and cornstarch in saucepan until blended and smooth. Add cinnamon stick. Place over low heat and cook, stirring, until mixture comes to a boil and thickens. Discard cinnamon stick. Stir in remaining cherries and remove from heat. Set aside to cool.

To make filling, beat cream with confectioners' sugar until firm. Spoon about half of cream into pastry bag fitted with ½-inch fluted tip. Place one sponge layer on serving plate and spread with thin layer of cream. Pipe four small rings of cream on top. Fill space inside rings with cherry mixture. Top with second sponge layer. Stir kirsch and sugar syrup until blended. Sprinkle half kirsch mixture over cake and spread with cream. Top with remaining sponge layer and sprinkle with remaining kirsch mixture. Spoon about 1½ cups remaining cream into pastry bag fitted with ½-inch open star tip and set aside for decoration. Spread remaining cream over top and sides of cake. Pipe reserved cream in rosettes around top edge of cake. Arrange chocolate rolls in center of cake and sprinkle with confectioners' sugar. Decorate rosettes with reserved cherries.

Frankfurt Ring

This cake is almost as popular in Germany as Black Forest Gâteau, although there are many opinions about the correct way to make it. The only thing on which everyone agrees is the shape of the cake. The cake can be made with a plain sponge or Genoise; the filling can be vanilla, coffee, or even cherry-flavored buttercream. The cake can be covered with chopped almonds, chopped hazelnuts, or crushed praline.

Obviously it is impossible to decide which version is best, but praline coating is one of the most popular ways to finish the cake. The crisp bits of caramelized almond complement the soft texture of the sponge and the flavor of the buttercream. In the following recipe we have choosen a sponge-flavored cake with cherry brandy and a coffee buttercream filling. The sponge is made in the same way in which the Genoise Mixture, page 28, is made.

Sponge:
4 eggs
1 egg yolk
½ cup granulated sugar
⅛ teaspoon salt
⅔ cup cake flour
⅓ cup cornstarch
¼ cup (½ stick) butter, melted

Filling:
German Buttercream, page 54
2 tablespoons confectioners' sugar
2 tablespoons powdered instant coffee
dissolved in 2 tablespoons boiling water
¼ cup kirsch
¼ cup sugar syrup

To decorate:
nut praline, see recipe in caption
8 glacé cherries, halved

8-inch ring mold, greased and floured

Preheat oven to 375°F

Prepare sponge according to directions on page 28. Pour into prepared pan. Bake in preheated oven 30 to 35 minutes. Cool in pan on wire rack 10 minutes. Remove from pan and cool completely on rack. Wrap cake in foil and let stand overnight. Cut cake into four layers. Set aside one third of buttercream. Stir confectioners' sugar and coffee into remaining buttercream. Fill cake as illustrated. Blend kirsch and sugar syrup and sprinkle over all but first layer.

To make praline, heat ⅔ cup granulated sugar in saucepan over low heat until caramel-colored. Stir in 1 cup toasted coarsely chopped almonds. Remove from heat and pour onto oiled marble slab. Brush rolling pin with oil to prevent praline from sticking. Roll out hot praline to about ⅛-inch thickness and let cool. Crush praline inside flan ring with heavy weight or meat tenderizer to prevent praline from scattering.

Cut sponge into four layers. Spread first layer with coffee buttercream. Cover with second layer. Blend kirsch and sugar syrup and sprinkle a little over layer. Spread with coffee buttercream. Repeat with remaining two layers. Refrigerate 1 hour. Spread with coffee buttercream and smooth with strip of parchment paper (see photo). Sprinkle with crushed praline, pressing in place lightly with hand. Pipe reserved plain buttercream into rosettes around top of cake. Decorate each rosette with glacé cherry.

Apricot Cream Gâteau

Sponge:
5 egg yolks
4 ounces marzipan
$\frac{1}{3}$ cup sugar
$\frac{1}{2}$ teaspoon vanilla
3 egg whites
$\frac{1}{2}$ cup sifted all-purpose flour
3 tablespoons cornstarch
2 ounces semisweet chocolate, grated

Apricot cream filling:
$\frac{1}{3}$ cup sugar
$1\frac{1}{4}$ cups milk
3 egg yolks
1 envelope plus 1 teaspoon unflavored
gelatin dissolved in $\frac{1}{4}$ cup water
2 ounces marzipan

3 tablespoons Amaretto liqueur
3 cups whipped cream
$1\frac{1}{2}$ pounds fresh apricots, stewed

Decoration:
1 cup heavy cream
2 tablespoons confectioners' sugar
1 Meringue Layer, page 34

2 10-inch springform pans, greased and
bottoms lined

Preheat oven to 425°F

Beat 1 egg yolk into marzipan until well blended. Gradually beat in remaining egg yolks, sugar, and vanilla. Beat egg whites until stiff. Stir flour, cornstarch, and grated chocolate together. Beat one third of beaten egg whites into marzipan mixture. Fold in remaining egg whites alternately with flour mixture. Divide mixture between prepared pans. Bake in preheated oven 8 to 10 minutes. Run tip of knife around inside edge of pans and remove sides. Invert cakes onto wire racks, peel off paper, and cool completely.

To make filling, cook sugar, milk, and egg yolks until thick enough to coat back of spoon following step-by-step directions on page 53. Stir in dissolved gelatin and strain mixture. Beat 3 tablespoons hot custard into marzipan. Add remaining hot custard and Amaretto and stir until well blended. Let stand until completely cool. Fold in whipped cream.

Return one sponge layer to a springform pan. Spread about one third of cream filling over layer. Set aside 4 to 5 apricots for decoration. Arrange remaining apricot halves over filling. Spread half of remaining filling over apricots. Top with second sponge layer and spread remaining filling over. Refrigerate 1 hour. Remove sides of pan carefully. Beat cream with confectioners' sugar until firm. Spoon half of whipped cream into pastry bag fitted with open star tip. Spread remaining whipped cream around sides of cake. Break meringue layer into pieces and sprinkle over cake. Pipe reserved whipped cream in large rosettes on top of cake. Slice reserved apricots and place on rosettes.

Flaky Choux Cake with Strawberry Filling

This light cream cake is made with crisp choux pastry. It should be eaten within 2 to 3 hours or the choux pastry will get soft quickly.

Choux paste:
¼ cup (½ stick) butter
1 teaspoon sugar
¼ teaspoon salt
1¼ cups all-purpose flour, sifted
5 eggs

Strawberry cream filling:
1 pint small strawberries
⅓ cup confectioners' sugar
1 tablespoon dark rum
3 cups heavy cream
5 tablespoons granulated sugar
confectioners' sugar for dusting

Preheat oven to 425°F

Grease and flour baking sheets and draw five 10-inch circles on them. Place butter, sugar, salt, and 1 cup water in medium-size saucepan and bring to a boil. Add flour, all at once, and stir until mixture forms a ball and comes away from sides of pan. Add eggs, one at a time, beating well after each addition. Spread choux paste thinly over circles, covering circles completely. Bake in preheated oven 12 to 15 minutes or until crisp and golden brown.

Select three best bases for cake and trim edges if necessary. Cut or break remaining choux bases into small pieces.

Reserve about ¾ cup strawberries for decoration. Place remaining strawberries in bowl, sprinkle with confectioners' sugar and rum. Crush strawberries coarsely with fork. Let stand 30 minutes. Beat cream with granulated sugar until firm. Spoon about 1 cup whipped cream into pastry bag fitted with open star tip and set aside. Fold 3½ cups whipped cream into crushed strawberries. Sandwich three choux bases with strawberry cream. Spread remaining plain whipped cream over top and around sides of cake. Sprinkle cake all over with choux flakes. Pipe reserved whipped cream in rosettes on top of cake and decorate with reserved strawberries. Dust top with confectioners' sugar.

Pischinger Cake

Praline:
1 teaspoon butter
¾ cup toasted, chopped hazelnuts
½ cup sugar

Buttercream:
1 cup (2 sticks) butter, softened
⅓ cup sugar
½ teaspoon vanilla
½ teaspoon powdered instant coffee
2 egg yolks

6 krumkake or pizelle wafers (both types of wafer can be made using most pizelle irons)

8 ounces semisweet chocolate, melted and cooled

To make praline, melt butter in medium-size saucepan. Add hazelnuts and sugar, and cook, stirring constantly, until sugar begins to caramelize. Remove from heat and pour onto marble slab. Let cool. Crush with rolling pin. (See praline, page 147.)

To make buttercream, beat butter, sugar, vanilla, and instant coffee in medium-size bowl until light and fluffy. Beat in egg yolks until well blended. Fold in crushed praline. Place one wafer on serving plate and spread with thin layer of buttercream. Repeat with remaining layers. Set aside ½ cup buttercream. Spread thin layer of buttercream over top and around sides of cake. Refrigerate 30 minutes. Spread reserved buttercream over cake and refrigerate 30 minutes. Spread melted chocolate over top and around sides of cake. Score cake into eight equal-size wedges with warm knife. Let stand until chocolate is set.

Pischinger Cake is an Austrian specialty that today has little in common with the original nut cake created by Oskar Pischinger, a well-known Viennese pastry chef. The original complicated cakes were mass-produced with great difficulty. Pischinger's fellow bakers have since developed more practical ways to make this cake, which is based on his original idea.

The story of a special Viennese cake

How could it be that a cake as modest as Sachertorte could become so famous and retain the fascination of food lovers for so many decades? Austrian bakers should consider themselves lucky to have such a cake—one that has made the headlines many times over the years. It is primarily thanks to the Sacher Hotel and the great Viennese bakery Demel that the cake has received so much public attention. They have never been able to agree on which one of them is entitled to the original recipe. In the end, it has been left to the courts to decide. The Sachertorte made at the Sacher Hotel is filled with apricot jam. At the Demel Bakery it is simply covered with chocolate. In any other situation a disagreement of this kind would be forgotten quickly, but not with the Sacher Hotel and the Demel Bakery, both deeply committed to old traditions. Tradition is no joking matter in the city of Vienna.

One of the nicest traditions of Vienna is to book a table for a late dinner at the Sacher Hotel following an evening at the world famous Vienna Opera House. They are located across the street from each other. And, at the end of a magnificent meal, there is no doubt about what to order: a piece of Sachertorte and coffee *met schlag* (whipped cream).

At the Demel Bakery (where there is no jam in the cake), amid the aroma of elegant pastries and freshly brewed coffee, one can feast on cakes and pastries that perfectly complement the chandeliers, mirrors, and ornate decor. Black dresses with white collars are always worn by Demel's attractive young ladies (it would somehow be inappropriate to refer to them as waitresses) who always avoid the personal pronoun when addressing a customer. "Has the gentleman ordered yet?" Or, "Does madame require cream?" They use a manner of speech that gives the whole proceeding something of the atmosphere of a Viennese stage set at the turn of the century. But this is the real world with a director in the background who knows something about both show business and art. Udo Proksch, alias Serge Kirchhofer, is the director. He preserves traditions passionately, and anyone who doubts it will soon be convinced by the quality of the pastries made at Demel's. No modern influences are tolerated and there is no other bakery that can claim to have resisted modern technology as consistently as Demel's. Master Leschanz, who runs the bakery, will not tolerate any compromises. Only the freshest and the very best is good enough.

There is something that these traditionalists share, curiously enough, with the proponents of nouvelle cuisine, although their recipes could hardly be adapted to fit the modern trend for low calorie food. Demel's makes their own jams and stewed fruit and they have their own mills to produce unbleached flour. In the basement there are old-fashioned machines producing nougat, marzipan, and even their own chocolate. Near by, quick-fingered girls make a variety of pralines by hand.

The following recipe for Sachertorte is, so to speak, *neutral*, and any similarity to the original is purely accidental!

Sachertorte

4½ ounces semisweet chocolate
½ cup (1 stick) butter, softened
1 cup sifted confectioner's sugar
5 egg yolks
1 teaspoon vanilla
4 egg whites
⅓ cup cake flour
¾ cup ground almonds
Apricot Glaze, page 60
Boiled Chocolate Icing, page 64

9-inch springform pan

Preheat oven to 350°F

Grease and flour springform pan. Melt chocolate in top of double-boiler. Remove from heat and set aside. Beat butter with ½ cup sugar and egg yolks until light and fluffy. Stir in vanilla and melted chocolate. Beat egg whites with remaining ½ cup sugar until stiff peaks form. Fold beaten egg whites into butter mixture with flour and ground almonds. Pour into prepared pan and smooth top. Bake in preheated oven 40 to 50 minutes. When cool, cover cake with apricot glaze and chocolate icing.

The Sachertorte represents all that is traditional in Viennese baking. The Sacher Hotel's version is filled with apricot jam and they claim their version is the original Viennese Sachertorte. The cakes are covered with delicious chocolate, one after the other, in their modern hotel kitchen. Sachertorte made at the Demel Bakery is made without jam. Their Anna Cake is also famous, partly because of its unusual turban shape. One of Demel's waitresses, dressed in the customary black dress and white collar, presides over the cake stands at the restaurant.

Small Cakes

Small cakes are a fairly recent innovation. In the past big was beautiful in baking. The larger and more sumptuous the better, and in keeping with the spirit of the times cakes were often made as large as wagon wheels.

It was not until Victorian times, with its emphasis upon the individual, that small cakes began to form the centerpoint of the window display of a patisserie. These delicate little cakes were entirely in keeping with an age in which hard physical labor was becoming a thing of the past and where it was becoming less necessary for food merely to satisfy hunger. It is hardly surprising that in modern times these small pastries make up an increasing proportion of patisserie's sales.

This new concept placed a different emphasis on the external appearance of the baker's creations, an emphasis that was even more important here than with the larger gâteaux. This explains why the products were sold both in the form of large cakes and in a miniaturized version as small cakes or slices. For the baker these slices were easier to divide into individual portions than the larger gâteaux. In home baking, quantities for large cakes could be halved to provide suitable sizes for the smaller family. Almost all "large recipes" could be reduced in this way, even the well-known Linzertorte, Sachertorte, or Baumkuchen. A more unusual example of the small cake is provided by the Swiss roll, in which a flat sponge is rolled with a lemon or chocolate cream, nut, fruit, or truffle filling. The roll is then cut into individual slices before serving to provide an attractive display.

Small, rum-soaked savarins with a variety of delicious fillings make excellent desserts while, despite the adverse effects of mass production, homemade Chocolate-covered Sponge Drops have remained a favorite with children for 150 years. These were invented in Vienna in 1822 when a magician called Kuton Bulchia Titescan was enjoying great popularity. A clever confectioner honored the Indian magician by creating a dessert whose chocolate coating and cream filling were meant to represent the brown complexion and dazzling white teeth of the conjuror. Even today these cakes are known as "Indians" in Vienna.

Small cakes are, or course, always a favorite with children as well as adults. Both like the idea of an individual portion, served up for instance in the form of éclairs or cream horns. Small cakes are usually especially attractive—for example the Strawberry Tarts or the Raspberry Meringues in this chapter. A combination of two or three different varieties of small cake on the table would serve equally well at an older child's party or at a morning coffee party for adults. Care should be taken to display the cakes as attractively as possible on pretty china with napkins as this will enhance their appeal.

Chocolate-covered Sponge Drops

This recipe serves as a basic recipe for small sponges that retain their shape during baking. Chocolate drops are one of the most popular small sponge cakes. They are usually filled with plain whipped cream, but can be filled with crème pâtissière.

5 egg yolks
⅓ cup sugar
7 egg whites
½ cup cornstarch, sifted
¼ cup all-purpose flour
Apricot Glaze, page 60
Boiled Chocolate Icing, page 64
1½ cups heavy cream, sweetened and whipped

Preheat oven to 400°F

Prepare sponge mixture as illustrated in step-by-step photos. This technique differs from the usual technique for making a sponge mixture because cornstarch is folded into beaten egg whites, and then beaten yolks are folded in rather than the more usual reverse procedure.

Brush baked sponge drops with apricot glaze, cover with melted chocolate and sandwich with whipped cream piped with ½-inch fluted tip. Alternatively, soak sponges in mixture of 1 tablespoon sugar syrup and 1 tablespoon dark rum. Prepare Simple Vanilla Custard, page 60, and sandwich sponges with custard. Brush with apricot glaze and cover with melted chocolate. (Makes 26 chocolate drops.)

2 **Beat egg whites** until stiff peaks form. Gradually add remaining sugar and continue beating until stiff and glossy. Fold in cornstarch.

3 **Pour half of egg yolk mixture** into beaten egg whites and fold in gently. Fold in remaining egg yolks.

1 **Beat egg yolks** and 1 tablespoon sugar until mixture is creamy and consistency of heavy cream. Do not overbeat.

4 **Fold in flour** very gently with wooden spatula to prevent mixture from loosing any volume or firmness.

5 **Line baking sheets** with parchment paper. Spoon mixture into large pastry bag fitted with ½-inch plain tip. Pipe mixture into rounded mounds onto lined baking sheets. Hold pastry bag vertically and squeeze mixture out in continuous motion. Space mounds about 1 inch apart.

6 **Dust drops lightly** with flour before baking to help drops rise evenly. Bake in preheated oven 5 minutes, lower oven temperature to 350°F and bake 8 minutes. Remove from baking sheets immediately and cool on wire racks.

7 **Place the drops** on a wire rack to cool. Press a spoon into the base of each drop while still warm to make a hollow for the filling, if required.

8 **Thinly brush drops** with apricot glaze. Alternatively, dip into glaze quickly and brush off excess. Place on wire racks and let stand until glaze is set.

9 **Prepare chocolate icing** according to step-by-step photos on page 64. Dip glazed drops into icing. Pierce drops with small pointed knife to remove from icing. Place on wire racks set over jelly-roll pan.

10 **Spoon whipped cream** into pastry bag fitted with open star tip. Pipe whipped cream onto uncoated side of half the sponge drops. Top with remaining drops, chocolate side up.

Marzipan "Potatoes"

This is typical of the kind of cake that can be made with sponge drops (see recipe opposite page). Round "potatoes" can be cut with a knife to make them look like open potato skins. To make oval "potatoes," pipe the sponge mixture into oval shapes. After baking, cut out a hollow in the base of the sponges and fill them with German Buttercream, page 54. Wrap in marzipan and roll in cocoa.

12 sponge drops, page 154
1 tablespoon dark rum
1 tablespoon sugar syrup
2 ounces semisweet chocolate, melted
$\frac{1}{2}$ recipe German Buttercream, page 54
$\frac{1}{3}$ cup pineapple jam
14 ounces marzipan
cocoa powder

Scoop out hollow in bottom of sponge drops. Blend rum and sugar syrup, and brush over bottom of drops. Let stand 15 minutes. Stir melted chocolate into one third of buttercream. Fill bottom of half the sponges with chocolate buttercream. Spread pineapple jam over bottom of remaining sponges. Sandwich buttercream filled sponges and pineapple sponges together. Spread remaining buttercream in thin layer over filled sponges. Thinly roll out marzipan and cut into 5-inch circles. Wrap marzipan circles around filled sponges, pinching edges of marzipan together to seal. Cut off excess marzipan with scissors. Roll marzipan-coated sponges in cocoa and shake off excess. Cut three slashes in top of marzipan with tip of sharp knife. Press marzipan back slightly so buttercream is visible. Place marzipan "potatoes" in small paper cups.

Oval marzipan "potatoes" can be made to look very realistic. Use oval-shaped sponge drops filled with buttercream. Wrap in marzipan and roll in cocoa. Make "eyes" with the point of a skewer.

5 egg yolks
½ cup sugar
pinch salt
grated peel of ½ lemon
4 egg whites
5 tablespoons cornstarch
½ cup sifted all-purpose flour
3 tablespoons butter, melted

Preheat oven to 425°F

Sponge Moons

These small sponge cakes can be filled with almost any kind of light custard, fruit, ice cream, or whipped cream. They are excellent cakes to have on hand when time is short because they can be made well in advance. They freeze well and will keep fresh for several days when wrapped in plastic wrap.

Line baking sheets with parchment paper. Draw eighteen to twenty 5-inch circles on paper about 1 inch apart. Beat egg yolks, ¼ cup sugar, salt, and lemon peel until foamy. Beat egg whites in separate bowl until stiff. Gradually add remaining ¼ cup sugar and beat until stiff and glossy. Fold egg yolk mixture into beaten egg whites. Sift cornstarch and flour and gently fold into beaten egg whites. Fold in melted butter. Spoon mixture into pastry bag fitted with ½-inch plain tip. Pipe mixture onto circles. Bake in preheated oven 8 to 10 minutes or until golden. (Do not allow edges to brown or they will be too crisp to fold.) Cool on paper on wire racks. Peel off paper, cover half of moons with whipped cream, custard, or fruit, and fold over (see photo). (Makes 18 to 20 small cakes.)

1 **Line baking sheets** with parchment paper. Draw 5-inch circles on paper about 1 inch apart. Spoon mixture into large pastry bag fitted with ½-inch plain tip. Pipe mixture onto circles in a spiral, starting at center of each circle and filling in circles completely.

2 **Sprinkle clean work surface** lightly with flour. Lift parchment sheets with baked cakes in place and invert onto floured surface and let cool completely. When cool, peel off parchment paper.

Éclairs

¼ cup (½ stick) butter · pinch salt
1¼ cups all-purpose flour, sifted
5 to 6 eggs
Apricot Glaze, page 60
2 teaspoons powdered instant coffee
2 teaspoons boiling water
Fondant, page 60

Coffee cream:
2 cups heavy cream
¼ cup confectioners' sugar, sifted
1 to 2 tablespoons coffee-flavored liqueur

Preheat oven to 425°F

Place 1 cup water, butter, and salt in saucepan and bring to a boil. Add flour, all at once, and stir vigorously with wooden spoon until mixture forms a ball and comes away from sides of pan. Remove from heat and place mixture in bowl. Let cool slightly. Beat in eggs, one at a time, beating well after each addition to incorporate thoroughly before adding next egg. Spoon choux paste into pastry bag fitted with plain tip (#11). Lightly grease baking sheets. Pipe twenty 4- to 5-inch long fingers onto baking sheets, spacing éclairs about 1½ inches apart. Bake 18 to 22 minutes or until golden brown. Cool on wire racks. Brush tops of éclairs with apricot glaze while still warm. Dissolve coffee in boiling water and stir into fondant until blended. Spread fondant over tops of éclairs and let stand until dry. Cut éclairs in half lengthwise, remove tops, and set aside.

Beat cream until soft peaks form. Add sugar and liqueur and beat until firm. Spoon whipped cream into pastry bag fitted with open star tip. Pipe whipped cream onto bottom of éclairs. Replace tops.

Strawberry Tarts

10 tablespoons butter, softened
1 cup confectioners' sugar
¼ teaspoon salt · 1 egg, beaten
2¼ cups all purpose flour

Filling:
¾ cup granulated sugar
5 tablespoons cornstarch
2 cups milk · 5 egg yolks, beaten
½ teaspoon vanilla · 4 egg whites
1 pint small strawberries

3 cups sweetened whipped cream

10 to 12 individual tart pans

Preheat oven to 400°F

Prepare pastry according to mixer method on page 37. Wrap and refrigerate 1 hour. Roll out pastry on lightly floured surface and line tart pans. Prick pastry all over with fork. Bake 10 minutes or until golden brown. Cool.

To make filling, stir half the granulated sugar, cornstarch, and milk in saucepan. Place over low heat and cook, stirring, until mixture comes to a boil. Stir a little hot milk mixture into beaten egg yolks. Return mixture to saucepan and cook, stirring, until thickened (do not allow to boil). Remove from heat and stir in vanilla. Beat egg whites with remaining sugar until stiff then fold into hot custard. Set aside about 1 cup strawberries for decoration. Puree remaining strawberries. Strain to remove seeds. Fold into custard mixture and spoon into tart shells. Cool completely. Decorate with piped whipped cream and reserved strawberries.

Chocolate Chimneys

10 ounces marzipan
½ cup all-purpose flour, sifted
4 egg whites, lightly beaten
½ cup plus 1 tablespoon milk
semisweet chocolate, melted and cooled
2 cups sweetened whipped cream

Preheat oven to 375°F

Work marzipan, flour, and a little beaten egg white together on clean work surface. Gradually work in remaining egg whites until thoroughly incorporated. Press mixture through fine mesh sieve into bowl. Cover and refrigerate overnight. Grease and flour two baking sheets. Remove marzipan mixture from refrigerator and let stand at room temperature 1 hour. Add milk and stir until well blended. Divide mixture in half. Spread half the marzipan mixture in thin layer over one prepared baking sheet. Spread remaining marzipan mixture over second baking sheet. Bake 4 to 6 minutes or until golden brown. Remove baking sheets from oven and cut marzipan into 4-inch squares. Return to oven and bake 5 minutes or until crisp and browned. Remove marzipan squares from baking sheets, one at a time and roll around metal cannoli tubes or thick handle of wooden spoon. Slide roll off tube and cool completely on wire racks. Repeat with remaining marzipan squares. Spread thin layer melted chocolate over marzipan rolls. Let stand until chocolate is set. Spoon whipped cream into pastry bag fitted with ½-inch plain tip. Pipe whipped cream into chocolate rolls at each end.

157

Dutch Cherry Slices

¾ pound Quick Puff Pastry, page 44
1 can (16 ounces) pitted tart red cherries
½ cup sugar
¼ teaspoon cinnamon
1 tablespoon cornstarch
2 cups heavy cream
⅓ cup red currant jelly
Fondant, page 60

Preheat oven to 425°F

Line baking sheet with parchment paper. Roll out pastry on lightly floured surface to 18- by 10-inch rectangle. Place on lined baking sheet and prick all over with fork. Refrigerate 15 minutes. Bake in preheated oven 12 to 15 minutes or until golden brown. Remove from baking sheet and cool on wire rack. Trim edges.

Drain cherries, reserving liquid. Place cherry liquid in saucepan. Add ¼ cup sugar, cinnamon, and cornstarch, and stir until blended. Place saucepan over low heat and

cook, stirring, until mixture thickens and comes to a boil. Stir in cherries and simmer 1 minute. Remove from heat and cool.

Cut pastry in half lenthwise. Spread cherries down center of one piece of pastry. Beat cream with remaining ¼ cup sugar until firm. Pipe whipped cream over cherries. Heat jelly until melted. Brush over second piece of pastry and let stand until set. Spread fondant over jelly-covered pastry and let stand until set. Proceed as illustrated.

Variation: To make coffee-cherry slices, flavour whipped cream with powdered instant coffee and 1 more tablespoon sugar. Flavor fondant with coffee and about 1 tablespoon coffee-flavored liqueur.

1 **Cut pastry lengthwise** into two equal-size pieces. Use ruler as guide. Brush melted red currant jelly over one pastry strip and let stand until set. Spread fondant over jelly-covered pastry strip and let stand until set. Cut into 2-inch-wide strips and set aside.

2 **Place remaining large pastry strip** between two pieces of wood (if available), 16 inches long and 2 inches high. Spread cherries down center. Spoon whipped cream into pastry bag fitted with large plain writing tip and pipe whipped cream on both sides and over top of cherries.

3 **Smooth whipped cream** with long flat icing spatula. Run tip of sharp knife along inside edge of wood and remove wood. Smooth sides.

4 **Place Fondant-covered strips** over whipped cream. Cut through filled slices with long sharp knife, wiping knife clean after each cut.

Raspberry Meringues

Meringue:
1 cup egg whites (about 8 egg whites)
1 cup superfine sugar
2 cups sifted confectioners' sugar
3 to 4 ounces semisweet chocolate, melted

Filling:
1½ tablespoons cornstarch
½ cup sweet red wine
⅔ cup sugar
1 pint fresh raspberries
2 to 3 tablespoons framboise (raspberry-
flavored liqueur)
2 cups heavy cream

Preheat oven to 225°F

Line baking sheets with parchment paper.
Draw thirty 3-inch circles on parchment.
Prepare meringue mixture according to
step-by-step photos on page 34 and spoon
into large pastry bag fitted with ½-inch open
star tip. Pipe meringue onto drawn circles.
Bake according to directions on page 34.
Remove meringues from lining paper and
dip tops of meringues into melted chocolate. Let stand until chocolate is set.

Stir cornstarch, wine and ⅓ cup sugar in
medium-size saucepan until blended and
smooth. Place saucepan over low heat and
cook, stirring, until mixture comes to a boil
and thickens. Add two thirds of raspberries
and return to a boil. Simmer 1 to 2 minutes.
Remove from heat and stir in framboise. Set
aside. Puree remaining one-third raspberries. Strain puree to remove seeds. Beat
cream with remaining ⅓ cup sugar until firm.
Fold in raspberry puree and spoon into
pastry bag fitted with ½-inch fluted tip. Pipe
raspberry cream in a ring over chocolate on
outer edge of half the meringues. Spoon
reserved raspberry-wine mixture into centers of piped cream. Top with remaining
meringues, chocolate side up. (Makes 15
filled meringue cakes.)

Cream Horns

These crisp puff pastry cases can be
shaped as horns or rolls. Metal tubes
are available to make both shapes. The
pastry is usually filled with a light
custard but is particularly delicious
when filled with sweetened whipped
cream, plain or flavored with vanilla,
brandy, kirsch, or your favorite
liqueur.

1 pound Puff Pastry, page 42
1 egg yolk beaten with 1 tablespoon
milk for brushing
sliced almonds (optional)
1 cup heavy cream
confectioners' sugar
1 teaspoon vanilla or liqueur
(optional)

Preheat oven to 400°F

Roll out pastry on lightly floured
surface to 18- by 10-inch rectangle.
Change directions frequently when rolling, rolling left and right and
then forward and backward. Cut
pastry into eight strips, 1¼ inches wide
and 18 inches long. Roll strips around
metal horns or tubes in spiral fashion,
overlapping edges slightly. Press edges
to seal. Brush with beaten egg yolk
mixture and roll in almonds if desired.
Place on ungreased baking sheet with
end of pastry on bottom and let stand
15 minutes. Bake in preheated oven
about 20 minutes or until golden. Slide
metal horns out and cool pastry
completely on wire rack. Beat cream
with 2 tablespoons confectioners'
sugar. Add vanilla or liqueur
if desired and fill horns.
Dust with confec-
tioners' sugar.

Strawberry Cream Roll

Sponge:

6 egg yolks · ½ cup granulated sugar
⅛ teaspoon salt
1 teaspoon vanilla · 3 egg whites
⅔ cup sifted all-purpose flour

Filling:

2 cups fresh small strawberries
¼ cup Sauterne wine
2 envelopes unflavoured gelatin
1½ cups heavy cream
½ cup granulated sugar

16- × 12-inch jelly-roll pan, greased and
lined

Preheat oven to 450°F

Beat egg yolks, ¼ cup sugar, salt, and vanilla
until thick and lemon-colored. Beat egg
whites until stiff. Add remaining ¼ cup sugar
and beat until stiff and glossy. Fold egg yolk
mixture into beaten egg whites. Fold in
flour. Pour into pan and smooth top. Bake 8
to 10 minutes or until cake springs back
when lightly pressed. Sprinkle clean towel
with confectioners' sugar. Invert cake onto
towel. Peel off lining paper and trim edges
of cake. Roll cake jelly-roll style and place
on wire rack to cool.

Puree strawberries and strain to remove

seeds. Place wine in small saucepan,
sprinkle gelatin over, and let stand 5
minutes. Place saucepan over low heat and
cook, stirring, until gelatin is dissolved.
Remove from heat and cool. Stir gelatin
into strawberry puree. Beat cream until soft
peaks form. Add sugar and beat until firm.
Fold whipped cream into cooled strawberry
mixture. Refrigerate 30 minutes. Unroll
cake and spread with strawberry cream.
Roll cake (without towel) and place, seam
side down, on serving plate. Refrigerate
until ready to serve. Dust with confectioners' sugar.

Hazelnut Cream Roll

Sponge:

6 egg yolks · ½ cup granulated sugar
⅛ teaspoon salt
1 teaspoon vanilla · 3 egg whites
⅓ cup all-purpose flour
3 tablespoons cornstarch
⅓ cup toasted ground hazelnuts

Filling:

2½ cups heavy cream
⅓ cup granulated sugar
⅔ cup toasted, ground hazelnuts

Praline:

½ cup sugar · ½ cup chopped hazelnuts

whole hazelnuts and chocolate candies

16- × 12-inch jelly-roll pan, greased and
lined

Preheat oven to 450°F

Beat egg yolks, ¼ cup sugar, salt, and vanilla
until thick and lemon-colored. Beat egg
whites until stiff. Add remaining ¼ cup sugar
and beat until stiff and glossy. Fold beaten
egg whites into egg yolk mixture. Sift flour
and cornstarch and combine with ground
hazelnuts. Fold into egg yolk mixture.
Spread mixture evenly in pan. Bake 8 to 10
minutes or until cake springs back when
lightly pressed. Sprinkle clean towel with
confectioners' sugar. Invert cake onto
towel. Peel off lining paper and trim edges
of cake. Roll cake in towel, jelly-roll style,
and place on wire rack to cool.

Beat cream with sugar until firm. Spoon
about one third of whipped cream into
pastry bag fitted with ½-inch open star tip
and set aside. Fold ground hazelnuts into
remaining whipped cream. Unroll cake and
spread with hazelnut cream. Roll cake
(without towel) and place, seam side down,
on serving plate. Pipe two or three
lengthwise strips of whipped cream onto
cake. Spread whipped cream with long icing
spatula, covering cake completely. Smooth
cream with strip of waxed paper (see
method, Frankfurt Ring, page 147).

Melt sugar in skillet. Add chopped
hazelnuts and proceed as directed on page
147. Crush praline and sprinkle over cake.
Pipe rosettes on top of cake with remaining
whipped cream and decorate with chocolate
candies and whole hazelnuts. Refrigerate
until ready to serve.

Lemon Roll

Sponge:
4 egg whites · ½ cup sugar
8 egg yolks · ¼ teaspoon salt
grated peel of 1 lemon · ⅔ cup cake flour
3 tablespoons cornstarch

Filling:
4 teaspoons unflavored gelatin
3 egg yolks · ½ cup white wine
½ cup granulated sugar · juice of 2 lemons
grated peel of 1 lemon
1 cup heavy cream
confectioners' sugar for dusting

16- × 12-inch jelly-roll pan, bottom lined

Preheat oven to 450°F

To make sponge roll, prepare according to step-by-step photos on page 30. Bake 8 to 10 minutes or until cake springs back when lightly pressed. Sprinkle clean towel with confectioners' sugar. Run tip of sharp knife around inside edge of pan to release cake. Invert cake onto sugared towel. Peel off lining paper and trim edges of cake. Roll cake in towel, jelly-roll style, and place on wire rack. Cool completely.

To make filling, soak gelatin in ¼ cup water 5 minutes. Beat egg yolks, wine, sugar, lemon juice and peel in saucepan until blended and smooth. Place over low heat and cook, stirring, just until thickened (do not allow to boil). Add gelatin and stir until completely dissolved. Remove from heat and cool completely. Beat cream until firm. Fold cream into cooled lemon-gelatin mixture gradually. Refrigerate 30 minutes. Unroll cake and spread lemon cream over cake. Roll cake and place on serving plate. Dust with confectioners' sugar.

Chocolate Roll

Cake:
8 egg whites · 1 cup sugar
1 teaspoon vanilla
3 ounces unsweetened chocolate, melted
and cooled
½ cup cake flour
½ cup seedless raspberry jam

Buttercream filling:
1½ cups (3 sticks) unsalted butter,
softened
¾ cup sugar
6 tablespoons cornstarch
3 egg yolks · 1¾ cups milk
2 tablespoons kirsch

sweetened cocoa for dusting
halved red glacé cherries

15- × 10-inch jelly-roll pan, lined

Preheat oven to 400°F

Beat egg whites in large bowl until stiff. Gradually add sugar and beat until stiff and glossy. Fold in vanilla and melted chocolate (egg whites will lose volume). Sift flour over chocolate mixture and fold in. Spoon mixture into large pastry bag fitted with ½-inch plain tip. Pipe mixture onto prepared pan (see photo). Bake 10 to 12 minutes. Cool in pan on wire rack 10 minutes. Invert cake onto large sheet of parchment paper. Spread jam over cake. Prepare German Buttercream according to directions on page 54. Spoon about 1 cup buttercream into pastry bag fitted with open star tip and set aside. Spread remaining buttercream over cake. Roll cake and place, seam side down, on serving plate. Dust with sweetened cocoa and decorate with rosettes of reserved buttercream and the glacé cherries.

1 **Line pan with parchment paper.** Spoon chocolate mixture into pastry bag and pipe strips lengthwise onto paper. Strips should barely touch.

2 **Cool cake in pan** on wire rack 10 minutes. Invert cake onto sheet of parchment paper and cool completely. Spread jam over cake. Spread buttercream over jam.

For variation, substitute orange juice and peel or lime juice and peel for the lemon juice and peel. If orange juice is very sweet, add a little lemon juice.

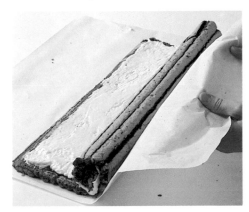

3 **Roll cake,** jelly-roll style, with aid of paper. Lift long edge of paper closest to you with both hands so cake rolls away from you. Move hands further down paper toward cake and lift paper so cake continues to roll.

4 **Dust cake** with sweetened cocoa. Cocoa provides a flavor contrast for unsweetened chocolate flavor of cake and sweet buttercream flavor of filling. Decorate cake with rosettes of buttercream and glacé cherries.

Traditional Holiday Baking

In Milan there lived an old confectioner who was very poor and whose only possession was a beautiful daughter who was the apple of his eye. His love for the beautiful Adalgisa was shared by a young nobleman with the picturesque name of Ughetto della Tella. If he was to win the daughter the young man had no choice but to go to the father's shop and offer his services as a baker, and he was able to win the old man's favor when he invented a cake that was to make the three of them rich and famous overnight. This was the world famous Milan Panettone.

This is a story that has been handed down through the generations, although at the time of its "discovery" the Panettone already had a long history. It was one of many Christmas cakes baked in ages past in celebration of the winter solstice, which also include the North German "Klaben" and the Christian "Stollen" (adapted into Christian symbolism in the form of a swaddled baby), English fruit cake, Central European fruit loaves, the French Bûche de Noël (a richly decorated sponge roll), the Danish "Kransekager" made of marzipan, and the Epiphany cake with its fascinating origins in the Roman Saturnalia. Throughout the Middle Ages it was customary to bake a pie for the feast of Epiphany. These contained a small object such as a bean or a small porcelain figure, and whoever found the bean in his portion became "king for a day." This is a custom that has recently been revived in Switzerland. These cakes also include the richly decorated "Grittibänzen," baked in Switzerland for St. Nicholas' Day, and the New Year pretzels, which are a good luck symbol.

Easter is the time for lambs and hares. Pagan spring fertility symbols were later adopted by the Christian world—the name Easter itself is derived from the name of a pagan god. A Russian specialty for Easter is the "Kulitsh," a yeast-dough cake that is cylindrical in shape and the taller the better.

It is not only for the established festivals of the Christian calendar that cakes have been baked over the centuries. Weddings are equally important and in many areas special cakes are made to celebrate the occasion. The most famous of these is the English Wedding Cake, which has now made its way to the Continent too. Photographs taken at the weddings of such cakes: temples, castles, cupids, doves, and flowers. And things have not changed greatly today: the modern wedding cake is usually of several tiers, covered in marzipan and then intricately decorated with sugar and icing. There is no other area of cooking so influenced by custom and tradition as the baking of cakes and pastries.

Kulitch

This is a traditional Russian cake baked in an unusual shape with very fine yeast dough. Like Pashka, which is made with cottage cheese and candied fruit, it is eaten at Easter. Since Kulitch and Pashka are usually eaten together, both recipes have been included.

¾ cup raisins
½ cup chopped mixed candied fruit

Kulitch and Pashka are traditional Easter dishes served in Russia and usually eaten together. Kulitch and pashka molds are difficult to find, but coffee cans and clay flower pots make excellent substitutes.

⅓ cup chopped almonds
2 tablespoons dark rum
about 3½ cups all-purpose flour
2 packages active dry yeast
⅔ cup granulated sugar
1 cup warm milk (105° to 115°F)
¾ cup (1½ sticks) butter, softened
1 teaspoon salt
1 teaspoon vanilla
pinch ground saffron
6 egg yolks
1¼ cups confectioners' sugar, sifted
1 tablespoon lemon juice
candied fruit to decorate

two 1-pound coffee cans

Preheat oven to 400°F

Generously grease two 1-pound coffee cans. Attach 2-inch foil collar to rim of cans and grease collar. Place raisins, candied fruit, and almonds in bowl. Stir in rum and set aside. Place 2 tablespoons flour, yeast, 1 teaspoon granulated sugar, and milk in large bowl, and stir to dissolve yeast. Cover bowl and let stand 10 minutes. Beat butter, remaining granulated sugar, salt, vanilla, and saffron until light and fluffy. Beat in egg yolks, one at a time, beating well after each addition. Add 2½ cups remaining flour to yeast mixture and beat vigorously with wooden spoon. Add butter mixture and remaining flour and beat to make soft dough. Stir in raisin-nut mixture. (Dough will resemble spongy batter.) Cover bowl and let rise 1 to 1½ hours. Stir dough down with wooden spoon. Spoon dough evenly into prepared cans, packing dough well into cans. Cover and let rise 20 to 25 minutes. Bake in preheated oven 15 minutes. Lower oven temperature to 350°F and bake 55 to 65 minutes or until long wooden skewer inserted in center of Kulitch comes out clean. Cool in cans on wire rack 15 minutes. Carefully remove foil collar and remove Kulitch from cans. Cool completely on rack. Blend confectioners' sugar, 2 tablespoons water, and lemon juice until smooth. Spoon over top of Kulitch and let icing run down sides. Decorate with candied fruit. Let stand until icing is set.

Pashka

Although it is not easy to find a traditional pashka mold, Pashka can still be made at home in a simple everyday household item—a clay flower pot. Use a clean flower pot with a hole in the bottom. The pot should measure 6 inches in diameter, 6 inches across the top, and 3½ inches across the bottom. Line the flower pot with a double thickness of cheesecloth and place a 2- or 3-pound weight on top of the Pashka before placing it in the refrigerator.

2 pounds cottage cheese
½ cup (1 stick) unsalted butter, softened
3 eggs
¾ cup sugar
grated peel of 1 lemon
1 cup dairy sour cream
½ cup chopped blanched almonds
⅓ cup raisins
¼ cup finely chopped candied lemon peel
¼ cup finely chopped candied orange peel

To decorate:
red glacé cherries
candied pineapple
candied citron
candied lemon and orange peel

Wrap cottage cheese in double thickness of cheesecloth and tie in center of handle of wooden spoon. Balance spoon across deep bowl so cheese is suspended over bowl. Let stand several hours. Discard liquid in bowl and place cottage cheese in fine mesh strainer. Press through strainer into bowl with back of spoon.

Line pashka mold or clean clay flower pot with double thickness of dampened cheesecloth large enough to cover top of mold. Set aside.

Beat butter, eggs, sugar, and grated lemon peel in large bowl until sugar is dissolved and mixture is thickened. Add cottage cheese and beat until smooth. Fold in sour cream, almonds, raisins, and candied lemon and orange peel. Spoon mixture into lined mold and smooth top. Fold cheesecloth over mixture and place mold in deep bowl. Place small flat plate on top of mold and weigh down with 2- or 3-pound weight. Refrigerate at least 24 hours. Unmold Pashka onto serving plate and carefully remove cheesecloth. Decorate with glacé cherries, candied pineapple, candied citron, and candied lemon and orange peels.

Easter Lamb

6 tablespoons ($\frac{3}{4}$ stick) butter, softened
$\frac{1}{3}$ cup granulated sugar
2 eggs, separated
grated peel of $\frac{1}{2}$ lemon
$\frac{2}{3}$ cup all-purpose flour
$\frac{1}{3}$ cup cornstarch
confectioners' sugar for dusting

small lamb-shaped cake mold, greased
and floured

Preheat oven to 350°F

Cream butter, granulated sugar, egg yolks, and lemon peel in medium-size bowl until stiff. Fold beaten egg whites into creamed butter mixture. Sift flour and cornstarch and fold into creamed mixture. Pour mixture into prepared pan and smooth top. Bake in preheated oven 25 to 30 minutes or until cake springs back when lightly pressed. Cool in pan on wire rack 10 to 15 minutes. Remove from pan and cool completely on rack. Dust with sifted confectioners' sugar.

Russian Easter Bread

about $4\frac{1}{4}$ cups all-purpose flour
2 packages active dry yeast or 1 cake (1 ounce) fresh yeast
$\frac{1}{3}$ cup sugar
1 cup warm milk (105° to 115°F)
$\frac{1}{2}$ cup (1 stick) butter, melted
1 teaspoon salt
grated peel of 1 lemon
3 egg yolks
1 cup raisins
1 egg yolk beaten with 1 tablespoon milk for glaze

Preheat oven to 375°F

Sift 3 cups flour into bowl and make well in center. Place yeast and 1 tablespoon sugar in well. Add milk and stir to dissolve yeast. Sprinkle a little flour over yeast mixture. Cover bowl and let stand 10 minutes. Beat butter, remaining sugar, salt, lemon peel, and egg yolks until blended. Stir butter mixture and raisins into flour-yeast mixture. Stir in enough remaining flour to make soft dough. Turn out dough onto lightly floured surface and knead until smooth and elastic. Place in greased bowl and turn to coat. Cover and let rise 1 to $1\frac{1}{2}$ hours. Grease baking sheet. Punch dough down and divide in half. Shape each piece into flattened ball and place on prepared baking sheet. Cover and let rise 1 hour or until doubled in bulk.

Shape dough into flattened rounds. Cover and let rise 1 hour or until doubled in bulk. Brush with beaten egg yolk mixture and cut cross, the symbol of Easter, in top of each loaf with sharp knife. Let rise 15 minutes. Bake as directed.

Brush loaves with beaten egg yolk mixture. Cut cross on top of each loaf. Bake in preheated oven 45 to 50 minutes or until golden brown and loaves sound hollow when tapped on the bottom.

Sift 4 cups flour into bowl and make well in center. Add yeast and 1 tablespoon sugar to well. Add milk and stir to dissolve yeast. Sprinkle a little flour over yeast mixture. Cover bowl and let stand 10 minutes. Blend remaining sugar, butter, and salt. Add butter mixture to flour-yeast mixture with 2 cups flour and beat with wooden spoon to make soft dough. Stir in enough remaining flour to make dough that comes away from sides of bowl. Turn dough out onto lightly floured surface and knead until smooth and elastic. Place in greased bowl and turn to coat. Cover and let rise 1 to 1½ hours. Punch dough down. Proceed according to photos below.

Easter Basket

Use a round, oval, or egg-shaped metal mold to make the basket. Special half-egg-shaped metal molds, used to make chocolate eggs, are ideal. Cover mold with aluminum foil. This will make it easy to remove the basket once it has been baked.

about 7 cups all-purpose flour
2 packages active dry yeast
⅔ cup sugar
1¾ cups warm milk (105° to 115°F)
½ cup (1 stick) butter, melted
1½ teaspoons salt
1 egg beaten with 1 tablespoon water for brushing
1 tablespoon crystal sugar or crushed sugar cubes
Royal Icing, page 64

11-inch-long egg-shaped metal mold

Preheat oven to 400°F

1 **Divide dough into thirds** and set one third aside. Cut remaining two thirds into thirty-four equal-size pieces. Roll out each piece into 14-inch rope. Place four ropes on work surface. Place next four ropes across them in opposite direction (right angle). Weave in lattice pattern starting at center.

2 **Add thirteen additional ropes** (three or four at a time) in one direction and remaining thirteen ropes (three or four at a time) in opposite direction. Weave together.

3 **Place mold on waxed paper** and draw outline of mold. Place waxed paper on baking sheet, grease paper, and set aside. Cover outside of mold with aluminum foil. Place lattice of dough over mold. Press edge lightly and trim off excess dough.

4 **Pinch off small piece** of remaining dough. Roll into two ropes each 16 inches long. Twist together, shape into ring, and press ends together. Brush one side with beaten egg yolk mixture and place on top of mold, brushed side down. Place on unlined baking sheet and set aside to rise 30 to 40 minutes.

5 **Shape remaining dough** into three ropes, 44 inches long. Braid ropes to make rim and place on outline drawn on waxed paper. Pinch ends together and set aside to rise 30 to 40 minutes.

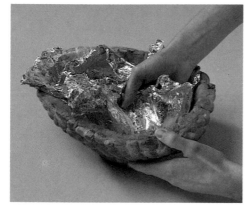

6 **Brush basket and rim** with beaten egg yolk mixture. Sprinkle crystal sugar over rim. Bake basket for 25 minutes. Bake rim about 20 minutes. Cool basket on baking sheet on wire rack. When basket is cool enough to handle, turn over and remove mold. Carefully peel off foil and cool completely. Remove rim from baking sheet and cool on rack.

7 **Spoon icing into pastry bag** fitted with small plain writing tip. Pipe icing around edge of basket. Place rim on bottom of springform pan and carefully slide rim onto edge of basket. Press gently and let stand until icing is set.

Austrian Braided Loaf

about 4 cups all-purpose flour
2 packages active dry yeast or 1 cake
(1 ounce) fresh yeast
$\frac{1}{3}$ cup sugar
1 cup warm milk (105° to 115°F)
$\frac{1}{2}$ cup (1 stick) butter, melted
1 teaspoon salt
grated peel of 1 lemon
1 egg · $\frac{2}{3}$ cup raisins
$\frac{1}{2}$ cup chopped mixed candied fruit peel
1 egg yolk beaten with 1 tablespoon
milk for glaze
Apricot Glaze, page 60
Fondant, page 60

Preheat oven to 375°F

Sift 3 cups flour into bowl and make well in center. Place yeast and 1 tablespoon sugar in well. Add milk and stir to dissolve yeast. Sprinkle a little flour over yeast mixture. Cover bowl and let stand 10 minutes. Beat butter, remaining sugar, salt, lemon peel, and egg until blended. Stir butter mixture, raisins, and candied fruit into flour-yeast mixture. Stir in enough remaining flour to make soft dough. Turn out dough onto lightly floured surface and knead until smooth and elastic. Place in greased bowl and turn to coat. Cover and let rise 1 to 1$\frac{1}{2}$ hours. Grease baking sheet. Punch

dough down and divide in half. Cut one piece of dough into four pieces. Shape into four 22-inch strands. Braid strands together (see photos, page 109). Place braid on prepared baking sheet. Brush with beaten egg yolk mixture. Cut second piece of dough into two pieces, one piece using two thirds of dough. Cut large piece into three equal pieces. Shape into three 18-inch strands. Braid strands together and place on top of large braid. Brush with beaten egg yolk mixture. Cut remaining piece of dough in half. Shape into two 18-inch strands. Twist strands together and place on top of loaf. Cover and let rise 1 hour, or until doubled in bulk. Brush with beaten egg yolk mixture. Bake in preheated oven 45 to 55 minutes or until golden brown. Brush with apricot glaze and frost with fondant while still warm.

Tirolean Fruit Loaf

A traditional fruit loaf is made with sour dough, which can be substituted for the plain yeast dough used below.

1 cup pitted prunes
¾ pound dried pears
½ pound dried figs
⅔ cup chopped hazelnuts
½ cup chopped walnuts
¼ cup chopped candied lemon peel
¼ cup chopped candied orange peel
⅔ cup raisins
⅔ cup currants
⅔ cup sugar
1 teaspoon ground cinnamon
½ teaspoon allspice
½ teaspoon aniseed
½ teaspoon salt
1 tablespoon dark rum
2 tablespoons lemon juice
1½ cups all-purpose flour, sifted
½ recipe Basic Yeast Dough, page 46
whole blanched almonds
glacé cherries

Preheat oven to 425°F

Place prunes, pears, and figs in bowl. Stir in 4 cups warm water, cover, and let stand overnight. Drain well and chop fruit. Dry bowl and return fruit to bowl. Add hazelnuts, walnuts, candied lemon and orange peel, raisins, currants, sugar, cinnamon, allspice, aniseed, salt, rum, and lemon juice. Stir well, cover, and let stand 1 hour. Add flour and mix well. Knead vigorously in bowl until mixture holds together. Divide mixture in half and shape into two loaves. Grease baking sheets. Cut yeast dough in half. Roll out each piece to thin rectangle large enough to wrap one fruit loaf. Wrap fruit loaves in dough, pinching seams to seal. Place loaves, seam side down, on prepared baking sheet. Cover and let stand 30 minutes. Brush tops with water and decorate with whole almonds and glacé cherries. Bake in preheated oven 10 minutes. Lower oven temperature to 350°F and bake 60 to 70 minutes or until crust is done. Remove from baking sheet and cool completely on wire rack.

Birnbrot

This loaf, which originated in farmhouse kitchens, was considered family fare rather than company food. Its main ingredient was dried pears. Modern recipes include so much dried fruit and almonds that the flavor of dried pears is less evident than it used to be. This is particularly true because it is now customary to flavor the fruit with kirsch, which may be added to the following recipe if desired.

¾ pound dried pears
⅓ pound dried figs
¾ cup pitted prunes
about 3 cups whole-wheat flour
1 package active dry yeast
½ cup sugar · ½ teaspoon salt
2 teaspoons cinnamon
¼ teaspoon ground cloves
grated peel of 1 lemon
⅓ cup chopped almonds
½ cup whole blanched hazelnuts

Preheat oven to 350°F

Place pears, figs, and prunes in bowl. Stir in 2 cups warm water and let stand overnight. Drain well, reserving ⅔ cup water. Coarsely chop fruit and set aside. Place flour in bowl and make well in center. Add yeast and 1 tablespoon sugar to well. Add reserved water and stir to dissolve yeast. Sprinkle a little flour over yeast mixture. Cover bowl and let stand 10 minutes. Add remaining sugar, salt, cinnamon, cloves, and lemon peel, and beat with wooden spoon to make stiff dough. Add chopped fruit, almonds, and hazelnuts, and stir until well blended. Grease baking sheet. Knead about ten to twelve strokes in bowl. Remove from bowl and shape into long loaf. Place on prepared baking sheet. Cover and let rise about 1 hour. Bake in preheated oven 60 to 70 minutes. Remove from baking sheet and cool on wire rack.

Grittibänz

This is a Swiss version of the German "Saint Nicholas loaf," a shaped loaf baked in many areas of Germany to celebrate Saint Nicholas' Day. These loaves are shaped into simple figures and the only decoration is 2 currants pressed into the dough for eyes. Saint Nicholas loaves from the Rhine area are rather elaborate, with Saint Nicholas often portrayed on horseback with an obligatory clay pipe in his mouth.

Swiss Grittibänz, originally called 'Chriddibenz'' when it first appeared in 1850, is intricate in shape, regardless of whether it comes from a bakery or is homemade.

about 6 cups all-purpose flour
2 packages active dry yeast
$\frac{1}{4}$ cup sugar
1½ cups warm milk (105° to 115°F)
$\frac{1}{3}$ cup butter, melted and cooled
2 eggs · 1 teaspoon salt
grated peel of 1 lemon
2 egg yolks beaten with 1 tablespoon
water for glaze

Preheat oven to 375°F

Sift 4 cups flour into bowl and make well in center. Place yeast and 1 tablespoon sugar in well. Add milk and stir to dissolve yeast. Sprinkle yeast mixture with flour. Cover bowl with clean towel and let stand 10 minutes or until cracks appear in flour layer over yeast mixture. Beat remaining sugar, butter, eggs, salt, and lemon peel until blended. Add to bowl with 1 cup flour. Beat vigorously with wooden spoon until smooth. Stir in enough remaining flour to make smooth dough that comes away from sides of bowl. Knead dough until smooth and elastic. Place dough in greased bowl and turn to coat. Cover and let rise about 1 hour. Grease baking sheets. Punch dough down and divide in half. Set once piece of dough aside. Divide remaining piece of dough into eight pieces: a large piece for the body, seven smaller pieces for the head, arms, legs, hat, and trimmings. Flatten large piece of dough, shape body, and place on prepared baking sheet. Brush with beaten egg yolk mixture. Shape head, arms, legs, hat, and trimmings. Attach to body with egg yolk mixture. Repeat with reserved piece of dough. Cover figures and let rise 20 to 25 minutes. Brush with beaten egg yolk mixture. Bake 30 to 35 minutes or until golden brown. Remove from baking sheets and cool on wire racks.

Panettone

This is a popular traditional Christmas cake and, like stollen, is sold in many bakeries at Christmas. Unfortunately, Panettone bought in a bakery, however good it may be, is rarely as good as the homemade cakes of Milan. Panettone cake pans are available at most specialty cookware stores, but if the traditional pan is not available, the cake can be made in a deep cake pan instead.

about 3½ cups all-purpose flour
2 packages active dry yeast
½ cup sugar
⅔ cup warm milk (105° to 115°F)
⅔ cup butter, melted and cooled
1½ teaspoons salt
grated peel of 1 lemon
¼ teaspoon nutmeg
6 egg yolks
1 cup raisins
⅓ cup chopped almonds
⅓ cup chopped candied orange peel
⅓ cup chopped candied lemon peel
1 egg yolk beaten with 1 tablespoon milk for glaze
Apricot Glaze, page 60
Fondant, page 60

Panettone cake pan or 3- to 4-inch deep 8-inch cake pan, greased

Preheat oven to 400°F

Sift flour into large bowl and make well in center. Place yeast and 1 tablespoon sugar in well. Add milk and stir to dissolve yeast. Sprinkle a little flour over yeast mixture. Cover bowl and let stand 10 minutes or until cracks appear in flour-yeast mixture. Beat butter, remaining sugar, salt, lemon peel, nutmeg, and egg yolks until blended. Stir butter mixture into flour-yeast mixture and beat vigorously with wooden spoon to make smooth dough. Stir in raisins, almonds, and orange and lemon peels. Turn out dough onto lightly floured surface and knead until smooth and elastic. Place dough in greased bowl and turn to coat. Cover and let rise 1 to 1½ hours. Punch dough down. Shape dough into flattened ball and place in prepared pan. Cover and let rise until doubled in bulk. Brush top with beaten egg yolk mixture. Bake in preheated oven 10 minutes. Lower oven temperature to 375°F and bake 50 to 60 minutes or until golden brown and cake sounds hollow when tapped on bottom. Remove from pan and cool completely on wire rack. Brush with apricot glaze and cover with fondant if desired.

Christmas Stollen

1⅓ cups raisins
¾ cup chopped almonds
⅓ cup chopped candied lemon peel
⅓ cup chopped candied orange peel
2 tablespoons dark rum
about 5¾ cups all-purpose flour
2 packages active dry yeast
½ cup sugar
1¼ cups warm milk (105° to 115°F)
¾ cup (1½ sticks) butter, melted
3 eggs
1½ teaspoons salt
1 teaspoon vanilla
grated peel of 1 lemon
4 tablespoons butter, melted and cooled
for brushing
confectioners' sugar for dusting

Preheat oven to 375°F

Place raisins, almonds, and candied lemon and orange peels in bowl. Stir in rum and set aside. Sift 4 cups flour into bowl and make well in center. Place yeast and 1 tablespoon sugar in well. Add milk and stir to dissolve yeast. Sprinkle a little flour over yeast mixture. Cover bowl and let stand 10 minutes or until cracks appear in flour-yeast mixture. Beat remaining sugar, ¾ cup melted butter, eggs, salt, vanilla, and grated lemon peel until blended. Add to bowl with 1 cup flour. Beat vigorously with wooden spoon until smooth. Stir in fruit-nut mixture and enough remaining flour to make soft dough that comes away from sides of bowl. Knead dough until smooth and elastic. Place dough in greased bowl and turn to coat. Cover and let rise 1 to 1½ hours. Grease baking sheets. Punch dough down and divide in half.

Roll out each piece of dough on lightly floured surface to oval 12 inches long. Press side of hand down center of oval to flatten. Brush with melted butter and fold in half lengthwise in traditional stollen shape. Place on prepared baking sheets. Cover and let rise 30 minutes. Bake in preheated oven 30 to 40 minutes or until loaves sound hollow when tapped on bottom. Remove from baking sheets and cool on wire racks. Brush with melted butter and sprinkle heavily with confectioners' sugar. Coating of butter and sugar will help keep Stollen moist.

Almond Stollen

about 3½ cups all-purpose flour
1 package active dry yeast
⅓ cup sugar
¾ cup warm milk (105° to 115°F)
⅓ cup butter, melted
1 teaspoon salt
grated peel of 1 lemon
¼ teaspoon grated nutmeg · 2 eggs
½ teaspoon almond extract
1¼ cups finely chopped blanched almonds
⅓ cup finely chopped candied lemon peel
¼ cup finely chopped candied orange peel
2 tablespoons butter, melted and cooled
for brushing
confectioners' sugar for dusting

Preheat oven to 375°F

Sift flour into bowl and make well in center. Place yeast and 1 tablespoon sugar in well. Add milk and stir to dissolve yeast. Sprinkle a little flour over yeast mixture. Cover bowl and let stand 10 minutes or until cracks appear in flour-yeast mixture. Beat butter, remaining sugar, salt, lemon peel, nutmeg, eggs, and almond extract until blended. Stir butter mixture into flour-yeast mixture and beat vigorously with wooden spoon to make smooth dough. Stir in almonds and candied lemon and orange peels. Turn dough out onto lightly floured surface and knead until smooth and elastic. Place dough in greased bowl and turn to coat. Cover and let rise 1 to 1½ hours. Punch dough down. Grease baking sheet.

Roll out dough on lightly floured surface to 14-inch oval. Press side of hand down center of oval to flatten. Brush with melted butter and fold oval in half lengthwise in traditional Stollen shape. Place on prepared baking sheet, cover, and let rise 20 to 30 minutes. Bake in preheated oven 30 to 40 minutes or until loaf sounds hollow when tapped on bottom. Remove from baking sheet and cool on wire rack. Brush with melted butter while still warm and sprinkle heavily with confectioners' sugar.

Pistachio Stollen

about 3½ cups all-purpose flour
1 package active dry yeast · ⅓ cup sugar
¾ cup warm milk (105° to 115°F)
⅓ cup butter, melted
1 teaspoon salt
grated peel of ½ lemon · 2 eggs
⅓ cup finely chopped candied orange peel
¼ cup finely chopped candied lemon peel
4 ounces marzipan
¾ cup chopped pistachios
1 tablespoon maraschino liqueur
2 tablespoons butter, melted and cooled
for brushing
confectioners' sugar for dusting

Preheat oven to 375°F

Sift flour into bowl and make well in center. Place yeast and 1 tablespoon sugar in well. Add milk and stir to dissolve yeast. Sprinkle a little flour over yeast mixture. Cover bowl and let stand 10 minutes or until cracks appear in flour-yeast mixture. Beat butter, remaining sugar, salt, lemon peel, and eggs until blended. Stir butter mixture into flour-yeast mixture and beat vigorously with wooden spoon to make smooth dough. Stir in candied orange and lemon peels. Turn dough out onto lightly floured surface and knead until smooth and elastic. Place dough in greased bowl and turn to coat. Cover and let rise 1 to 1½ hours. Blend marzipan, pistachios, and maraschino liqueur. Shape into ½-inch-thick roll. Cut into small cubes and set aside. Punch dough down then knead in marzipan-pistachio cubes quickly so they remain whole. Grease baking sheet.

Roll out dough and shape according to directions for Almond Stollen, this page. Place on prepared baking sheet, cover, and let rise 20 to 30 minutes. Bake in preheated oven 30 to 40 minutes or until loaf sounds hollow when tapped on bottom. Remove from baking sheet and cool on wire rack. Brush with melted butter while still warm and sprinkle heavily with confectioners' sugar.

Chocolate Christmas Cake

1 cup heavy cream
14 ounces semisweet chocolate
6 tablespoons (¾ stick) unsalted butter, softened
5 tablespoons dark rum
Chocolate Genoise, page 30
1 tablespoon Cointreau

To decorate:
chocolate fans, page 66
finely chopped chocolate
marzipan St. Nicholas
chocolate leaves

Prepare Ganache Cream with heavy cream, chocolate, butter, and 3 tablespoons rum following directions on page 57. Cut genoise into three layers. Spread one layer with Ganache Cream and top with second layer. Sprinkle with 2 tablespoons dark rum and spread with Ganache Cream. Place third layer on top. Sprinkle top layer with Cointreau. Spread remaining Ganache Cream over top and around sides of cake. Sprinkle finely chopped chocolate around bottom edge of cake.

Decorate cake with overlapping circles of chocolate fans. Place marzipan St. Nicholas in center of cake and arrange chocolate leaves on plate around cake.

Bûche de Noël

The chocolate log is a traditional French Christmas Cake that can be decorated in a variety of ways. The basic cake is always a plain sponge, usually filled with chocolate or mocha buttercream. It is sometimes decorated with green marzipan leaves, chocolate flowers or, as illustrated above, meringue mushrooms.

Sponge:
8 egg yolks
½ cup sugar
¼ teaspoon salt
grated peel of 1 lemon
4 egg whites
⅔ cup cake flour
3 tablespoons cornstarch

Buttercream filling:
1 cup superfine sugar
1 vanilla bean
6 egg yolks
⅓ cup unsweetened cocoa
3 ounces semisweet chocolate, melted
1 to 2 tablespoons powdered instant coffee
1½ cups (3 sticks) unsalted butter, softened

To decorate:
marzipan leaves
meringue mushrooms

Prepare sponge roll according to step-by-step photos on page 30. Prepare buttercream according to directions for French Buttercream, page 55. Cream cocoa, chocolate, and coffee with butter (step 3). Spread half the buttercream over cake. Roll cake and place on serving plate, seam side down. Spread thin layer of buttercream over cake. Spoon remaining buttercream into pastry bag fitted with open star tip. Pipe buttercream in lengthwise strips on cake, covering cake completely. Decorate with marzipan leaves and meringue mushrooms.

Galette des rois

This flat puff pastry is a traditional dish served for Twelfth Night in the region of France north of the Loire Valley. Its popularity is rapidly spreading to southern France as well.

1⅓ pounds Puff Pastry, page 42
2 cups Almond Cream, page 56
1 egg yolk beaten with 1 tablespoon milk for brushing
¼ cup sugar
1 tablespoon dark rum

Preheat oven to 450°F

Galette des rois is made in the same way Pithiviers, page 136, is made. Roll out pastry and cut into two 10-inch circles. Spread almond cream over one pastry circle on ungreased baking sheet to within 1 inch of edge. Brush pastry edge with beaten egg yolk mixture. Place second pastry circle over filling and press edges firmly together to seal. Hold blade of sharp knife at right angle to edge of pastry and draw blade up quickly to flute. Refrigerate 30 minutes.

Brush top of galette with beaten egg yolk mixture. Cut leaf designs in top layer of pastry with sharp pointed knife. Be careful not to make cuts too deep or filling will run out during baking. Refrigerate 15 minutes. Bake in preheated oven 15 minutes. Lower oven temperature to 400°F and bake 20 to 25 minutes or until golden brown.

Place sugar and 3 tablespoons water in small saucepan and bring to a boil, stirring until sugar is dissolved. Boil until mixture is syrupy. Remove from heat and stir in rum. Brush syrup over top as soon as it comes out of oven.

Twelfth Night Cake

Baking a special cake on January 6 to celebrate Epiphany of Twelfth Night is an old custom that has its origin in Roman Saturnalia, the feast in honor of the god Saturn. This "festival of gluttony," in which everyone could take part, was carried over into early Christian Europe. One custom of the feast was the choosing of a king. A bean was hidden in a cake, and whoever found it became king for a day. The tradition of including a bean in a cake—or a coin—still survives today. The custom of making an Epiphany cake was revived in Switzerland after World War II and remains popular today.

⅔ cup raisins
⅓ cup chopped almonds
1 tablespoon dark rum
about 3½ cups all-purpose flour
1 package active dry yeast
⅓ cup sugar
¾ cup warm milk (105° to 115°F)
6 tablespoons (¾ stick) butter, melted
1 teaspoon salt
grated peel of 1 lemon
⅛ teaspoon nutmeg
2 eggs
1 egg yolk beaten with 1 tablespoon milk for glaze

Preheat oven to 375°F

Place raisins and almonds in small bowl. Stir in rum and set aside. Sift flour into bowl and make well in center. Place yeast and 1 tablespoon sugar in well. Add milk and stir to dissolve yeast. Sprinkle a little flour over yeast mixture. Cover bowl and let stand 10 minutes or until cracks appear in flour-yeast mixture. Beat butter, remaining sugar, salt, lemon peel, nutmeg, and eggs until blended. Stir butter mixture into flour-yeast mixture and beat vigorously with wooden spoon to make smooth dough. Stir in reserved raisins and almonds. Turn dough out onto lightly floured surface and knead until smooth and elastic. Place dough in greased bowl and turn to coat. Cover and let rise 1 to 1½ hours. Punch dough down and divide in half. Shape one piece of dough into flattened ball, about 6 inches in diameter. Place on large greased baking sheet and brush with beaten egg yolk mixture. Cut remaining dough into seven equal-size pieces. Shape each piece into flattened ball, pinching and tucking ends under. Dip tops of balls in beaten egg yolk mixture and attach around large ball on baking sheet, glazed side up. Let rise, uncovered, 20 to 30 minutes. Brush with beaten egg yolk mixture. Bake in preheated oven 30 to 35 minutes or until golden brown. Remove from baking sheet and cool completely on wire rack.

English Wedding Cake

It is difficult to determine whether this cake is simply something to eat or a work of art. Cakes decorated in this way are part of a traditional wedding ceremony in many parts of the world. However, in Britain, part of the tradition is that the cake served is always a rich fruit cake, whereas in the United States, a bride often serves her favorite kind of cake. It is the icing and decoration that is similar throughout much of the world. One reason fruit cake is so popular in England is that the cake will keep for months. In addition, the cake is firm enough to permit two, three, or even four cakes to be arranged in tiers, one above the other. Because fruit cake keeps so well, it is customary in Britain to set aside one tier and serve it at the christening of the first child or on the first wedding anniversary.

The following recipe will make one 12-inch round cake or one 11-inch square. Cut the recipe in half to make a small tier. Cover the cake with several layers of Royal Icing.

$1\frac{1}{2}$ cups dark raisins
$2\frac{3}{4}$ cups golden raisins
4 cups currants
1 cup chopped mixed candied fruit
$\frac{2}{3}$ cup chopped almonds
$\frac{1}{3}$ cup brandy
$1\frac{1}{2}$ cups (3 sticks) plus 2 tablespoons
butter, softened
2 cups firmly packed light brown sugar
$\frac{1}{2}$ teaspoon salt
8 eggs
grated peel of 3 lemons
2 teaspoons cinnamon
1 teaspoon nutmeg
2 tablespoons molasses
$3\frac{1}{4}$ cups all-purpose flour
1 teaspoon baking powder
Apricot Glaze, page 60
$2\frac{1}{2}$ pounds marzipan

Royal icing:
5 egg whites
$12\frac{1}{2}$ cups confectioners' sugar, sifted
juice of $\frac{1}{2}$ lemon

12-inch deep cake or springform pan,
greased and lined

Preheat oven to 275°F

Christmas Cake

This is a traditional British Christmas cake and, like the wedding cake, it is made from a dark, heavy fruit cake. Christmas cakes are usually more highly spiced than wedding cakes but, like the wedding cake, they are covered with marzipan and Royal Icing.

A Christmas cake can be a genuine work of art as shown on a cake decorated by Susan Greenway in the photograph above. After the second layer of icing has been applied, the sides are given a rippled effect with an icing comb. The decorative edge is made in several stages because the icing must be allowed to harden between each step. Santa Claus is outlined with a stencil and then filled in with white and tinted icing. A simple decoration can be made instead by spreading the second layer of icing on roughly with a knife to create the effect of deep snow.

Soak raisins, currants, candied fruit, and almonds in brandy overnight in covered bowl. Cream butter, brown sugar, and salt in large bowl until fluffy. Beat in eggs one at a time. Stir in lemon peel, cinnamon, nutmeg, and molasses until blended. Sift flour and baking powder and fold in butter-egg mixture. Fold in fruit-brandy mixture. Pour into prepared pan and smooth top. Bake in preheated oven 3 hours or until cake tester inserted in center of cake comes out clean. If top of cake browns too fast, cover with double thickness of greased waxed paper during last 30 minutes of baking. Cool cake in pan on wire rack 1 to 2 hours. Remove from pan and cool completely on rack. Peel off lining paper and prick bottom of cake with metal skewer. Spoon brandy over bottom of cake, wrap in waxed paper, and overwrap with aluminum foil. Store in airtight container at least two weeks before proceeding to next step. Brush top of cake with apricot glaze. Roll out about one third of marzipan to $\frac{1}{2}$-inch thickness and use to cover top of cake. Brush sides of cake with apricot glaze. Roll out remaining marzipan in long strips and place around sides of cake.

To make icing, beat egg whites in large bowl until frothy. Gradually beat in confectioners' sugar and lemon juice, beating constantly. Beat until icing is very stiff and shiny. Keep bowl of icing covered with damp cloth to prevent it from drying out. Cover cake with thin layer of icing (see photos alongside). Let cake stand several hours or until icing is firm and dry. Repeat process two or three more times.

When iced cake is completely dry, decorations can be added. Mark patterns with stencils. Use rotating cake stand to make the job as easy as possible. An assortment of very small piping tips are essential.

Susan Greenway is the wedding cake specialist at the London Inter-Continental Hotel. The decorations on this two-tier wedding cake clearly illustrate her artistic talent. She used parchment paper piping bags and an assortment of small tips. The cake was placed on a rotating cake stand to make icing and decorating as easy as possible.

Almond Buttercream Cake

This buttercream cake has been decorated with amusing marzipan figures. These figures are available in some specialty candy shops. They can also be made at home with a good supply of marzipan, food coloring, and a talent for creativity. Use them to turn a simple cake into something truly unique.

Cake:
6 eggs separated
2 ounces marzipan
1 teaspoon vanilla
¼ teaspoon salt
½ cup sugar
⅔ cup sponge cake crumbs
½ cup ground almonds
⅓ cup all-purpose flour

Buttercream:
¾ cup sugar
5 tablespoons cornstarch, sifted
3 egg yolks
2 cups milk
1 teaspoon vanilla
1½ cups (3 sticks) unsalted butter,
softened
1 ounce semisweet chocolate, melted and
cooled
1 tablespoon Amaretto liqueur
1 tablespoon sugar syrup
2 tablespoons toasted ground almonds
marzipan figures
glacé cherries

10-inch springform pan, greased and
bottom lined

Preheat oven to 375°F

Beat 1 egg yolk into marzipan until creamy. Add remaining egg yolks, vanilla, salt, and sugar, and beat until well blended. Beat egg whites until stiff and fold into marzipan mixture. Stir cake crumbs, ground almonds, and flour, and fold into marzipan mixture. Pour into prepared pan and smooth top. Bake in preheated oven 30 to 40 minutes or until center springs back when lightly pressed. Cool in pan on wire rack 10 minutes. Remove from pan and cool completely on rack. Wrap cake and let stand overnight. Prepare buttercream according to directions for German Buttercream, page 54. Add melted chocolate to one quarter of buttercream. Cut cake into three layers. Place one cake layer on serving plate and spread with chocolate buttercream. Top with second layer. Blend Amaretto and sugar syrup and sprinkle 1 tablespoon over cake layer. Spread with buttercream and top with third layer. Sprinkle remaining 1 tablespoon Amaretto mixture over top of cake. Spoon about ⅔ cup buttercream into pastry bag fitted with open star tip and set aside. Spread remaining buttercream over top and around sides of cake. Refrigerate 30 minutes. Run icing comb around sides of cake and sprinkle top with toasted ground almonds. Pipe buttercream in rosettes on top of cake and decorate with marzipan figures and glacé cherries.

Chocolate Hedgehogs

These jolly hedgehog cakes illustrate the fact that there are more ways to use sponge cake than just to make the usual round cake. Cut a round sponge cake to make the hedgehogs or bake them in heatproof mixing bowls. This recipe makes two hedgehogs.

Cake:
5 eggs
2 egg yolks
¾ cup sugar
½ teaspoon grated lemon peel
1 cup cake flour
¼ cup cornstarch
6 tablespoons butter, melted and clarified

Buttercream:
¾ cup sugar
5 tablespoons cornstarch, sifted
3 egg yolks
2 cups milk
1 teaspoon vanilla
1½ cups (3 sticks) unsalted butter,
softened
3 ounces semisweet chocolate, melted and
cooled

Decoration:
about ¾ cup slivered almonds
18 ounces semisweet chocolate, melted
marzipan
Royal Icing, page 64

two 1-quart heatproof mixing bowls

Preheat oven to 375°F

Grease and flour mixing bowls. Prepare cake according to directions for Genoise Mixture, page 28. Pour mixture into prepared bowls. Bake in preheated oven 25 to 35 minutes or until center springs back when lightly pressed. Cool in bowls on wire rack 10 minutes. Remove from bowls and cool completely on rack. Prepare buttercream according to directions for German Buttercream, page 54. Add 3 ounces melted chocolate to buttercream and beat until blended. Cut each cake into four layers. (Trim and shape cakes to resemble hedgehogs, see photo.) Spread chocolate buttercream between layers. Cover hedgehogs with thin layer of buttercream. Refrigerate 30 minutes. Push slivered almonds into cake. Place on wire rack set over jelly-roll pan. Pour melted chocolate over hedgehogs, covering them completely. Let stand until set. Make nose and eyes with marzipan and cover marzipan with Royal Icing. Attach to hedgehogs with dab of icing and finish eyes with dab of chocolate.

Glossary

A

Agar-Agar, jellying agent made from several types of East Asian seaweeds.

Agen prunes, semi-dried plums, a specialty of Agen, a French town on the Garonne.

Almond Cream, an almond confectioners' cream made with butter, ground almonds, icing sugar, eggs, and cornstarch. Used for cake fillings and also in flans either alone or with fruit, see page 56.

Almond essence, finely ground, sweet almonds are heated in milk or water and then drained through a muslin cloth. Used for almond milk, blancmange, etc.

Almond liqueur, an aromatic liqueur made by distilling pulped almonds.

Almond paste → Marzipan.

Almond sponge mixture, a sponge mixture made by beating the egg yolks and whites separately and adding ground almonds or marzipan with the flour.

Amaretto → Almond liqueur.

Angelica, a plant classed as an herb, the stalks of which are candied and used as a decoration for desserts.

Antilles rum, type of rum distilled in the Greater and Lesser Antilles.

Apostle cake → Brioches, see pages 116–17.

Apricot brandy, a brandy-based fruit liqueur made with fresh or dried apricots.

Apricot Glaze, a glaze made with apricot jam, sugar, water, and lemon juice. Used mainly as an insulating layer between the cake and the icing or other covering, see page 60.

Arancini, dried and candied orange peel cut into round slices.

Armagnac, famous brandy from southwest France with minimum alcohol content of 38 percent proof. It matures in oak vats and its flavor is excellent for cake fillings.

Arrak, a brandy with three different methods of preparation. Usually made from rice, but occasionally from molasses and in Southeast Asia from palm wine (made by tapping the sap of the coconut palm). Excellent for flavoring cream fillings.

B

Baba, ring-shaped yeast cake soaked in spirits or syrup.

Baiser, meringue mixture of egg whites and sugar, see page 34.

Baumé, Antoine, French chemist (1728–1804), inventor of the saccharometer. The scale is divided into units known as Bé, a shortened version of his name.

Bavarian Cream, type of custard made with egg yolk, sugar, milk, vanilla, gelatine, and whipped cream, see page 53.

Bavaroise → Bavarian Cream.

Beef suet, once used in the baking of Christmas Stollen and mixed with butter to make puff pastry.

Bénédictine, strongly-flavored, French herb liqueur.

Bergamot liqueur, pear liqueur.

Bienenstich, flat yeast cake spread with a mixture of butter, sugar, honey, and flaked almonds before baking and filled with whipped cream once cold. See Almond and Custard Slices, page 119.

Binding agent, a substance that thickens a liquid and makes it smooth. Examples include: corn, rice, and potato starch, Agar-Agar. gelatine, tragacanth, pectin, and gum arabic.

Biscuits à la cuiller → Sponge fingers.

Biskotte, Austrian term for sponge fingers.

Black bun, Scottish fruit cake with extremely high currant content.

Bremen Klaben, a kind of stollen made with yeast dough and containing almonds, raisins, and currants. Baked for special occasions particularly at Christmas.

Bun cases, paper cases with pleated sides in various sizes for small cakes, petits four, or sweets.

Butter pastry, Austrian term for puff pastry.

C

Calvados, French apple brandy which matures for about six years in oak casks. Named after the area in which it originated.

Cannelle, cinnamon bark.

Cannelons, tubes of marzipan filled with whipped cream or light buttercream.

Caramel, brown, burnt sugar.

Chaudeau, a frothy wine sauce, served hot.

Chocolate, cooking, a substitute for eating chocolate, made basically from vegetable fat and with a low cocoa content.

Cherry brandy, sweet, brandy-based liqueur, made from cherry juice and crushed cherry stones.

Chestnut → Marron.

Chestnut puree → Marron puree.

Christmas log → Bûche de Noël, see page 172.

Coffee essence, extremely strong extract of coffee beans.

Glossary

Cognac, French brandy from the Charente region, which has to mature for several years in oak casks.

Cointreau, light French liqueur, flavored with orange rind.

Confectioners' cream, *crème patissière*, made with sugar, egg yolk, flour or cornstarch, milk, and vanilla, see page 50.

Copra, dried kernel of the coconut which is rich in fat.

Cordial Médoc, French liqueur made from Cognac, peel of curaçao oranges and dessert wine.

Cornstarch, swells in liquid at 140–150°F. Used as a binding agent in the making of custards, sweet sauces, etc.; binds at simmering point, see page 12.

Cream of tartar, sour potash of tartaric acid which during fermentation precipitates the production of alcohol.

Crème, term applied to a number of very sweet French liqueurs, made generally from fruit, for example:
Crème d'ananas – pineapple liqueur
Crème de cacao – chocolate liqueur
Crème de cassis – blackcurrant liqueur
Crème des fraises – strawberry liqueur
Crème de menthe – green mint liqueur
Crème de moka – coffee liqueur
Crème de prunelle – sloe liqueur.

Crème bavaroise – Bavarian Cream, see page 53.

Crème Chantilly, sweet whipped cream, see page 51.

Crème de truffes, another name for Canache Cream, see page 56.

Crème fouettée, whipped cream.

Crème patissière, confectioners' cream, see page 50.

Crème Saint-Honoré, Chiboust Cream, a light cream for cake fillings, see page 51.

Crumbs, grated bread, sponge, or biscuits.

Curaçao, orange liqueur, made originally with the rinds of curaçao oranges, cane sugar, and brandy; made nowadays with a base of wine brandy, gin, and other brandies.

Curds, the cheeselike substance produced when milk turns sour.

Custard sauce, eggs beaten with sugar and milk (flavored with vanilla or lemon rind). Used with fruit pies, for example.

D

Diplomat cream, cold vanilla custard (confectioners' cream) flavored with a liqueur and mixed with an equal quantity of whipped cream.

Doughnuts, balls of yeast dough which are deep fried. English and American term.

Duchesses, small choux pastries.

E

Éclair, long French cakes of choux pastry, filled with custard or cream and then iced, see page 157.

Egg Canache, a Canache Cream made with milk chocolate and egg yolks.

English cream → Vanilla sauce.

Essence, concentrated liquid used for flavoring.

F

Feuillantines, small cakes of puff pastry.

Fig cake, ground hazelnuts beaten with sugar, butter, and egg yolks and then egg whites followed by flour, cinnamon, grated nutmeg, chopped dates, walnuts, and figs and grated lemon rind folded into the mixture. The cake pan is lined with Linz pastry, filled with the mixture and baked.

Florentines, flat cakes which keep well, made with butter, sugar, honey, cream, almonds, and candied orange peel. These round cakes are coated with chocolate after cooking and decorated with an icing comb.

Fondant, fondant icing. A thick white icing of boiled sugar, in contrast to Royal Icing, which is made cold from egg whites and sugar. To use, fondant should be warmed to body temperature over a pan of hot water, see page 60.

Frangipane, cooked cake filling made with flour or cornstarch, eggs, milk, and vanilla mixed with finely crushed macaroons. A mixture of Almond Cream and confectioners' cream is also known as frangipane.

G

Galette, plain flat cake containing a lot of butter and cooked on a baking sheet.

Gâteau, French term for any type of large cake. They can vary in shape, be filled or unfilled, iced or uniced, but are usually decorated in some way, although this is not essential.

Gaufres, French term for waffles.

Gelatine, pure, tasteless substance derived by prolonged boiling of animal or fish bones. A jellying agent in powder or leaf form. Its main use in baking is for custards and jellies. There is no difference in strength between leaf or powder gelatine. Leaf gelatine should be soaked in cold water for 10 minutes, squeezed out, then added to the hot liquid. Powdered gelatine should be dissolved in a little hot water in a bowl over a saucepan of hot water.

Genoise, fine sponge mixture, see pages 28–9.

Gingerbread glaze, edible starch heated and boiled with water. Used to give a shine to gingerbread, macaroons, etc.

Glacé fondante → Fondant.

Glacé icing, sugar stirred to a thick paste with hot water and flavored.

Glacé royale → Royal Icing.

Glucose, grape sugar or dextrose, together with fructose, a natural sugar found in fruit.

Grand Marnier, French Cognac-based liqueur, flavored with bitter oranges.

Grappa, Italian grape brandy.

Grillage, Austrian term for melted sugar with coarsely chopped nuts.

Gum arabic (Senegal gum, acacia gum). Obtained from the sap of tropical acacia trees. Comes as a colorless powder to be diluted in twice the amount of water and used to glaze macaroons, etc.

Fruit brandy, made from fermented fruit or fruit juice, either berries, core, or stone fruits. Unfermented fruit distilled with alcohol produces a spirit, e.g., raspberry spirit.

Fruit puree, pulped and strained fruit.

Fruit syrup, fruit juice and sugar.

H

Hazelnut cake, mixture of Genoise sponge with ground hazelnuts, baked in round or square pan. The cake is cut into four or five rounds, then sandwiched together and coated in hazelnut buttercream. Decorated with chopped, toasted hazelnuts and icing sugar.

Hutzelbrot, highly spiced fruit loaf of yeast dough with prunes and stewed pears. An Advent specialty.

I

Icing, sugar or chocolate coating for desserts, or small and large cakes.

Indians, Austrian name for Chocolate-covered Sponge Drops, see pages 154–5.

Irish Mist, name of a liqueur which consists of Irish whiskey flavored with herbs.

Italian meringue, whisked egg whites sweetened with sugar syrup, used in buttercream.

J

Jelly, jellified fruit juice, eaten plain or with a filling.

K

Kipferl, Austrian term for croissants.

Kirschröster, easy cherry cake, made with cherries, grated bread crumbs, and an egg custard.

Kirsch, brandy made with the fermented pulp of small black cherries. Made in the Black Forest and Vosges areas and in Switzerland.

Kithul palm (*Caryota urens*), type of sugar palm; sap is tapped from the trunk and flower buds to make sugar.

Klöben, crescent-shaped yeast cakes, filled with chopped almonds, currants, and candied peel.

Königskuchen, a cake made by creaming butter with egg yolks, sugar, and grated lemon peel before folding in flour, whisked egg white, and dried fruit. Baked in greased, paper-lined loaf pan. See Rum-Raisin Cake, page 76.

Kransekager, Danish specialty. Rings of macaroon mixture decorated with piped Royal Icing and put together to form a tall, towerlike cake.

L

Lebkuchen, general term covering spice cake, gingerbread, and honey cake.

Lemon sugar (orange sugar), cube or loaf sugar used to grate the rind of citrus fruit.

Liebesknochen, German name for éclairs.

Linzertorte, almond shortcrust, see pages 40–1.

M

Macaroons, small cakes made with ground almonds, sugar, and egg whites.

Mandarinette, a liqueur flavored with mandarin peel.

Maraschino, Italian liqueur made with a brandy of fermented Marasca cherries (Dalmatia) and spices.

Margarine, butter and fat substitute, originally usually made from beef suet but nowadays from vegetable fats.

Marille, Austrian name for apricots.

Marron, edible chestnut (*Castanea sativa* or *C. vesca*). Cultivated chiefly in the Mediterranean region. Available fresh in autumn and winter, but all the year round sweetened or unsweetened in cans or in puree form.

Marron puree, butter and sugar are heated and then used to caramelize peeled chestnuts before milk is added and cooked until the chestnuts are soft. It is then pureed in a blender and mixed with whipped cream.

Marsala, Italian dessert wine, sweet or dry. Excellent for flavoring of custards.

Marzipan, preparation made with sweet almonds and sugar. Used to decorate and cover cakes, in almond cream and in a variety of cake mixtures.

Melon or pumpkin seeds, these dried seeds can be used instead of almonds, particularly to sprinkle on cakes.

Meringue, whisked egg white that contains no trace of yolk. Sugar is gradually added during whisking. Also small cakes of sweetened whisked egg whites which are dried out in the oven rather than baked, see page 34.

Mikado Gâteau, consists of three genoise sponges and three meringue bases, sandwiched together and coated with rum buttercream, sprinkled with chopped, toasted almonds, and dusted with icing sugar.

Mince pie, filled with a mixture of raisins, sultanas, chopped almonds and apple, suet, sugar, spices, and rum or brandy. Baked between two layers of puff pastry to make small tarts, eaten hot. British specialty particularly for Christmas.

Mirabell, a brandy made with mirabelle plums which can be produced either by the fermentation process or by distilling unfermented fruit.

Mirliton, small puff pastry tarts.

Mostacciole, small, rectangular, Italian cakes, flavored with cloves and nutmeg and covered in chocolate.

Muffins, English yeast-dough cakes.

Muffkuchen, cinnamon and almond sponge cake from Germany.

N

Napfkuchen, cakes, usually of yeast mixture, baked in a deep, round (Gugelhupf) pan.

Necci, Italian chestnut cake.

Negerküsse, small sponges or cookies sandwiched with meringue as whipped cream and coated in chocolate.

Nid de Pâques, French Easter basket. A sponge ring sandwiched with buttercream and piped all over with a spaghetti piping nozzle. Decorated with sugar eggs.

Nonpareilles, hundreds and thousands; tiny, colored sugar sweets.

P

Palmier, small puff pastry cakes, also known as pigs' ears.

Paris-Brest cake, choux mixture piped in a thick ring onto a baking sheet and baked. Cut through horizontally and filled with Saint-Honoré cream mixed with crushed praline. Dusted with icing sugar.

Paris cream, a chocolate cream, made by boiling ½ pint double cream and stirring in 8 ounces plain chocolate. When cold it is whisked (Canache, see page 56).

Pâté à choux, Choux Pastry, see page 36.

Pâté brisée, rub-in pastry, see page 37.

Pâté feuilletée, Puff Pastry, see pages 42–3.

Pâté levée, yeast pastry, see page 44.

Pâté sucrée, sweet shortcrust, see page 38.

Peach Brandy, a liqueur with brandy base, made with fresh or dried peaches.

Pectin, a soluble jellying agent obtained from plants, which combines with fruit acids and sugar to form a jelly. Extracted from unripe fruit such as apples, quinces, currants, lemons, and sugar beet. Commercially prepared apple or beet pectin comes in liquid or powder form. Used in flan glazes and to make jellies and jams.

Persipan, marzipan substitute, made by heating the ground kernels of apricot or peach stones with sugar.

Petits fours, small cookies served with after-dinner coffee, can be filled with cream or iced, or served plain.

Pie, a pastry dish, either savory or sweet, made in a ceramic dish with a filling and lid of shortcrust, puff, or rub-in pastry.

Pigs' ears, puff pastry rolled on sugar, folded twice into the center and cut into thick slices. Caramelizes during baking, see page 127.

Pinza, Italian yeast-dough Easter bread which has a deep cross cut into the top.

Piping Icing, a very thick sugar icing applied with a piping bag to make delicate sugar decorations such as whirls, flowers, etc.

Pithiviers, thin round base of leftover puff pastry, with puff pastry rim and lid and filling of Almond Cream, see pages 136–7.

Platz, yeast cake from Thuringia.

Platzek, flat Polish cakes of various flavors.

Port, red or white Portuguese dessert wine. Matures for three years in oak casks. Maximum alcohol content 25 percent. Dry to semisweet.

Potato flour, potato starch.

Praline, confection of almonds and burnt sugar, see page 147.

Profiteroles, small choux pastry cakes with cream or custard filling.

Prophet cake, large yeast dough cake (Brioche).

Puree, pulp of various kinds of fruit.

Putitz, type of Strudel cake made with yeast pastry.

Q

Quillets, small sponge cakes.

R

Raffinade, refined sugar, see page 17.

Rahm, name for cream in southern Germany and Switzerland.

Regent Cake → Prince Regent Cake, see page 142.

Rehrücken, chocolate sponge baked in a long pan, spiked with almond sticks and covered in melted chocolate, see page 77.

Rodonkuchen, kind of Napfkuchen.

Roquille, preserved peel of Seville oranges.

Roulade, sponge roll, see pages 30–1.

Royal Icing, white sugar icing made with icing sugar, egg white, and lemon juice, see page 64.

Royale, egg custard.

Rum, distilled spirit of which the best types are made from fresh sugarcane. Other types are made from molasses. As well as classifying rums by country of origin as in Jamaica or Cuba rum, there is also either light (colorless) or dark rum, colored with sugar coloring.

S

Sabayon, frothy wine sauce made with egg yolks, sugar, spices, and white wine which are whipped in a bain-marie. An accompanying sauce to desserts.

Saint-Honoré cake, Gâteau Saint-Honoré, named after the patron saint of French bakers, see page 140.

Salambos, short, wide cakes filled with vanilla confectioners' cream. The top is dipped in sugar and sprinkled with chopped pistachio nuts.

Sand cake, plain round sponge cake.

Sauce, mixture of milk, egg, and sugar which is poured over a variety of cakes or puddings.

Savarin, ring-shaped yeast cake, baked in a special savarin pan, soaked in syrup and liqueur while still hot and with a variety of fillings.

Savoy sponge, a fine sponge cake baked in a sandwich pan which is eaten plain with fruit or chocolate sauce or stewed fruit.

Schlotfeger (Chocolate Chimneys), a marzipan mixture which is rolled into a tube around a rolling pin after cooking, before covering with chocolate and filling with whipped cream, see page 157.

Sherry, Spanish dessert wine from Jerez, available either dry or sweet.

Shoe Soles, rounds of thinly rolled puff pastry, rolled over granulated sugar into ovals. Caramelized during baking, see page 126.

Slivovitz, fine plum brandy, with crushed plum stones added during distillation.

Spanish wind, small half-spherical meringues.

Sponge, light cake made either with or without butter and baked in various shapes.

Sponge fingers, light cookies used in the making of several cakes and puddings. An essential ingredient of making some desserts.

Spritzkuchen, balls of choux pastry formed by piping and then fried in hot oil, see French Crullers, page 129.

Starch, edible, finely ground wheat, corn, or potato flour. Used in cake mixtures, custards and for binding.

Strauben, sweets fried in fat.

Striezel, long plaited, yeast-dough cake, see page 167.

Strudel, a dessert made with pastry stretched extremely thin, covered with a filling, rolled up and baked in a flat pan.

Stuten, long cakelike loaf made with raisins and currants.

Sugar, boiling:
Thread: 230°–234°F, wet your index finger and thumb and pinch a little syrup between them. When you separate your fingers a thread forms.
Soft ball: 234°–240°F, take a little syrup from a wooden spoon and dip immediately into iced water. The sugar should easily form a ball. Used for Italian meringue or buttercream.
Firm ball: 244°–248F, when syrup is dipped into water it forms a firm but pliable ball.
Hard ball: 250°–266°F, syrup forms a much firmer ball that remains slightly sticky.
Soft crack: 270°–290°F, when dropped into iced water the syrup separates into threads that are hard but not brittle.
Hard crack: 300°–310°F, threads formed in iced water are hard and brittle.

Sugar, crystallized, white sugar in fairly large crystals used mainly to sprinkle on loaves and cakes.

Sugar, spun, sugar boiled with 3 percent glucose to 290°F and then pulled to and fro with a whisk to make extremely fine threads of sugar.

Sugar coloring, dark-brown sugar syrup. Caramel is heated to over 350°F, i.e. burnt. Hot water is then added and the liquid brought to a boil. Used to color cream fillings, fondant, etc.

Sugar syrup, made by boiling 1 pound sugar with 1 pint water for 1 minute to 220°F on the sugar thermometer. Can be made in advance and stored until needed. Used to moisten cakes, to stew fruit, as a glaze, or to dilute fondant.

Süster, yeast-dough cake with almonds.

Syrup, thick, concentrated sugar solution sometimes with fruit juices or extracts added. Also glucose syrup obtainable from chemists. Also homemade boiled sugar made by dissolving 1 pound sugar in ½ pint water.

T

Tarte, French name for flat fruit flans (baking sheet flans), whereas gâteau refers to a taller cake.

Tartelette, French term for small shortcrust cases which are baked blind. Can be filled with custard, jelly, fruit, and cream.

Tia Maria, coffee liqueur.

Tiered cake, cake made by combining two cakes of different size.

Thousand-leaf cake → Gâteau Mille-feuille, see page 136.

Treacle, syrup made from the tapped sap of the sugar palm.

V

Vacherin Chantilly, filling of whipped cream and vanilla. Decorated with whipped cream, candied cherries, and angelica.

Vacherin glacé, Vacherin with ice-cream filling, decorated with whipped cream.

Vanilla cream, whipped cream flavored with vanilla: Chantilly Cream, see page 51.

Vanilla sauce, custard; sauce made with milk, egg yolks, sugar, and vanilla. Served separately with various desserts or as the basis for a range of flavored custards.

Vanilla sugar, flavoring of sugar with at least 5 percent vanilla pod pith.

Vanillin, flavoring which tastes and smells of vanilla. Forms naturally in vanilla pods through fermentation. Also manufactured synthetically, but of lower quality.

W

Wafers, thin, pale-colored biscuits made by baking a mixture of flour and water. Used as a base for cakes made with delicate almond sponge. Sometimes used to form layers for cakes.

Wähe, Swiss flans, both sweet and savory.

Weinbrand, brandy made in the same way as Cognac by distilling wine.

Whisky, spirit made by distilling fermented barley, rye, wheat, and maize. Scottish Whisky is made chiefly from barley malt and has a slightly smoky flavor. A similar grain spirit from Ireland is spelled *Whiskey*, as is that from America which is, however, made almost exclusively from maize. Minimum alcohol content 43 percent.

Wiesbaden pineapple cake, waffles sandwiched together with nougat, marzipan, and pineapple jam and covered with chocolate.

Windmasse, meringue mixture usually made with boiled sugar.

Z

Zabaglione, Italian wine dessert, usually made with Marsala.

Technical Terms Explained

A

au four, baked or browned in the oven.

B

bain-marie, a container partially filled with hot water over which custards or cake mixtures are beaten warm or foods kept warm.

batterie, a set of kitchen utensils, e.g., bowls or pans in assorted sizes.

batterie de patisserie, baking utensils.

beurre manié, a mixture of flour and butter.

binding, to make a liquid thicker by adding eggs, gelatine, or starch.

blanching, to plunge almonds or pistachio nuts in boiling water and then to peel off the skins; to boil briefly; to plunge fruits (e.g., peaches) into boiling water to loosen the skin.

blind, bake, the baking of pastry cases unfilled or lined with parchment paper and weighted with dried beans which are removed after baking.

browning, to quickly color a cake or mixture (meringue) in a hot oven.

C

candying, covering fruit or fruit rind with a thick sugar solution and then drying.

caramelize, coating or mixing (e.g., nuts) with sugar cooked to a caramel.

chemise, outside coating.

clarifying, (of butter) to remove impurities by heating over a gentle heat and straining the clear fat into a separate bowl leaving the sediment behind.

coating, to cover cakes, flans with butter cream, whipped cream, flaked almonds, etc.

confectioner, baker of sweet cakes that are often sold on the premises with tea or coffee.

couleur, coloring, particularly brown sugar coloring.

creaming, beating butter or fat with some other ingredient or alone until light and fluffy.

D

decoration, embellishment of a cake or flan.

deep frying, frying pieces of dough or fritters in plenty of hot fat until golden brown.

dough, general term for mixtures of ingredients made by the kneading process (unlike cake mixtures which are beaten).

drain, to remove liquid by pouring through a sieve.

dunking, dipping cakes or praline in melted chocolate.

F

fashion, to give shape to, to form.

fermenting, the ripening process in a yeast mixture.

filter, to drain off liquid through a fine sieve or paper.

flaming, pouring alcohol over a dish (e.g., Christmas pudding) and then setting light to it, so that the alcohol is burned off to leave only the flavor of the spirit.

flouring, dusting pans, molds with flour after greasing with butter; sprinkling the worktop with flour.

fluted, with a ribbed or pleated edge, e.g., pans.

folding in, combining whisked mixtures such as egg whites with other ingredients so that the volume is not lost. Best achieved with a metal spoon.

frappé, chilled in ice.

friture, deep fat for frying doughnuts or fritters.

G

gimblettes, rings of choux pastry.

glazing, to cover a cake or pastry with a substance which gives it a shiny surface; used specifically of boiled, strained apricot jam, or egg yolk.

gratinate, to brown the top of a dish.

greasing, to coat the inside of a pan with butter or oil to make it easier to remove the food from the pan after baking.

I

icing, sugar coating spread over cakes or pastries.

L

liaison, thickening.
lining, covering the insides of a pan or dish with thinly rolled pastry.

M

macerate, to soak chopped or whole fruits, pieces of sponge cake, etc., in a liqueur or spirit sweetened with icing sugar.
marinate, to season and make tender by soaking.
masking, to cover a mold or pan with a thin covering of jelly before adding the filling.
mixture, general term for sponge, meringue, etc., in uncooked state. A preparation made with eggs which is mixed by the beating process (unlike dough which is kneaded).
model, old-fashioned baking mold often of carved wood; to shape, form, e.g., marzipan.
moisten, to soak sponges and small cakes with sugar syrup (flavored with fruit juice, liqueur or spirit).

O

oily, used to describe marzipan when it has been handled too much and the almond oil separates from the other ingredients.
oxidize, when raspberries, currants, or black cherries turn blue or purple after stewing in pans that contain lead or are zinc-coated. Use only enamel or steel pans for cooking these fruits.

P

panaché, striped in various colors.
patisserie, section of a hotel kitchen in which fine cakes are made, or place where they are baked, sold, or eaten.
patissier, pastry cook, chef, responsible for the making of desserts.

perfuming, to give a dish a particular flavor and smell by adding an aromatic ingredient such as an essence, liqueur, or spirit.
piping, shaping a mixture before cooking by using a piping bag and nozzle.
poaching, slow cooking in liquid without boiling.
praline, chopped almonds cooked in sugar to caramelize (see page 147).
pulp, fresh fruit mashed then passed through a sieve, liquidizer, or blender.

R

ratafia, collective name for all sweet fruit liqueurs.
reduce, boiling a liquid to thicken it. Reduces the volume and increases the flavor.
refreshing, cooling hot food quickly by dipping in cold water.
renversé (e), upside down, turned out of the pan.
rolling out, making pastry thin evenly by rolling to and fro with a wooden rolling pin.
royal (e), made with egg jelly.

S

sandwiching, joining together two cakes by means of cream, etc.
separating, dividing eggs into yolks and whites.
serving, preparing for presentation at the table.
setting, point at which a jelly, custard, mixture begins to thicken or become firm.
simmering, to boil very gently and slowly.
skimming, removing the scum which rises to the top of a liquid in order to clarify a sauce, for example.
strain, to pass through a sieve in order to reduce to a pulp or remove lumps.

T

temper, to warm chocolate slowly to 90°F before use, to produce an even texture, and give a good flavor.
thickening, to partly bind a liquid with starches (e.g., fruit juice); to heat a custard to just below boiling point so that it coats the back of a spoon, or forms ripples when you blow on it.
turning out, removing food from the container in which it has been cooked or allowed to set.
turns, repeated rolling and folding of puff or croissant pastry.

V

vanilla, flavored with vanilla.

W

whipping, beating cream, a sauce, or custard with a whisk to make it lighter by working in air.
whisking, to beat until light and stiff.

Z

zest, thinly peeled rind of oranges, lemons, or limes.
Zuckerbäcker, originally a tradesman who made refined cane sugar into loaf form. The term later came to be applied to any chef who made pastries with sugar decorations. Still used in Austria for a confectioner.

Dividing cakes into portions

Round cakes and gâteaux can be divided into equal portions simply and exactly by using a special cutter in plastic or tin (see overleaf). However, most people do not have a cutter of this kind and have to rely on a long knife and judging by eye. The diagrams on the right should prove helpful in this case.

The basic rule is that the deeper and richer the cake, the more slices you can get from it. When deciding how many portions you are going to divide the cake into, you should also bear in mind that a fragile or soft cake cannot be cut into very small portions without breaking. Flat cakes such as fruit flans will usually cut into twelve portions. Cakes of medium depth (poppy-seed or lemon cake) will usually make fourteen portions. Cream or buttercream gâteaux can be cut into sixteen or eighteen portions depending on size and depth. For twelve portions you need to make six diagonal cuts. The first cut divides the cake in half. The second and third cuts will divide the cake into sixths. These segments are then halved with three further cuts.

For fourteen portions you need seven diagonal cuts. First cut the cake in half. The second cut makes two fourteenths. The third cut halves the two large segments. The next two cuts divide the two remaining large segments into thirds, and the sixth and seventh cuts divide the remaining two large pieces in the same way.

For sixteen portions you need eight diagonal cuts. The first two cuts divide the cake into quarters. The next two cuts halve each quarter. The cake is now in eighths and four further cuts will divide each of these in half again.

For eighteen portions you need nine diagonal cuts. Divide the cake in half. The second cut marks off two eighteenths. The next three cuts divide the large segments into quarters and then these are in turn halved with the remaining four cuts.

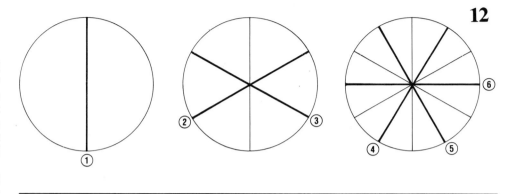

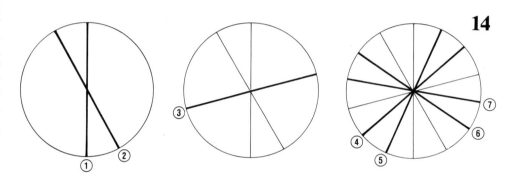

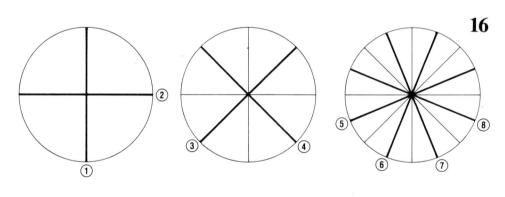

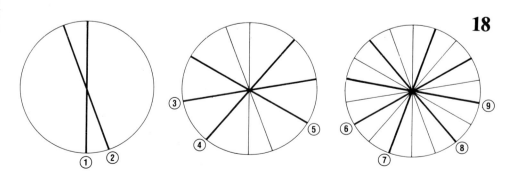

Utensils and equipment

Nowadays there is no limit to the amount of baking utensils and equipment that are available and every cook must decide for him or herself what utensils are needed. A lot of the manual processes, and even the complete process in some cases, can now be done mechanically.

The photographs on the right cover almost the complete range of equipment for a domestic kitchen, but are restricted to manual processes. Just as the step-by-step photographs at the beginning of the book deal mainly with manual preparation, the choice of utensils here has been limited by the same considerations. Most people will be familiar enough already with the mechanical and electrical appliances found in most modern household kitchens.

It is hoped that the photographs and descriptions of the utensils and pans will demonstrate the wide choice available and make the job of choosing what to buy easier. Baking requires special utensils and especially pans which do not form part of "standard" kitchen equipment. But even with standard equipment one can make a start on baking and success does not depend entirely on having the right equipment.

If you begin on the path of home baking by making the simplest recipes (the basic recipes that are explained by series of photographs in this book) you will only need a minimum of equipment. The main thing is to have a reliable oven that functions properly and a large work top.

The choice of further equipment and utensils will depend on whether you want a kitchen on professional lines and on how often you intend to bake. If you are only going to make cakes occasionally there is no need to buy equipment that will only be required once, or at the most twice, a year.

It is possible to improvise in baking, but not at every stage. For the inexperienced success depends on following the recipe and method exactly, and here weighing and measuring correctly are very important and the relevant equipment is indispensable. You need scales that are accurate, a measuring jug to measure larger liquid measures while for small liquid measures you can use a graduated measuring cylinder. Very small quantities are given in the recipes in teaspoons and the smallest of all in pinches. This does not call for the fingertip sensitivity of the professional chef and should not worry the beginner unduly.

The experienced chef should not need detailed advice on equipment for most will have learned all they need to know from past experience. They will no doubt have bought a marble slab already, having found that no other material is as good for working with chilled pastries or marzipan, and they will know where to use electrical appliances to save their muscle power without affecting quality. And only if this requirement can be met should the pastry cook consider using mechanical aids.

Electrical equipment is not included in this section, since there are no appliances exclusive to baking that have not already been dealt with in the section on basic recipes.

Stainless steel saucepan, especially designed for an electric burner, stainless steel can be used to cook any ingredients. Copper saucepans with stainless steel lining. Ideal for cooking on gas. Conduct heat excellently. The best pans for working with sugar. Wood-framed sieve with metal or plastic mesh. For sifting flour or similar ingredients. Ideal for straining custards and fruit puree. Measuring cylinder, graduated glass tube for measuring small volumes of liquid.
Plastic measuring cup for larger liquid measures.
Stainless steel measuring cup has the added advantage of being suitable for measuring hot liquids or for heating liquids.
Saccharometer, for measuring the density of sugar when making syrup.
Sugar thermometer, in degrees Celsius and Fahrenheit, with protective wire casing, for measuring temperature when boiling sugar.

Tartlet pan, plain or fluted, available in different diameters.
Fluted flan pans, 1-inch deep.
8 to 10 inches in diameter. Pans with loose bases are ideal.
Aluminum sponge or flan rings, available in different depths and sizes. Stand on baking sheet and paper for baking or hold filled cake in shape.
Parchment paper, excellent base for baking any type of cake.
Pie pans, for round tarts or pies with sloping edge.

Rolling pin with moving center.
Available up to 4 inches in diameter.
Pyrex rolling pin, comes with rings of various thickness that fit over the ends and allow easy rolling to a given thickness.
Plain rolling pin, helpful when lining pans with pastry; the most common rolling pin in France.
Patterned rolling pin. Used to produce a checked effect on marzipan or pastry. Also available to produce grooves.
Pastry wheel, plain or fluted.
Ruler, for marking rolled pastry.
Pastry stencils, domed pan shapes with a central hole through which they are held, are ideal for drawing circles.
Cake bases in aluminum or cardboard.
Sugar dredger for icing sugar, for kitchen use.
Cake cutter in plastic or tin.
Available for 12–18 portions.
Wire rack with pan. Used as base when covering large or small cakes with melted chocolate.

Balloon whisk with steel or wooden handle in various sizes. For beating sponge mixtures, egg whites, and cream and stirring small quantities.
Wooden spoon, for stirring and binding custards.
Wooden spatula, for beating.
Wide-topped mixing bowl in copper, the ideal bowl for whisking meringue.
Stainless steel bowls, rounded shape with slightly flattened base makes whisking easier than in flat-bottomed basin.
Plastic mixing bowl set. These inexpensive bowls are ideal for beating and whisking providing they are kept away from direct heat.
Shallow plastic bowls, ideal for mixing small quantities and good for the refrigerator if covered in cling film or aluminum foil.

Piping bags in four sizes, in fabric or plastic.
Piping nozzles used with piping bag.
Most common are plain and fluted versions. There are also a range of more specialized nozzles for piping leaves, flowers, etc.
Icing comb in plastic, for decorating cream and buttercream coatings.
Plain and fluted round cutters, basic baking equipment.
Special cutters, available in any shape imaginable.
Heart-shaped cutters can also be used as baking mold.
Cream-horn molds, available as tubes or narrow cones.
Leaf-cutters for making pastry or marzipan decorations.
Kitchen scales, for precise weighing of ingredients.

Cake knife, straight blade for cutting and spreading all types of cake.
Palette knife in four sizes, for spreading custards and icing.
Angled palette knife, easier to use for spreading flat sheets of pastry particularly on baking sheet.
Fruit knife, pointed knife for all kinds of fruit.
Small pointed knife, used whenever intricate cutting is required.
Metal spatulas, for loosening cakes from baking sheet.
Brushes in various sizes. For thin application of glazes or icings.
Rubber spatula and plastic pastry scraper. Indispensable when making sponge mixtures or custards.
Grater, for finely grated citrus peel.
Citrus knife or zester, removes uniform strips of rind.

Springform cake pans, popular for domestic use. Available in several diameters. In tin, sheet-iron, or nonstick finish. Smooth ring mold in various sizes and materials, e.g., aluminum, sheet-iron, tin, and nonstick finish.
Loaf pans in nonstick finish, in 10- and 12-inch sizes.
Loaf pan in sheet-iron or tin, available in four different sizes. Adjustable loaf pan, adjusts in size from 9- to 15-inch aluminum.
Brioche pans, fluted tin molds that can also be used for other types of cake.

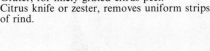

The ceramic gugelhupf mold, available in many sizes, bakes very evenly. Only disadvantage is that they are breakable.
Rehrücken or Balmoral pan in copper and also in other materials.
Marguerite pan, a copper mold with fluted top. Traditional pan for marguerite cake, but can of course be used for other cakes.
Ring mold in copper or tin; ideal for baking ring sponges, but also good for blancmanges and custards.
Old-fashioned German gugelhupf mold in copper. Available in a variety of sizes and other materials, e.g., tin, enamel, or ovenproof glass.

Index